As If Already Free

"A fundamental contribution containing precious insights into what made David Graeber the most innovative social thinker of our time, and why the legacy of his ideas will continue to inspire projects of emancipation, for generations to come."
—David Wengrow, Professor, University College London, co-author with David Graeber of *The Dawn of Everything*

"In this stimulating collection of "slow cooked" essays, the editors reflect on the enduring enchantment of David Graeber's ideas. They remind us that there is always hope in today's troubled world and that the activist pursuit of hope can be fun as well as rewarding."
—Chris Gregory, Emeritus Professor of Anthropology, Australian National University

"Uncovers the critical contributions of Graeberian thought to contemporary education, politics, economy, reproduction, and power relations writ small and large. A must-read for anyone who believes in the power of academia as activism."
—Sophie Chao, environmental anthropologist, University of Sydney

"A simultaneously rigorous and personal tribute to a giant in public anthropology and activism ... destined to serve as an invitation to further conversation, action, and friendship."
—Hirokazu Miyazaki, Northwestern University

"From *Game of Thrones* and *The Idiots* to free birth and megafires in Australia, this book's writers honour Graeber's legacy, while revealing their own original voices. Informing, provoking and imagining alternatives, they testify to people's lives and struggles today. [It] will find a broad readership among thinkers and activists for social and economic justice, along with urgent climate action."
—Lorraine Mortimer, independent anthropology scholar

Anthropology, Culture and Society

Series Editors:
Holly High, Deakin University
and
Joshua O. Reno, Binghamton University

Recent titles:

Vicious Games:
Capitalism and Gambling
REBECCA CASSIDY

Anthropologies of Value
EDITED BY LUIS FERNANDO ANGOSTO-
FERRANDEZ AND GEIR HENNING
PRESTERUDSTUEN

Ethnicity and Nationalism:
Anthropological Perspectives
Third Edition
THOMAS HYLLAND ERIKSEN

Small Places, Large Issues:
An Introduction to Social
and Cultural Anthropology
Fifth Edition
THOMAS HYLLAND ERIKSEN

What is Anthropology?
Second Edition
THOMAS HYLLAND ERIKSEN

Anthropology and Development:
Challenges for the Twenty-first Century
KATY GARDNER AND DAVID LEWIS

Seeing like a Smuggler:
Borders from Below
EDITED BY MAHMOUD KESHAVARZ
AND SHAHRAM KHOSRAVI

How We Struggle:
A Political Anthropology of Labour
SIAN LAZAR

Private Oceans:
The Enclosure and Marketisation of the Seas
FIONA MCCORMACK

Grassroots Economies:
Living with Austerity in Southern Europe
EDITED BY SUSANA NAROTZKY

Caring Cash:
Free Money and the Ethics of Solidarity
in Kenya
TOM NEUMARK

Rubbish Belongs to the Poor:
Hygienic Enclosure and the
Waste Commons
PATRICK O'HARE

The Rise of Nerd Politics:
Digital Activism and Political Change
JOHN POSTILL

Ground Down by Growth:
Tribe, Caste, Class and Inequality in
Twenty-First-Century India
ALPA SHAH, JENS LERCHE, ET AL

Audit Culture:
How Indicators and Rankings
are Reshaping the World
CRIS SHORE AND SUSAN WRIGHT

The Paradox of Svalbard:
Climate Change and Globalisation
in the Arctic
ZDENKA SOKOLÍČKOVÁ

Watershed Politics and Climate Change
in Peru
ASTRID B. STENSRUD

When Protest Becomes Crime:
Politics and Law in Liberal Democracies
CAROLIJN TERWINDT

As If Already Free

Anthropology and Activism
after David Graeber

Edited by
Holly High and Joshua O. Reno

First published 2023 by Pluto Press
New Wing, Somerset House, Strand, London WC2R 1LA
and Pluto Press, Inc.
1930 Village Center Circle, 3-834, Las Vegas, NV 89134

www.plutobooks.com

Copyright © Holly High and Joshua O. Reno 2023

British Library Cataloguing in Publication Data
A catalogue record for this book is available from the British Library

ISBN 978 0 7453 4845 2   Paperback
ISBN 978 0 7453 4850 6   PDF
ISBN 978 0 7453 4846 9   EPUB

Typeset by Stanford DTP Services, Northampton, England

Simultaneously printed in the United Kingdom and United States of America

Contents

Illustrations

Series Preface

As people around the world confront the inequality and injustice of new forms of oppression, as well as the impacts of human life on planetary ecosystems, this book series asks what anthropology can contribute to the crises and challenges of the twenty-first century. Our goal is to establish a distinctive anthropological contribution to debates and discussions that are often dominated by politics and economics. What is sorely lacking, and what anthropological methods can provide, is an appreciation of the human condition.

We publish works that draw inspiration from traditions of ethnographic research and anthropological analysis to address power and social change while keeping the struggles and stories of human beings center stage. We welcome books that set out to make anthropology matter, bringing classic anthropological concerns with exchange, difference, belief, kinship and the material world into engagement with contemporary environmental change, capitalist economy and forms of inequality. We publish work from all traditions of anthropology, combining theoretical debate with empirical evidence to demonstrate the unique contribution anthropology can make to understanding the contemporary world.

Holly High and Joshua O. Reno

Preface

Holly High and Joshua O. Reno

There are many things those who knew David Graeber miss about him, but perhaps the most remarked upon is the conversation. David was a wonderful conversationalist. This volume started when we (Holly and Josh) learned of David Graeber's unexpected passing on September 2, 2020. David is the one who first introduced us.[1] Emailing from a world away, we reflected on just how extensive David's network of friends, former students, collaborators, and comrades had become over the past two decades. We will always fondly remember the person we knew, and part of that is connecting with the other people he knew, those who he also had an enormous impact on. In many ways, that is the focus of this volume: the influence David Graeber has had on the intellectual work of the contributors, and the influence he may yet have in an anthropology and activism yet to come. But this volume is not intended as a hagiography, biographical account or a memorialization of David the man. Rather, it is an active engagement with Graeber's intellectual legacy, not as celebration, but as conversation.

This book is a product of a "slow workshop." Rather than one meeting held over consecutive days, we held a series of Zoom sessions throughout 2021, sometimes separated by weeks, sometimes months. The benefit of maintaining a year-long dialogue was that it allowed people to participate who otherwise would not have been able to: this was a time when COVID-related lockdowns and disruptions were impacting many scholars' work and lives. The format also made it possible to schedule events so that people from radically different time zones could join. Usually two contributors per session workshopped essays with the group in real time. The attendees came from different areas of scholarly expertise, different parts of the world, and different generations. Not all, in the end, could contribute a chapter. But all of them knew Graeber's work and wanted to discuss what it meant and what it could still mean, in and out of academic life. At our editorial suggestion, many suggested different pieces by Graeber for us to discuss as a conversation starter, before moving on to engaging with a draft contribution. These conversations allowed us time to identify and cultivate shared themes across the papers (Graeber's and our own). All the chapters were workshopped, slowly, in this way.

Those themes included, especially, an interest in how Graeber's ideas bring together academic scholarship and activism, for imagining new ways to live and not only to think; use of a personal and accessible mode of writing that tries to bring anthropological and philosophical ideas to the broadest possible audiences; an exploration of unexpected and comparative juxtapositions, across time and space, to inspire these projects; and an attraction to writing about oneself and the world as twin, opposed yet interwoven registers of anthropological reflection. Our collective goal was to, slowly, consider what it means to further the conversation in anthropology after David Graeber. We will have more to say about what such expanding means in the introduction. Suffice to say here that each of these themes expresses one dimension of what that furthering might look like now and in years to come.

Beginning with the first, contributors to the slow conference often alluded to the politics of education and the academy, sometimes making that the direct focus of their papers. Interpreting Graeber's very specific combination of political anarchism and anthropological scholarship seemed to give us license to brandish activist sensibilities (anarchist or otherwise) against what could often seem like overly rigid and harmful structures (Graeber might have said, "bullying") in academic life. At the same time, anthropological activism was often taken in the other direction, meaning some contributions focused on the specific politics of everyday human existence: anthropologists as active humans, not people who passively study the human in general. It was such concerns, after all, that had driven us to the slow conference model to begin with. Thinking and writing for life is, in this sense, an activist project, one that Graeber showed can make anthropology a vital tool outside of the stuffy halls of academic power and privilege.

This leads to the second theme, an interest in more personal and accessible writing. Graeber cultivated a distinctive writerly voice. He included personal anecdotes, jokes (of varying quality) and evocative vignettes from the archives. At times he appeared to be writing for the greatest number of possible readers, as if the goal were to touch lives and inspire others with new appreciations for their own capacities for creation. On the other hand, many of his books are tomes: rambling and hard to summarize. Although he could write in an accessible and fun way, often Graeber chose not to, choosing instead exhaustive detail and long-winded recounts of ethnographic observations or old and half-forgotten anthropological debates (about string games in the Pacific, for instance). Our slow conference reflected on, but never really explained, the appeal of this second writerly style. If there was no single "message" to be found across this large corpus, there was pleasure to found there, along with a familiar pattern—an almost mischievous or defiant tendency to bring up hoary and forgotten bits of ethnographic data long since rendered obsolete if not outright politically suspicious, and discuss these as if they were anthropological commonplaces. Some of us adopted a similar style in our drafts, giddy, as he had been, to see where such paths would lead us.

This brings us to our final theme, which arguably moves through all the papers; that sense of fit between our selves and the world, as it is and as it could be. Each chapter articulates something about how Graeber's work touched on the author's own, that sense of both resonance and difference that is the joy of a good conversation, even if this can perhaps never be fully pinned down.

Another dimension of our project was a systematic reading of Graeber's works, conducted by Josh and Holly. We included in our study all of Graeber's books, including co-authored and most recent, posthumous ones; namely, *False Coin of our Own Dreams* (2001),[2] *Fragments of an Anarchist Anthropology* (2004), *Lost People* (2007), *Possibilities* (2007), *Constituent Imaginations* (2007), *Direct Action* (2009), *Debt* (2011), *Revolutions in Reverse* (2011), *The Democracy Project* (2013), *The Utopia of Rules* (2015), *On Kings* (2017), *Bullshit Jobs* (2018), *Anarchy—In a Manner of Speaking* (2020), *Dawn of Everything* (2021) and *Pirate Enlightenment* (2023). Together, these amounted to over 5,000 pages of text. We included his articles, media reports and other literature at a later stage and as appropriate. But with the books, our method was systematic: taking a leaf from Graeber's own playful use of structuralism, we approached these as a corpus of myth-work and thus applied a structural analysis using Excel spreadsheets, which quickly grew to awkwardly vast proportions.

Lévi-Strauss's approach to myth turned out to be very appropriate to the daunting task of thinking across David Graeber's oeuvre. As many have commented, he left an unusually large amount of significant writings. These are like myths in that they are, self-consciously at times, stories that he proposed as new truths to guide new possibilities for social action. They are also like myths in being "sprawling" (his own description) rather than linear in form and intention. As we note, Graeber tends to take his readers on a ramble through ideas, facts and theories, his enthusiasm consistent but the landscape varied, with the reader sometimes lost in detail and sometimes led to brilliant vistas. Like myths, his works are also repetitive: the same quip or memorable story is often told again, slightly differently, in another work. We also believe his works can be treated as myths insofar as they return to and offer a series of different solutions to repeating contradictions. Like the workshop, this analysis was a slow process. And like the workshop, it was incredibly enriching. It brought the realization that, in his writing, perhaps what Graeber expressed more than anything was not a kind of statement ("this is what I think") but a kind of provocative conversation ("what about this?"). We argue that the overriding approach of his work was dialogic: dialogism characterized his understanding of humanity, politics, ethnography and the potentials of activism and anthropology. An activism and anthropology after David Graeber, we therefore argue, would be just that: a conversation.

We had set out in shock and grief over an unexpected death, mourning conversations that would not be had with a lost friend. For both editors the depth of the grief came as somewhat of a surprise. Part of our motivation behind the workshop and analysis was a desire to better know what it was we were grieving. What was it we enjoyed so much about David Graeber and his work? After all was said and done, what was it that he had wanted to say in those thousands of pages of text? And the product of this process was itself conversation: the enriching conversations of the workshop, and the appreciation of his writings as a form of conversation. This volume is offered as another contribution to the conversation: about anthropology, about activism, and about Graeber's writing.

The editors thank their two partners and families, in the U.S. and Australia, for help and encouragement (as well as general respite) during the slow process of completing this book. We also thank all of those who participated in the slow conference over 2021 for the wonderful conversations of which they were a part. This includes the contributors to this volume as well as those who could not contribute a chapter in the end, including Chris Gregory, Sophie Chao, Luiz Costa, Oana Mateescu and Keir Martin. Their commentary on papers, shared memories of David Graeber and his work, and general solidarity during that challenging year were vital. We also thank Mark Treddinick for his constructive guidance on writing this unusual book. Our thanks, too, to Pluto Press, especially David Castle for his unwavering support, the anonymous reviewers of the book for their helpful and productive insights, and Jamie Cross for his initial encouragement. Portions of this book have appeared elsewhere in a past issue of the journal *Zilsel*. We thank *Zilsel* for allowing our thoughts to appear in both places, and for their lively interaction with the material. Finally, we sincerely thank Amelie Katczynski, who provided crucial support in bringing this manuscript to completion.

Notes

1. Or, rather, he invited Josh, then his colleague at Goldsmiths, to a London pub where Holly (then finishing an appointment at Cambridge) was joining him for drinks.
2. This is more widely known as *Toward an Anthropological Theory of Value* but among his friends, Graeber made it known that he always wanted this title.

Introduction
David Graeber in the Library Stacks

Holly High and Joshua O. Reno

In November 1991, a cold wind blew in across Chicago, and a graduate student with unkempt hair and an unassuming sweater pushed a trolley through the university library. He was happy to have the job, but struggling to keep it and also write up the results of his fieldwork in Madagascar. It was common in those days for the university not to offer financial support to students. But he noticed that students from middle- and upper-class backgrounds had little trouble securing grants and other funds to support their writing. Not him, though; he was stuck in the library stack. At least it was warm here.

His tongue returned to a tooth that had been bothering him. He could not afford the dental care that would save it. So, this is my life of privilege, he thought. He had come back from fieldwork to a department absorbed in an ethical crisis about the privileged position of anthropologists as compared to the people in their field sites. Some students had decided the only ethical thing to do was to avoid fieldwork altogether, or to focus only on groups more powerful than themselves, or write *about* dialogical ethnography—often in anguished tones—rather than simply writing it. But wasn't the point of anthropology, he thought, to trouble the point of view we all privilege, our own, by really listening to other people's points of view? Wasn't the lesson of all fieldwork that no one has all the right answers, holds the full picture, of what life is or should be like—along with the discovery, the little jolt of excitement, that reality, that the world, is unfinished? That's what he thought he'd learned.

Far from coming home to accolades for his long and sometimes difficult fieldwork in Madagascar, he walked back into a sense of dire suspicion about that kind of fieldwork and indeed about the entire endeavor of anthropology. Perhaps it was his working-class background (his mother was a garment worker and his father a plate stripper). Partly because of his upbringing, he was more interested in identifying the value of anthropology for social change than joining his largely class-privileged classmates in what looked to him to be a mostly self-concocted ethical crisis, all played out to a soundtrack of French theorists from the 1970s on constant replay—as if the radio was jammed on the Classic Rock station. He also could not shake the feeling that his graduate supervisors were tuning him out.

His hands trailed across the spines of the books on the trolley. Each one needed to be reshelved, but no one seemed to mind how long it took him. He saw no reason to hurry. He had grown up in a house full of books and ideas and all the time in the world. School had been difficult: both he and his brother had been bullied in primary school. His parents had tried to help, but they were left feeling powerless, and he gradually realized that they were traumatized by their experience of being unable to protect their children. At home, talk and books had offered not only escape from that situation, but also a way to think about it. The young David came across the ideas of anarchism—which he later described as "an absolute rejection of all forms of bullying"—in that home filled with books.[1] When he was 14, his hobby—translating Mayan texts—had earned him an invitation to attend a new high school, and eventually paved the way for his university studies. And more subtle bullying.

He picked up a book from the trolley to reshelve. The title caught his eye, and he flipped it open. He could lose hours in the library stacks this way, especially when he found books that spoke in detail about other cultures or medieval history or some other obscure corner of human experience. When this happened, he would forget his loneliness and the nagging dental pain in his mouth. He especially loved books that compared across such detailed accounts: those grand, old, ambitious books of anthropology like Hubert and Mauss's *General Theory of Magic* and *Sacrifice: Its Nature and Function*. These books showed their age—loose spines, yellowing pages, and speaking to an audience that seemed to have stopped listening. But to his reading, they threw wide open the possibilities of what human being could be. There could be something misleading in books, too: he smiled as he thought of how a theory he had been developing about narrative during his Master's studies, had crumbled when he listened to actual narratives in Madagascar. But that, he saw now, was a theory made of other theories entirely. The books that truly inspired him weren't based on theories; they were built on evidence of different ways of life. These books were based on treating ordinary people, no matter where they come from, as equal to the most esteemed philosopher. As he saw it, if you weren't prepared to go out and encounter people and treat them as equals, you were stuck in the labyrinth of the library stacks forever.

It worried him that these books in particular—the books that recorded some of the most startling findings of anthropology—were being ignored or even rendered "taboo" in the ethical crisis anthropology was mired in. Politics mattered deeply to him, but it was as if there was only one right way to merge it with anthropology, and a fairly class-privileged one at that. As it was when anthropologists and their students rallied around their favorite cult theorist or "-ism," and decried or ignored anyone else. It was just like sectarianism he had seen at the few activist meetings he had attended. There were so many squabbling egomaniacs, inside the university and outside. Surely there was a better way to work together. He slid the book into its correct place on the shelf, and reached for another.

*   *   *

We have imagined this scene, based on the notes and reflections David Graeber left in his books and interviews, and on things he said to us. This unassuming graduate student would go on to become arguably the most influential anthropologist of the twenty-first century, at least to date. As we write, we also imagine future readers in the aisles of library stacks around the world, and that magical moment when their hands will hold one of David Graeber's books for the first time. We imagine the reader avidly consuming one, and then scanning the shelf for another. What they won't see, if they come across that wonderful and weird voice in the wilderness, is a guide intended to help them make sense of the enormous output from this renegade scholar. This book is for them. It is for any reader who wants to know more about David Graeber's work and the influence it has had, or could have, on anthropology.

This book is about the books David Graeber left "in the stacks" and their importance for anthropology. In this introduction, we provide a uniquely comprehensive survey of David Graeber's books, explaining how these emerged over the arc of his career and were related to specific historic moments in the discipline and global politics more generally. Taking a nod from his own playful uses of structuralism, we provide a synchronic reading of these, drawing out some of the most salient themes of his work that emerge when it is taken as a whole. In the chapters that follow, the contributors to this volume show how elements of David Graeber's work have been taken up and expanded in their ongoing scholarly work.

It is important to separate between Graeber the myth and David the man. We are dealing in this book with the former. The fictional account of him in the stacks above is based on comments, mostly in Graeber's own books, about himself. These have myth-like qualities: even if they are rooted in facts, their story-like repetition supported the creation of a writerly persona. This is not to be confused with David, the human person. Here, we are not writing a biography or hagiography of the funny, weird, occasionally impolite, always clever man himself, but about the possibilities his writings offered for an anthropology and a world to come. Hereafter we will refer to "Graeber" or "David Graeber" to reflect that distinct focus. We will have occasion to talk about Graeber's life below, but we do so with the purposes of constructing a diachronic analysis of his books as they relate to chronological events.

Writing an introduction and an overview of Graeber's work is an ambivalent exercise. Each contributor to this volume has found inspiration for their own work in that of Graeber, but they could all name books and articles by him that they did not care for. This is fitting since, as we explain here, Graeber also had an ambivalent relationship with his role in the discipline of anthropology and the game of intellectual recognition more broadly. The prestige games of academia brought Graeber a great deal of unhappiness, and he actively wrote against "Great Man" approaches to intellectual history towards the end of his life, even as he seemed unable to shake his fascination with prestige. This is not a pattern we wish to repeat ourselves. As we will conclude, one inspiration we take from Graeber is the possibilities of what we call his dialogic approach to understanding people and being human. A commitment to dialogism means recognizing that ideas and insights never emerge whole from the mind of one scholar, but are learned from and shared as part of ongoing dialogue with others, including everyday people. That dialogue, for Graeber, included not only engagement with his contemporaries, but also and especially with the ideas of those who came before and, he hoped, those still to come. As he wrote in one of his posthumously published books: "I hope the reader has as much fun as I did."[2]

We read Graeber as both a mythmaker and a mythbuster (we elaborate further on this in chapter 3). By this we do not mean that he trafficked in untruths, but rather that his aim in intellectual work was often to enable social action towards solving some kind of problem, and he understood the role that stories play—the stories we tell ourselves and the stories we live by—in motivating action, and even as the goal of political action. Graeber worked to create new stories that were not only supported by the best evidence, but also that opened up new horizons of possibilities. If his work can be read as myth-work, it follows that the tools of myth analysis can be used to understand his legacy. Below, we describe first the story arc of Graeber's work (in Lévi-Strauss's terms, a diachronic reading) and then an analysis of some recurring themes (a synchronic reading).

David Graeber: The Story Arc

Graeber's publishing career can be roughly divided into two distinct decades which, though equally productive, were radically different to live through. The first, from the publication of his first book, *Towards an Anthropological Value* in 2001 to the cusp of the appearance of *Debt* in 2011, can be described as his "years in the wilderness" (High and Reno, ch. 3 this volume); in these years he deepened his activism and experienced difficult losses in his personal life, as well as a sense of exile and exclusion from the discipline he loved.[3] The second decade, from the publication of *Debt* to his death in 2020 at the age of 59, saw his combined activism and intellectual work earn him global recognition as an important public intellectual.

   The first decade saw the publication of five books that together articulated a distinct vision for anthropology and ethnography that Graeber passionately believed in, but which he felt was ignored. He described his book, *Toward an Anthropological Theory of Value* (see Pedersen, ch. 9 this volume), as an attempt to make Terence Turner's ideas about value available outside the University of Chicago's select circle: for years Turner's unpublished book "Critique of Pure Culture" was circulated and much discussed among University of Chicago students and colleagues. Graeber's book on value attempted to bring these ideas to a wider audience and, more than that, to show the value he strongly believed anthropology could have for the world. A 2004 pamphlet, *Fragments of an Anarchist Anthropology*, was published in a Prickly Paradigm Press, an imprint run by his PhD supervisor, Marshall Sahlins.[4] The 2007 collection, *Possibilities: Essays on Hierarchy, Rebellion and Desire*, appeared in anarchist publisher AK Press, with a blurb from Sahlins.[5] The co-edited volume *Constituent Imaginations* emerged in the same year with the same press.[6] All of these texts derive from his education at Chicago, including some Master's level essays. And all are arguably written in a hopeful tone, with what appears to be the eagerness of someone relatively new to anthropology, who wants to articulate what it was that attracted him to it (interesting gems he has unearthed from the library stacks). These books can be read as communicating something quite personal: the dearly held hopes that had led Graeber to anthropology, not as the discipline existed, but as it could be. It was understandable, then, that Graeber felt it sharply when all these publications received what he felt was a lukewarm reception.

His two ethnographies were also produced in this period: *Lost People* in 2007, based on his fieldwork in Madagascar, and in 2009 *Direct Action*, which described the Global Justice movement.[7] Long and descriptive, both defiantly bucked the trend towards theory (theoretically ambitious, single-issue ethnographies) and, perhaps for this reason, they were slower than he'd hoped in finding a readership.

Graeber credits his first real encounter with anarchism to his PhD fieldwork in a region of Madagascar: at that time, the state had, for all practical purposes, ceased to function due to austerities imposed by the International Monetary Fund (IMF). Graeber's involvement with the global justice movement began when he had already completed his doctorate and begun a tenure-track position at Yale. He was a commentator for the journal *In These Times*, which tasked him with understanding what was happening in Seattle in 1999. As a result of this experience, Graeber became a regular at the Direct Action Network meetings in New York. He did not initially intend this activism as a research project, but he came to recognize the importance both of the historical moment and the anarchist processes, such as consensus building, taking place in these meetings. Crucially, he identified these as similar to what he had seen in Madagascar and as a vital experiment in what democracy could look like.

By Graeber's own account, his growing activism was a decisive factor in his being ousted from Yale University and his intellectual "exile" from the United States.[8] At Yale he worked alongside luminaries Immanuel Wallerstein and James C. Scott. Graeber would later radically develop his own versions of both Wallerstein's world systems and Scott's notion of anarchist history. But his time at Yale was also remembered by him as extremely difficult: while his job was under threat, his brother became seriously ill and died. This led to him becoming the sole carer for his mother during her illness and then death. He would later reflect on this in his Malinowski lecture and in his book *Utopia of Rules*.[9] The dismissal from Yale had brought him, if not fame, then at least notoriety. Even those who had not read his work were aware that he was known as a potentially controversial activist anthropologist. There is a shift here, too, in his writing. If his vision for how activism and anthropology could drive one another had been more conceptual in *Fragments*, *Theory of Value* and *Possibilities*, now it would inform his focused projects on contemporary issues, including debt, sovereignty, employment, bureaucracy, activism, and freedom.

With his 2011 *Debt: The First 5,000 Years*, his publishing career entered a new phase, one he would barely live long enough to enjoy. *Debt* was the first book he produced in exile. He wrote it largely while working at Goldsmiths College, New Cross. While he wrote, he was plagued by his sense of exclusion from the United States Ivy League and the lack of recognition of his books in wider anthropology. In particular, it troubled him that people did not seem that interested in the alternative approach to anthropology he thought he had clearly and cogently presented in the *Theory of Value* book and *Possibilities*. It was like being alone in the library stacks at Chicago all over again.

In England he did find new comrades and friends, of course, as he did seemingly everywhere he travelled. Brian Morris, for instance, was at Goldsmiths and had also written on anthropology and activism.[10] But the issue was not about who was there, but what was expected of academic staff. Goldsmiths assumed as a matter of course that professors would manage Master's programs and do other administrative work, regardless of their status. As Graeber said to Josh and others while working at Goldsmiths, and later wrote in *Bullshit Jobs*, the scenario was "one possible vision of hell": anthropologists were offered jobs based on one skill (writing) but then expected to do entirely different tasks. He likened it to a group of skilled cabinet makers who were then required to fry fish. What is worse, not all that many fish actually needed frying. Still, "somehow they all become so obsessed with resentment at the thought that some of their coworkers might be spending more time making cabinets and not doing their fair share of the fish-frying responsibilities that before long, there's endless piles of useless, badly cooked fish piling up all over the workshop, and it's all that anyone really does."[11] That Graeber produced *Debt* in this emotional and material context is remarkable, and can perhaps be read as another act of defiance.

In his own words, *Debt* was "an attempt to see if it was still possible to use the intellectual tools available to someone like myself—historical, ethnographic, theoretical—to actually influence public debate on issues that really mattered."[12] It was also intentionally "a grand, comparative effort" and "a big, sprawling, scholarly book—the kind that people don't write anymore."[13] The book opens with a conversation between Graeber and an unnamed woman at a garden party at Westminster Abbey. They are discussing the IMF austerity packages, the kind that had caused epidemics of deadly malaria in Madagascar when Graeber was there. Still, the woman exclaims, "Surely one has to pay one's debts." The rest of the book dismantles such moralisms. The reason Graeber was there at the garden party, surrounded by London notables, was because he was living near the Abbey at the time. He'd met a gregarious Anglican priest who had taken vows of poverty and therefore spent whatever funds he came into on lavish parties. Graeber had found in London and at Goldsmiths, if not a place exactly conducive to his writing, then at least pockets of eccentric and non-alienated existence, where defiant writing and thinking were possible.

With the assistance of a literary agent, Melissa Flashman, he published *Debt* with a large New York trade publishing house (Melville House) and successfully promoted the book to a broad readership globally. In the Afterword to the 2014 edition of *Debt*, he noted wryly that his career up until this point seemed to have been characterized by bad timing: first he published an ambitious book addressing comparative theory in anthropology just when the discipline had decided it no longer produced that kind of theory, and then he produced two long, descriptive ethnographies just when these went out of style, and then he came out openly as an anarchist just when 9/11 broadened the definition of and concern with terrorism. With *Debt*, however, his timing was impeccable. It appeared a couple of years after the 2009 financial crisis; on the one hand, people no longer believed the crisis had been a momentary blip; on the other, outrage about the response to the crisis around the world was commonplace. People wanted answers. Many, across the political spectrum, watched wealthy private banks bailed out with public money and felt they had been and were being lied to. Graeber explains that when he originally set out to write this book in 2008, he deliberately approached the topic as a matter of political importance and with the aim of reaching a larger audience.

According to Semanticscholar.org, *Debt* is Graeber's most cited work.[14] However, it is not really citations in scholarly publications that mark this book as Graeber's most recognized success. Rather, at least in Graeber's eyes, it was that it shifted public debate. This was the same accomplishment that he and others would later credit to the Occupy Wall Street movement that he was engaged with shortly thereafter, a movement with which *Debt* was allied in spirit. When *Debt* attracted wide attention and catapulted him to recognition as a public intellectual, he was thrilled. He spent 2011 busy figuring out his next project. He applied for and received a Leverhulme grant to return to Madagascar, but instead went to work with Adbusters in Canada and helped with the Occupy Wall Street action. Both Occupy and *Debt* argued that debts are promises, but that some promises seem made to be broken (New Year's resolutions, wedding vows, or a politician's election promises) while other promises are kept at all costs, making otherwise unthinkable cruelty not only possible but seemingly inevitable (such as austerity after the financial crisis, and IMF packages familiar throughout the Global South).

Serendipitously, when Graeber returned from exile to promote *Debt*, he helped cofound the Occupy movement, then in its nascent stages. He went on to become a key figure in this movement. While he is often credited with coming up with the slogan "we are the 99%", in his own account the slogan came from a collective conversation to which he was only one of the contributors (that is, it was a product of mutual dialogue). A couple of years after the publication of *Debt*, the Bank of England produced a video on the origin of money which eschewed the myth of barter altogether, and instead proposed that money is based on the kind of promises people make to one another. This sounds very much like the kind of argument Graeber made in *Debt*. Graeber did not think this shift in conversation was attributable to his work alone: indeed, he often derided "Great Man" approaches to intellectual work. True to the dialogic approach he generally took, he instead saw all ideas as emerging from countless conversations and social interactions. Dialogism was basic to his understanding of human nature, and also informed his approach to ethnography, his politics, and his vision for anthropology (High and Reno, ch. 3 this volume).[15]

Debt was published the same year as *Revolutions in Reverse*.[16] The latter is arguably a defiantly optimistic book. A collection of essays, it outlines and enacts a vision for what anthropology, and intellectual work more broadly, could be. Like *Debt*, it was written while Graeber was under the impression that anthropology as a discipline was rejecting him. *Revolutions*, however, seems to fight back against this bleakness with love. Of his own style of writing Graeber says his method is to: "start out from some aspect ... that seems particularly bleak, depressing ... some failure, stumbling block ... and to try to recuperate something, some hidden aspect we usually don't notice, some angle from which the same apparently desolate landscape might look entirely different."[17] Arguably, he applied this approach not only in his writing, but also in his vision for anthropology and his own place in that discipline.

In the afterglow of *Debt* and Occupy, Graeber took up a professorship at the London School of Economics and Political Sciences, London, and published several popular salvos. In 2013, *The Democracy Project* was released as a description of his involvement in the Occupy movement, but also as a rethinking of democracy.[18] *The Utopia of Rules* appeared in 2015, again aimed at a broad audience, this time highlighting the spread of bureaucracy and its implications. This included wry observations and real hurt based on his experience of bureaucracy when he was the sole carer for his dying mother.

On Kings, co-authored with Marshall Sahlins, appeared in 2017.[19] *Kings* is in the style of *Debt* but arguably better: in organization, coherence, and significance. It deals with the emergence of states and sovereignty from ritual and the supernatural. The project began when he set out to engage with Fraserian ideas about mythical regicide and an in-depth exploration of ethnography of the Shilluk. But this project also allowed him to revisit his Madagascar and even Mayan material. We might see it as an attempt to make good on some of the promise that he saw in anthropology when he was younger: what can be achieved through broad comparison of the ethnographic record? How can we make it relevant to the pressing questions of our day? This book signals the height of his collaboration with the HAU project (it was published with HAU books and the project began with an essay on the divine kinship of the Shilluk in that journal's inaugural issue) (see High and Reno, ch. 3 this volume, for more on this episode) and it is the first of his co-authored books (though he had co-edited another before). Despite being a free, open access volume, Graeber thought *Kings* did not attract the attention it deserved. Not nearly as much, to be sure, as the #hautalk campaign that questioned the repute of HAU. He contributed to #hautalk with comments about his falling out with the journal he had co-founded. #hautalk grew into a broader set of discussions, on and offline, about privilege and exploitation in higher education, decolonizing anthropology, and more.[20] While none of this accounts for the lack of success of *Kings* when compared with *Debt*, it does perhaps indicate some of the context. This was not the moment for the turn to ethnographic and comparison-derived theory that Graeber had imagined.

Bullshit Jobs, appearing in 2018, returns to popular writing, this time addressing core assumptions about the value of work, possibly indicating a shift away from anthropological theory towards more classically anarchist-inspired topics. In the Preface to this book, there are traces of his growing happiness in his so-called exile. He describes, seemingly surprised, the popularity of his article in *Strike* magazine. Instead of theory from ethnography, *Bullshit* was ethnography from theory: his short polemic in *Strike* led readers to share their lived experiences with him which then formed the basis of his book. The importance of conversation is evident again here in his work: David was an avid user of social media, especially Twitter, and encouraged these kinds of unexpected dialogues. There is also here another articulation of what he meant by his self-identification as an anarchist:

> I'm personally an anarchist, which means that, not only do I look forward to a day sometime in the future when governments, corporations, and the rest will be looked at as historical curiosities in the same way as we now look at the Spanish Inquisition or nomadic invasions, but I prefer solutions to immediate problems that do not give more power to governments or corporations, but rather, give people the means to manage their own affairs.[21]

Nevertheless, *Bullshit Jobs* ends with an endorsement of the Universal Basic Income. That can be further seen as an acknowledgment of the positive role states can play in some circumstances. This tallies with his increasing role in politics in his new home of the United Kingdom, where he was a vocal supporter of Jeremy Corbyn. His open identification as an anarchist often drew critique or even ridicule on points like this, and he was called often to explain his anarchism. In this volume, we discuss his anarchism specifically in chapter 3.

His final three books—*Anarchy—In a Manner of Speaking*, *Dawn of Everything*, and *Pirate Enlightenment*—all appeared posthumously, in 2020, 2021, and 2023 respectively.[22] The first is a transcript of a broad conversation between Graeber, his wife Nika Dubrovsky, Mehdi Belhaj Kacem, and Assia Turquier-Zauberman that covers diverse aspects of Graeber's thought. The second is co-authored with archaeologist David Wengrow and considers evidence about humanity's past as an affirmation for the possibilities for the future. The third is a chapter excised from *Kings*, presented here as a relatively short and contained historical exploration that reconsiders a supposedly "failed kingdom" in eighteenth-century Madagascar as instead a successful political experiment. It shows the influence of both Sahlins and Wengrow on his thinking. The first two books even more explicitly depict Graeber in rewarding friendships cultivated through open dialogue and boundless curiosity. It is only in these two books that Graeber mentions his Jewish identity, and both times it appears as an identity he shares with his co-author (Wengrow) and interlocutors (Dubrovsky). He is clear in both cases that being Jewish has been one of the influences on his intellectual work.

Dawn is worth singling out as a particularly remarkable piece of writing. It weaves together evidence from prehistory and ethnography to shatter baseless myths and create a new story to tell ourselves about human nature, one that affirms the human capacity to imagine and create new ways of being. Thinking diachronically, it is tempting to see this final book as a synthesis of the kind of world historical ethnographically derived theory of books like *Debt* and *Kings* with the more popular, anarchist-inspired writings like *Bullshit Jobs*. Like *Kings*, it is again co-authored, and like *Debt* it is again aimed at speaking to a wide audience on a matter of public importance, but this time combining the ambition of comparative ethnology with the expertise of a co-author and the reach and savvy of a major New York press. If the books on value, debt, and kings could be seen, in a sense, as working through Graeber's tumultuous relationship with the discipline of anthropology, *Dawn* seems to step back from that struggle to look at an even bigger picture: the entire enterprise of the human. While the release of *Pirate Enlightenment* assures that *Dawn* will not be his last book—and it is possible more will be published posthumously—the latter is certainly easy to read as a culmination or an opus. But there are other ways to read this entire collection of books, to which we now turn.

Recurring Themes: A Synchronic Analysis of Graeber's Books

Imagine for a moment the books by David Graeber that we have described above arranged on a library shelf diachronically, in the order of publication date. Imagine someone in the stacks looking them over, guided by call number order. Read that way, one can trace how certain thoughts changed or developed in concert with events of the time. But there is another way of reading them. Imagine the books stacked now one on top of the other, with threads running through the entire stack, as if some awful pest has burrowed through them creating unexpected channels through the layers of worn pages. When each of the books is read as part of a whole, the characteristics of each take on new significance: what is a minor refrain in one is a major theme of another. What seems like an offhand comment in one is revealed as an echo of a much larger train of thought explored elsewhere. Below, we read Graeber's books like an orchestral score, not browsing along the library shelf, but worming our way, burrowing through all Graeber's books at once, as if the thousands of pages formed a single stack. Put differently, we provide a synchronic reading. Such a reading reveals many recurring themes in Graeber's work, but our intention is specifically to answer the question: What does anthropology and activism after David Graeber entail? We mean "after" here not only in the diachronic sense, of an anthropology and activism going on subsequent to or later than his own contributions, but also in the synchronic sense: what does anthropology and activism "in the manner of" or "consistent with" David Graeber entail? Anthropology and activism "after" David Graeber in this sense furthers or expands on his own.

The answer we discovered, and which we unpack below, is that anthropology after David Graeber would entail a dialogic anthropology. Some of Graeber's books were dialogic in the sense of containing very long accounts of dialogues and discussions (*Direct Action*, *Lost People*) and these were the books Graeber himself was most proud of. Yet his "popular" books, we argue, are also dialogic. Even if they are not written in the style literally of dialogues, they retain his commitment to dialogue on a theoretical level, such as his repeated defense of the viability of collective decision-making through open discussion, of anthropology as a potential contribution to ongoing conversations, and the power of these conversations to genuinely change people and the world. Even books that are largely works of history, like *Pirate Enlightenment*, *Dawn* or *Debt* are dialogic in the sense that he argued people throughout the world and throughout time are worth listening to, with ideas worth taking seriously.

For this reason, we argue that consistently throughout his work, Graeber promoted a dialogic approach. This was true of his ethnography, his politics, his vision for intellectual work and his understanding of human beings. It is a theme that runs from his earliest ethnography to his posthumously published works. He consistently argued that human beings "always retain their capacity to surprise you."[23] He saw people as capable of intentional social change, creativity and unexpected solutions, or, as he glossed it early on, "possibilities." This had implications for his understanding of human being, his writing, his activism, and his understanding of the role of anthropology. We will turn to each of these below.

Human Being

Graeber's dialogism is underpinned by a particular understanding of human experience. This understanding reflects a model, dominant in

United States anthropology, where a basic characteristic of human experience, on a group level, is the capability of generating strikingly different cultural concepts and practices which can be very difficult for an outsider to understand. And yet, understanding is possible, at least for some people some of the time (see Reno, ch. 1 this volume). Where Graeber differs from this dominant view is that he also suggested that individuals are no less capable of generating radically new concepts and practices. This means that within any given context, no matter how much is assumed among a group, there will also be room for dialogue between its members. We might say that his dialogism assumed both that underlying commonality made a conversation possible, and that difference made the conversation interesting.

He was fascinated by the idea that what we apprehend as cultures may actually be the effects of social movements of cultural refusal. For instance, speaking favorably of Marcel Mauss, he noted:

> Algonkians in Alaska refuse to adopt Inuit kayaks, despite their being self-evidently more suited to the environment than their own boats; Inuit, similarly, refuse to adopt Algonkian snowshoes. Since almost any existing style, form, or technique has always been available to almost anyone, he (Mauss) concluded, cultures—or civilizations—are based on conscious refusal.[24]

Graeber also offered detailed descriptions of the divine kingship of the Shilluk,[25] the advent of the concept of a "fetish" among European merchants operating in West Africa,[26] and wampum.[27] In the first instance, he examined these examples as part of ongoing struggles, sometimes violent ones that could be thought of as social movements, or moments of refusal and rejection. Cultural creativity is a possibility in any given culture or intercultural context. At another level of abstraction, however, these analyses were aimed not only at grappling with the dynamic life of the given concept or practice, but also at identifying the significance of these for overcoming current day ethnocentric assumptions in relation to some overarching theme, such as sovereignty, commodity fetishism, and value. Graeber examined difference and diversity in pursuit of insights that would assist in rethinking human being more generally: that is, as a contribution to ongoing cultural refusal and creativity.

His dialogism, then, is rooted in a basic commitment to something like a "psychic unity of mankind." Early on, he argued that it was very possible

that every language in the world had a word for "oppression," or at least
had the tools available for making thinkable a concept linking a sense of
weight and heaviness with the notion of the power of some over others.[28]
He understood oppression as formative of much of what we take to be
the everyday. He was fond of pointing out that very little of our everyday
lives can be explained without eventual recourse to admitting that ultimately, things like property rights and public conduct are backed by the
sanctioned use of violence by police. While oppression explained a lot
for Graeber, he always viewed people as able to think critically about and
beyond oppression. While such thought can lead to familiar debates over
freedom and equality (see Maurer's Afterword, this volume), for Graeber
domination is more fundamentally about a loss of creativity. His insistence on an underlying commonality in human experience was not simply
a rejection of cultural relativism. It was a defense of human creativity. He
was scornful of approaches that assumed it was only the theorist who was
capable of creating analytical frameworks and thinking from a new angle
about any given situation. He believed that all people held creative potential not only for providing commentary on their own lives, but also for
imagining the world anew.

At times, his view of humanity strayed into a kind of implicit psychology.
While Graeber early on sounded a note of skepticism about psychoanalysis
(for instance, in parts of *Value* and in a footnote in *Lost People*), over time
his work deployed more overtly psychological explanations. For instance,
he argued that debt relations can create a situation where honor is the
highest value, but where most people are unable to maintain their honor:
debtors faced with debts they cannot reasonably pay become indignant at
best, or at worst capable of atrocities which would otherwise have been
unthinkable. He gives an extended description of the genocidal cruelty of
Cortes and his men, arguing that only the psychology of debt could explain
their inhumanity (Cortes began his mission heavily indebted and seeking
to repay his debts, and all his party ended up heavily indebted). He links
this explicitly to the woman at Westminster Abbey who, despite her obvious
care for those suffering under IMF-imposed austerity measures, could still
insist that debts must be paid, whatever the costs. This argument is linked
to another of his key assumptions about human psychology, which is that
people often wish to see themselves as good people doing good things,
and that when denied this, people often become either despondent or
resentful, and are more likely to tend towards extreme acts or beliefs. He
argued in *Bullshit Jobs* that this value—much more than money—is what

motivates much human activity, including work. In this volume, Michael Ralph argues that the Eritrean independence movement was motivated by deeply held notions of sacrifice, liberation and debt (all key themes in Graeber's work). This approach is also one way of understanding Graeber's argument in *Value*, where he argued that money is another abstraction of human creative potential in pursuit of what is held dear. In this volume, David Pedersen contextualizes Graeber's theory of value in larger conversation of which it was an important part.

Graeber also employed psychological arguments in *Bullshit Jobs* to argue that doing meaningless work caused emotional suffering, as reported by the people who shared their stories with him. Bullshit jobs create sadistic working conditions, he commented, where the meaninglessness of the work can be deliberately used to increase suffering. The rejection of *Bullshit Jobs* by economists was premised on the a priori assumptions: (a) that bullshit jobs could not possibly exist because if a job exists, it could only be to serve some purpose, in which case it would not be bullshit, and (b) even if such a job did exist, everyone would want to do it because humans are assumed to be out to do as little as possible for the most gain. It is here that it is possible to see Graeber's myth-making at work once again. If Graeber made the occasional psychologizing argument, it was typically in support of his claim that disciplines like economics themselves are based on a handful of very simplistic and unrealistic assumptions about human psychology, none of which stand up to sustained empirical observation. Graeber's psychologizing, then, was not so much a fully fleshed out model of the human mind and emotions, but another example of his key assumption that people always have a capacity for possibilities, and so any discipline based on a narrow set of assumptions about human psychology will be bound to misrepresent. His dialogism is thus rooted in an axiomatic assumption that humans are capable of diversity and are, in fact, diverse. Even today, in a period he characterized as one as a "war on the imagination," where neoliberalism has increasingly come to be a political project of convincing people that the system we have now is the only one possible (even if it is leading to extinction), he saw reservoirs of human possibilities all around us. In this volume, Holly High (ch. 2) uses this concept of possibilities to rethink the anthropology of birth.

Misfits, unconventional figures, clowns, and oddballs are a recurring figure in Graeber's books. This makes his books apt for an unexpected dialogue with critical disability studies, as Reno argues in his chapter. In Graeber's first ethnography he described the "eccentrics and oddballs" he met in Madagascar as "both the main way we define what we consider normal, and also a reservoir of possibilities during moments of change."[29] He took time in *Value, Possibilities, Kings* and *Dawn of Everything* to talk about clowns and (in the latter in particular) people categorized as having non-normative bodies. He argued that these formed a kind of reservoir of diversity that some societies turn to in times of social change for new ideas or leadership,[30] rehearsing an argument originally made by Paul Radin in relation to the tolerance of skeptics among the Winnebago and by T.O. Beidelman about the importance of "Bulls" in Nuerland.[31] It was increasingly clear that he identified with this persona of the oddball who nonetheless provides the inspiration needed for a social movement when the time comes. He quipped, "They're probably who we'd be if we happened to have been turn-of-the-century Nuer."[32] In *Utopia of Rules*, he suggested that bureaucracy has eroded the space in which oddballs and eccentrics could live in peace, with a concomitant decline in innovation.[33] We might say that part of the direct action he took against the "war on the imagination" was to himself be a misfit, an oddball, an eccentric, insisting on pointing the way to other social possibilities precisely at the point of history when we were supposed to have stopped believing that revolutions were possible at all.

Graeber also pointed to reservoirs of possibilities in everyday life, for all people, everywhere. He developed the concept of "baseline" or "elementary" communism as a way of describing the vast majority of social interactions, even in societies that consider themselves governed by capitalist principles.[34] "Mythic communism," by contrast, is the idea that true communism lay either in the very distant past (some Garden of Eden or lost prehistoric times) or in the very distant future (through the heroic efforts of social engineering or a Great Leader). For some, communism is mythic in the sense that, even if it were to be realized in the current day, it would never work anyway because it is somehow contrary to human nature. In place of mythic communism, Graeber conceived of communism as a very everyday concept, here with us already in the small gestures of everyday life, and "the foundation of all human sociability." [35] Communism is the collaboration people show when working towards a common goal, even if they work for Goldman Sachs, and that baseline level of mutual aid which is a shared expectation in everyday life (and without which everything else would grind to a halt). In this volume, Gustav Peebles (ch. 8) uses the concept of the commons to, unexpectedly, rethink the role of Central Banks.

Graeber also saw an affirmation of possibilities in the mere fact of seasonality (following Robert Lowie): the seasons, and the way we adapt our lives to them, now as ever, remind us that we do move in and out of varied ways of being.[36] Rituals, too, could be "laboratories of social possibility."[37] And play, so fundamental to human development, tends to throw up possibilities. What begins as free play often generates its own rules and could be the beginning of a game which solidifies into a new arrangement. This processual view of human being, which he once described as "Heraclitean," assumes that "what is most essential about human beings is not what they are at any given moment, but what they have the capacity to become."[38] It follows from this view of human experience that social movements and revolutions cannot be a European invention. In *Dawn of Everything*, he argued that all people everywhere have the capacity for intentional social change, and this fact likely explains much of the diversity we see in the ethnographic record, history, and prehistory. In his latest, posthumous book, Graeber characterizes an enigmatic episode of Malagasy, pirate history as a form of "proto-Enlightenment." This was part of an effort, also motivating much of *Dawn and Kings*, to recognize that all people, everywhere, are capable of radical self-conscious experimentation.[39] However, rules or social movements here and elsewhere can solidify so that "We tend to become slaves of our own creations." [40] Graeber was not opposed to rules: he saw them as an inevitable part of everyday human experience, and a necessary part of any play that remains fun long term. His vision for freedom was not a freedom *from* rules, but rather a freedom *to choose* the rules one lives by, and to live in awareness that one has that potential, knowing new rules could always be erected and old ones torn down. In this volume, Michael Edwards (ch. 6) expands on Graeber's conceptualization of imagination to rethink the uprising in Myanmar's "Spring Revolution." Meanwhile, Sharad Chari (ch. 5) examines the broken promise of public education to offer such spaces of rule-bound freedom in the present moment.

Ethnography

Lost People, Graeber's first ethnography, is long. It is also incredibly hard to follow. We suspect this is in large part because of the "dialogic" style Graeber consciously adopted. He presented scenes, events, and sometimes entire conversations in a quite raw style, retaining much of their original complexity. It was as if he wanted to retain in his writing a strong flavor of the provisional and shifting nature of social life, or, in his words, "the haphazard, unpredictable nature of fieldwork."[41] But this was not the main point of his dialogic ethnography. Rather, this style of writing appears to have been adopted, above all, as a way of staying true to his understanding of human being, particularly his understanding of cultural difference as significant but not an absolute divide between self and other. Divides make dialogue a challenge but also a pleasure. Graeber wanted the people in his ethnography to come across as convincing individual characters, with their own quirks and idiosyncratic takes on things, telling stories and creating speculative frameworks of their own. *Lost People* is dense with local terms. This can be quite disorientating for a reader not familiar with Madagascar, but it also conveys some of the implications of the dialogic approach: that, with time and commitment, it *is* possible to gain fluency with such strange words, and to understand another context without reducing people to cardboard cut-outs, and without erasing their history.

Graeber's second and final ethnography, *Direct Action*, was, somewhat defiantly, even longer and even more committed to a dialogic style. Flagrantly bucking the trends in global anthropology at the time, he wrote "there is no particular argument to this book."[42] He makes generalizations rarely and only once the reader has been immersed in real-time descriptions of multiple meetings and actions (around approximately page 247). He saves his caricatures for the World Bank, IMF, and police. In the preface, he effortlessly glosses the global situation when the alter-globalization movement arose, showing that he was more than capable of making glosses. It is just that, when he came to writing ethnography, he quite clearly did not want to. In this respect, he defended ethnography as a form of detailed description.[43] Even then, Graeber writes, ethnography only captures at most 2 percent of what is going on. Theory, he argued, was an even further simplification.[44] But what Graeber wanted to convey in his ethnographic writing, at least, was something "somewhat true to the integrity of its object," by which he means the uncertainty of much of what he experienced, the sense of long planning and then a confused flurry of action, and then the process of making meaning of that action afterwards.[45] He refers to this open-endedness throughout the book in terms of narrative: activists plan events that they hope will be narrated in certain ways, contest alternative narratives, and have arguments about how the story should be told. This concern with narrative is a continuation from *Lost People* and reinforces the sense that, for Graeber, when it came to writing dialogic ethnography, what he meant largely was literally dialogue: in media reports, the stories people told, and the conversations they had.

Politics

Graeber's approach to political theory was informed by dialogism, but not exactly the same as that which shaped his ethnographies. For instance, Graeber argued for the possibility of political pleasure, by which he meant the realization of a democratic yearning—widespread across cultures and among individuals—for a politics where "humans are fundamentally equal and allowed to manage their collective affairs in an egalitarian fashion, using whatever means appear most conducive."[46] Notably, democracy for Graeber is not an invention of "the West" (a concept which he lampoons as spurious): in fact, it has been practised by many people in different times and places. Furthermore, it is not defined by majority voting, professional politicians, heroic competition, or the existence of political parties. Rather, it involves "collective deliberation on the principle of full and equal participation."[47]

Graeber was particularly interested in consensus decision-making as a path to democracy (dialogism in yet another form). His interest in consensus was clearly triggered by his experience with the Direct Action Network (DAN; first as an activist and then as an ethnographer), although through that process he realized that he had witnessed consensus decision-making during his time in Madagascar, but in a much less self-conscious form. That only inspired him more when, after his experience with the Direct Action Network (DAN), he helped in the early days of the Occupy movement. For Graeber, importantly, consensus did *not* require bringing everyone around to holding the same view, and much less was it about forcing everyone to agree.[48] Rather, it was a "process" (this term is critical) that starts out by assuming that there will be differing and perhaps incommensurable views in any gathering of people. This difference is approached not as a problem to be overcome, but as a potential that is useful for solving a problem. He argued that consensus decision-making—or any collective decision-making—is most effective when it is aimed at an action (solving a problem, planning an event, etc.).[49] Consensus-based decision-making involves organized deliberation, where different views can be worked with such that the creative potential inherent in this diversity is unleashed.[50] Critically, it involves no threat of force.[51]

The "pleasure" of politics, for Graeber, resided precisely in this sense of oneself eclipsed. This is an idea that first appears in his writing in words attributed to "Jessica," a DAN member. She says:

> There have been times I've been at meetings and there's a proposal I didn't even like all that much, but over the course of the discussion, it became obvious that just about everyone else thought it was a really good idea. I found there's actually something kind of pleasurable in being able to just let go of that, realising that what I think isn't even necessarily all that important, because I really respect these people, and trust them. It can actually feel good. But, of course, it only feels good because I know it was *my* decision, that I could have blocked the proposal if I'd really wanted to. *I* chose not to take myself too seriously.[52]

By contrast, Graeber described majoritarian decision-making as largely unenjoyable, noting that most people in so-called democracies never get to experience politics as a pleasure.[53] Instead, they experienced entrenched positions, competition, and conflict.[54] Majority decision-making tends to produce "Great Men" with groups of followers, and groups locked into endless struggles. Graeber developed a detailed account of "sectarian groups" in his ethnography *Direct Action*. Sectarian groups feature hierarchical organization, a charismatic (invariably male) leader, a theory which is the reason for the group's existence, and the production of position papers applying that theory to virtually any topic imaginable. These position statements are printed in a newspaper, which the party members are duty-bound to sell. This is very much an etic description (he notes that no one identifies *themselves* as "a sectarian"—this is instead how sectarians were described to Graeber by anarchists, many of whom had firsthand experience of participating in cult-like sectarian groups before coming to anarchism).

Another aspect of his politics is apparent in a synchronic assessment of his non-ethnographic books (which is to say, most of what he wrote and will be remembered for). Here it is helpful we find to return to Lévi-Strauss's take on myth as containing, sometimes in the same telling, a transformation of elements such that one set of terms and relations are flipped and exchanged.[55] This was famously and confusingly encapsulated in Lévi-Strauss's formula fx(a), fy(b) $\simeq$ fx(b), f a-1(x). We are not concerned with making sense of this, per se, except to point out that one way to see Graeber's initial mythical project is as a transformation of this sort.

So, if political change (a) is for him a function of creative freedom (x) and anthropology (b) is a function of ethnographic description (y), then it follows that he would endeavor to show anthropology itself (b) over time to be primarily characterized in terms of possibilities (x) which could best be realized by engaging in apolitical readings (a-1) of the ethnographic record.

What does this mean? Well, it is one way of explaining a curious but compelling dimension of Graeber's political anthropology, namely that his radical approach was premised on an occasional impatience for those questioning the politics of ethnographic representation, a concern that flared up during his graduate years and again during #hautalk. In these moments, he seems to have felt that something was lost of the creative possibilities of the ethnographic record if, for instance, Fraser's or Lowie's or Evans-Pritchard's descriptions were thought to be of *no value* except as bad examples of unethical or outmoded research or writing. In other moments, he provided very detailed accounts showing how sexism, racism, and colonialism produced systematic misreading of the ethnographic evidence. For instance, *Dawn* examines how contributions to the history of ideas by women, indigenous interlocutors, and Black scholars had been similarly dismissed. This is an explicit theme of *Pirate Enlightenment*. At the same time, he has also argued that suspicious or cynical readings of past texts, readings that cast them as fictional by-products of the power relations of their time and nothing more, also can paradoxically reproduce racist narratives about "the West" as the point of origin for all ideas worth knowing about. He wrote:

> the blanket condemnation of Enlightenment thought is in its own way rather odd, when one considers that this was perhaps the first historically known intellectual movement organized largely by women, outside of official institutions like universities, with the express aim of undermining all existing structures of authority. What's more, if one examines many of the original sources, Enlightenment thinkers were often quite explicit that the sources of their ideas lay outside what we now call "the Western tradition" entirely.[56]

There are no doubt many ways that Graeber's relationship to knowledge and (de)colonization can be read and will be read in the future. In this volume, Georgina Tuari Stewart (ch. 4) discusses how Graeber's politics and approach to the ethnographic record can be read as compatible with a Māori philosophy. Sharad Chari's (ch. 5) contribution, meanwhile, examines elements of race as they factor in higher education. Michael Ralph (ch. 7) retells the recent history of Eritrea in dialogue with Graeber's writing on radical democratic experiments and against neocolonial appraisals of "African" countries.

The politics of anthropological representation relate to our next theme, which is the importance of seeing the possibilities of anthropology beyond mere criticism and dismissal of Bad Men or, on the other hand, an effusive praise for Great Men. Such thinking—which individualizes (and often racializes) credit rather than acknowledging dialogism—is, in fact, deeply connected to the projects of colonization and empire.[57] If Graeber the mythbuster and mythmaker is worth engaging with at all, it is creatively, playfully, irreverently, lest we fall back on the trope and into the trap of Great Man thinking.

Vision for Intellectual Work, Particularly Anthropology

Graeber used his understanding of how sectarian groups operate to sound a warning about the role of vanguardism in academic work, including anthropology. In a memorable passage, he characterized intellectual debate at Chicago, where he gained his PhD, as a "twilight of the vanguard": social theory had been reduced to little more than belittling, ridiculing, or dismissing what others had said. Listening was only sustained until one could work out which "-ism" the speaker fell into, at which point they could be disregarded with impunity.[58] Graeber explicitly likened these to the sectarian groups he had witnessed in activist circles: the same cult-like structure, the same focus on a core figure or leader, and the same robotic production of position papers from the theoretical standpoint that is the reason for the group's existence. Graeber advocated instead for a model of intellectual work where it was accepted at the outset there will be differences, perhaps incommensurable in nature (for instance, it is difficult to see how the layered levels of emergences assumed by Critical Realism can be tallied with the rather flat structure of Actor Network Theory).[59] But he argued that the point of intellectual work is not to try to convince everyone to come around to your point of view (and, if they don't, ignore them). The point is to work towards a pragmatic goal and the values inextricable to that pursuit. When working towards a shared goal, he reiterated, diversity of views within the group is a strength.

Related to his anti-sectarian approach to academic work, Graeber also wryly repeated Bourdieu's observation that, in intellectual work, one knows one has won the game when "other scholars start wondering how to make an adjective out of your name."[60] Graeber characterized this as a Great Man approach to intellectual work: even scholars who might scoff at the idea of a Great Man approach to history, he noted, still go ahead and trace ideas back to a single man's genius—Foucault or Trotsky—instead of treating ideas as the products of "endless conversations and arguments in cafes, classrooms, bedrooms, and barber shops, involving thousands of people inside and outside the academy (or Party)."[61] Moreover, this can occur even when the genius in question is singled out for scorn:

> It's as if history, and especially radical history, has become some sort of moral game where all that's really important is to make clear just how much one is not letting the Great Men of history off the hook for the (obviously, very real) racism, sexism, and chauvinism they displayed, without somehow noticing that a four-hundred-page book attacking Rousseau is still a four-hundred-page book about Rousseau.[62]

His emphasis on gender here is deliberate, as is the implicit comparison between intellectuals and kings. It is common for political figures (ancestors, martyrs, founders, institutions) to be far more important after death than when they were living. He argued that mourning is an important part of "people-making," with the fact that the person concerned can no longer be directly involved in it itself "underlining how much of the work of making and maintaining a career is always done by others."[63] This work of mourning and making Great Men out of mere men is often done by social subordinates and women, people who are unlikely to have the same work done for them. The negation of the self in mourning thus has similarities to the negation of self by people who subordinate themselves to a sectarian group or an intellectual vanguard Great Man theorist. Graeber acknowledged that his idea of "political pleasure" likewise involved a negation of the self, but the crucial difference was that it was done in a process that first ensured one's freedom to cease playing the game at any point.

While this point is significant for many parts of Graeber's thought, including the link he often came back to between people-making, care, and domination, the aspect we underline here is its significance for the question we put to ourselves in creating this volume: "What does anthropology and activism after David Graeber entail?" How do we offer a response to this question without contributing to the mythical manufacturing of yet another Great Man? We can say that such an effort would definitely not involve an attempt to find a way to make an adjective out of his name, or a new "-ism." It would also not involve any attempt to make a Great Man myth. Taking a dialogic approach, it would place his thoughts among streams of conversations, inspirations, and events, and would carry these onwards, particularly towards action aimed at solving some kind of problem. Graeber's dialogic approach assumed that everyone has great ideas, particularly when the right processes are in place to allow these to emerge and be heard. Through dialogue, groups can produce ideas that no individual would have come up with. Unleashing this potential for human creativity is a matter of urgency, given the many problems currently facing our species and the world. In short, "a Graeberian approach to anthropology" is a contradiction in terms. But an anthropology in conversation with David Graeber is thoroughly consistent. Anthropology after David Graeber can be—and we hope will be—an anthropology carried on by each of us from our own unique perspectives, with purpose, and in dialogue with one another. That is, it will not be him: it will be us.

Notes

1.   David Graeber, Mehdi Belhaj Kacem, Nika Dubrovsky, and Assia Turquier-Zauberman, *Anarchy—In a Manner of Speaking* (Belgium, France and Luxembourg: Diaphenes, 2020).
2.   David Graeber, *Pirate Enlightenment, or the Real Libertalia* (New York: Farrar, Straus and Giroux, 2023), xiii.
3.   David Graeber, *Toward an Anthropological Theory of Value: The False Coin of Our Own Dreams* (New York: Palgrave, 2001); David Graeber, *Debt: The First 5,000 Years* (Brooklyn and London: Melville House, 2011).
4.   David Graeber, *Fragments of an Anarchist Anthropology* (Chicago: Prickly Paradigm Press, 2004).
5.   David Graeber, *Possibilities: Essays on Hierarchy, Rebellion, and Desire* (Oakland, CA and Edinburgh: AK Press, 2007).
6.   Stevphen Shukaitis and David Graeber with Erika Biddle (eds.), *Constituent Imagination* (Oakland, CA and Edinburgh: AK Press, 2007).
7.   David Graeber, *Lost People: Magic and the Legacy of Slavery in Madagascar* (Bloomington, IN: Indiana University Press, 2007); David Graeber, *Direct Action: An Ethnography* (Oakland, CA and Edinburgh: AK Press, 2009).
8.   David Graeber, *Bullshit Jobs: A Theory* (London: Penguin Books, 2018), 274–275; David Graeber, *The Democracy Project: A History, a Crisis, a*

Movement (New York: Spiegel & Grau, 2013), 5; Graeber, *Direct Action*, xvii–xix.

9. David Graeber, *The Utopia of Rules: On Technology, Stupidity, and the Secret Joys of Bureaucracy* (Brooklyn and London: Melville House, 2015).

10. Brian Morris, *Anthropology and Anarchism: Their Elective Affinity* (London: Goldsmiths College, University of London, 2005); Brian Morris, *Anthropology, Ecology, and Anarchism: A Brian Morris Reader* (Oakland, CA: PM, 2014).

11. Graeber, *Bullshit Jobs*, 12–13.

12. Graeber, *Debt*, 393.

13. Ibid.

14. As of October 12, 2022.

15. See also Dennis Tedlock and Bruce Mannheim, *The Dialogic Emergence of Culture* (Urbana and Chicago: University of Illinois Press, 1995).

16. David Graeber, *Revolutions in Reverse* (London and New York: Minor Compositions, 2011).

17. Ibid., 4.

18. Graeber, *The Democracy Project*, 5.

19. David Graeber and Marshall Sahlins, *On Kings* (Chicago: University of Chicago Press, HAU Books, 2017).

20. David Graeber, "Here's a Thought re #hautalk—Why Not Take the Occasion to Ask What is Going on in our Own Departments?" Twitter, June 17, 2018, available at: https://twitter.com/davidgraeber/status/1008309 270188843008 (accessed March 6, 2023).

21. Graeber, *Bullshit Jobs*, 275.

22. David Graeber and David Wengrow, *The Dawn of Everything* (Great Britain: Allen Lane, 2021).

23. Graeber, *Possibilities*, 31.

24. David Graeber, "Culture as Creative Refusal," *Cambridge Journal of Anthropology* 31, no. 2 (2012): 1–19.

25. Graeber and Sahlins, *On Kings*; Graeber, *Possibilities*.

26. Graeber, *Possibilities*.

27. Graeber, *Toward an Anthropological Theory of Value*, 117–150.

28. Graeber, *Possibilities*, 255.

29. Ibid., ix.

30. For example, Graeber et al., *Anarchy*; Graeber and Wengrow, *Dawn of Everything*, 97, 248.

31. Thomas O. Beidelman, "Nuer Priests and Prophets: Charisma, Authority and Power among the Nuer," in *The Translation of Culture: Essays to E.E. Evans-Pritchard*, ed. Thomas O. Beidelman (London: Tavistock Publications, 1971), 375–415.

32. Graeber et al., *Anarchy*.

33. Graeber, *Utopia of Rules*, 80–81.

34. Graeber, *Toward an Anthropological Theory of Value*, 231; Graeber, *Debt*, 94–102; Graeber, *Revolutions in Reverse*, 35; Graeber et al., *Anarchy*.

35. Graeber, *Debt*, 96.
36. Graeber, *Lost People*, 286; Graeber et al., *Anarchy*, 97.
37. Graeber and Wengrow, *Dawn of Everything*, 116–117; Graeber, *Pirate Enlightenment*, 101–105.
38. Graeber, *Possibilities*, 258.
39. Graeber, *Pirate Enlightenment*, 88.
40. Graeber, *Possibilities*, 143.
41. Ibid., 323.
42. Graeber, *Direct Action*, viii.
43. Ibid., 14–15, 509.
44. Ibid., 519.
45. Ibid., 14.
46. Graeber, *The Democracy Project*, 184.
47. Ibid., 186.
48. Graeber et al., *Anarchy*, 48.
49. Graeber, *Direct Action*, 205.
50. Ibid., 320; Graeber et al., *Anarchy*, 48.
51. Graeber, *Direct Action*, 185.
52. Ibid., 305.
53. Graeber, *Fragments*, 73.
54. Graeber, *Direct Action*, 304.
55. Claude Lévi-Strauss, "The Structural Study of Myth," in *Structural Anthropology* (New York: Basic Books, 1963), 206–231.
56. Graeber, *Pirate Enlightenment*, x.
57. Joshua Reno and Britt Halvorson, "The Gendering of Theory in Anthropology since 2000: Ontology, Semiotics and Feminism," *Current Anthropology* (forthcoming).
58. Graeber, *Possibilities*, 302.
59. Ibid., 324.
60. Ibid., 304.
61. Ibid.
62. Graeber, *Pirate Enlightenment*, xi.
63. Graeber, *Possibilities*, 99–100.

1

On Morons

Joshua O. Reno

Introduction

> I was curious. Why was he smashing all those beetles? What did he get
> out of it? First thing I did was ask him. "Orson, why are you smashing
> all those beetles?" He gave me an answer. "Smash the beetles! Smash
> them! Kun kun kun!" I wasn't deterred. I was the smartest person I
> knew, certainly I had the wherewithal to unravel the mysteries that
> lay at the heart of a moron. So I went to Maester Valeric's library…
> Turns out far too much has been written about great men and not nearly
> enough about morons. Doesn't seem right.
>
> —Tyrion Lannister[1]

The fictional Tyrion Lannister, played here by actor Peter Dinklage, is
not wrong when he decries the paucity of literature on "morons" when
compared with "great men." But it would also be true to say that stories
of great men and morons are actually thoroughly intertwined. Sometimes
great men turn out to be morons, sometimes morons are also great men.
Sometimes they spend time together. Taking note of their connection
requires that the ideas behind "great man" and "moron" be explored in
greater depth.

We owe a debt to David Graeber for examining the former category
in one of the last books published during this lifetime, and arguably one
of the more neglected by his readers, critics, and admirers—*On Kings*,
co-written with Marshall Sahlins.[2] In this chapter I want to argue that performing an identical exercise on morons, that is, a comparative account
of morons beside kings, is also worth doing. Moreover, I think that this is
worthwhile for both anthropology and for activist projects, two things that
Graeber was deeply committed to.

Following pathbreaking work by Robert Edgerton and Jani Klotz, among others, Patrick McKearney and Tyler Zoanni have recently noted that cognitive disability is not just another form of social or cultural difference that anthropologists should attend to.[3] Rather, this way of being different challenges many of the taken-for-granted epistemological and methodological assumptions of the field itself. Specifically, I am interested in the third set of questions that McKearney and Zoanni argue are raised by the "thorny issue" of cognitive disability: "how should we study cognitive difference anthropologically? Can we use existing models of social and cultural construction to capture the experiences of those living under the description of cognitive difference and disability? Or does it require new anthropological tools?"[4]

In truth I am not trying out new anthropological tools in this chapter but, like Graeber, playing with some old ones. But can there be an anthropology of morons and what might that look like?

Full disclosure: my son Charlie is a moron. Or, to use the more neutral-sounding parlance of our times, he is an American adolescent diagnosed as a low-functioning person on the autism spectrum. I don't like calling him a moron and am only doing so for the purposes of this chapter. After all, the term "moron" was invented in 1910 at the same time as "feeble-minded" by a eugenicist who wanted to eradicate people like my son from the Earth.[5] I am taking that word back and will explain my motives for doing so in a moment. But it is not like saying he "has autism," which can mean a million things, helps people understand him better. As Zoanni rightly points out, various "ecological" factors in government, medical care, culture and circumstance conspire to shape the kinds of diagnoses and life experiences that people with radically different "minds" end up having.[6] In Charlie's case, being disabled involves not being able to talk—he cannot speak one word nor sign one gesture of ASL (American Sign Language). This also means that he has a lot of trouble adopting many of the ordinary forms of acceptable social behavior that are expected in day-to-day life, that he will likely never have a calling or profession, make lifelong friends or have romantic affairs, convert to a religion or protest for collective change.

Charlie is different. He is so different, in fact, that I wager it probably would not matter what people might come across him, from what time in history and from whatever cultural world of experience, they would share at minimum an understanding that he was set apart, separate from them. They might not think of "minds" as things individual people have, they might not separate medical from cosmological understandings (as moderns supposedly do), they might or might not have a local term available like "moron" at their disposal ... but they would still reckon that Charlie was different than most people they knew and at that point they would then alter their expectations, rethink their ordinary social judgments about what constitutes appropriate or inappropriate ethical behavior, whether toward him or from him. This might seem somewhat banal—though some anthropologists will find such a universal claim scandalous—but it actually hints at the connection between so-called morons and kings.

My guiding question, in a sense, is what if Graeber and Sahlins had written a book called *On Morons* instead of *On Kings*. For one thing, they would have made editors and readers very uncomfortable with their language. "Great person," even "great man," is easier to say and to equip as a cross-cultural tool of comparison than "moron."[7] Currently, the agreed upon umbrella term for the condition of people with cognitive limitations is "cognitive, intellectual and/or developmental disabilities" (or sometimes I/DD). Believe me, I know how moron sounds. I feel like I am betraying Charlie even uttering the words, but language is so alien to him that my precious discomfort is in a way laughable. Half the time, I don't know what to call my teenage son, to indicate that he does not, cannot, and may never talk. "Moron" was for a time a way of indicating that kind of inability, whereas the term "autism," on its own, does not.

I am not the first to suggest an affinity between David Graeber's approach to anthropology and that of Edmund Leach (see Edwards, ch. 6 this volume). If there is a lack of fit between entities in the world and the names we apply to them, as Leach argued in an article Graeber was fond of, then it is also true that names for anomalous experiences, things, and people are quickly taken up and appropriated for multiple uses.[8] In another time, not so long ago, I would have learned to call my son mute, dumb, a fool, an idiot, an imbecile, retarded, schizophrenic and, yes, *moron*. Gradually, however, these names for anomalous behavior (that is, intellectual and/or linguistic in-ability) were absorbed into casual terms of verbal abuse to use against *anyone*, including ourselves (I call myself an idiot at least once a day, for example). This has led to the paradoxical situation where terms of abuse for people diagnosed with cognitive disabilities are now utilized to critique, ironically, forms of bigotry and oppression:

Thus, very progressive teachers, researchers, and even activists will use words like moron or idiot even when critiquing racist, sexist, or otherwise offensive behavior, all the while refusing to admit or realize that they are channeling one form of bigotry to attack another.[9]

My use of "moron" is meant to call attention to a widespread history of forgetting, to the stupid historiography of stupidity, whereby people are marked as mentally deviant for social discipline and/or death, only to have these very labels ignorantly appropriated, with seemingly no awareness of the processes that made such labels possible.

I am exploring the utility of Graeber's writing and research partly because some of his work touched on disability in ways that have not been widely recognized (but might have been, see Introduction, this volume. Moreover, there is something useful, I believe in rethinking morons in parallel with his work with Sahlins on kings in particular since it arguably opens up new ways of complicating dominant notions of disability. These assumptions include taking for granted that disability is everywhere considered to be an unfortunate or inauspicious tragedy above all else. As "crip theorists" argue, associating disability with tragedy is less a universal truth, than it is a common morality tale that harms both disabled and able-bodied people alike.[10] My use of "moron" in this chapter is meant to cover cognitive, developmental and/or linguistic disabilities of different kinds. It is rather like a cognitive answer to the term "crip," which disability theorists and activists have also recently re-appropriated (in a direct parallel to other reclaimed words like "queer"). Using "moron" and "crip" as terms of art is meant to call attention to the discomfort these utterances can create and moral assumptions which lie behind that discomfort.[11]

In this chapter I outline the contours of one possible anthropology of people like Charlie (though by no means the only one). I do so to show what this actually reveals about the anthropology of everyone else and so can shed light on ideas from personhood to power and creativity. McKearney and Zoanni point out that taking cognitive disability seriously in ethnographic research challenges assumptions about "the process of ethical subject formation."[12] Thinking in terms of personhood is one way of getting beyond the critique of disability as nothing more than social labels for non-normative behavior. The point of their intervention and mine is not only that our ideas about humankind are wrong, but also that we are making anthropology worse, and by extension the world, by not supporting and talking more about people with disabilities of all kinds.

While it may come as a shock, one of the first and only anthropologists of cognitively disabled persons, Edgerton, was also quite influential in shifting political policies toward them. And, as Klotz notes, this had some negative consequences, specifically insofar as disability justice has normally excluded people who are profoundly intellectually disabled, that is, morons.[13]

More than talk about an alternative anthropology of morons, therefore, I want to push the limits of thinking of moron as a kind of being, and consider ways in which it is also, and more interestingly, a mode of action and a way of becoming. My focus will be on people diagnosed with cognitive disabilities in very different contexts (thus involving very different forms of diagnosis and ideas of bodies and minds). This already complicates my comparative approach. At the same time, people with these diagnoses also present a more challenging "other" with whom anthropologists have yet to adequately reckon and, as Tyrion Lannister said, that doesn't seem right.[14] I start by outlining one way that this might be done, in terms of concepts of morality and personhood, and then turn to a different, more historically, comparatively informed approach. I conclude by considering becoming moron as a challenging and even desirable way forward, against assumptions that stupidity is only ever to be denigrated as unproductive and limiting. We'd certainly do better, I believe at least, to have more morons than more kings.

Exemplary Persons and Moral Imagination

One night we arranged for the dancers of Siem-reap to come and perform in front of the temple. After dinner fifty small torch-bearers came to fetch us at the *sala*, and we traversed the long causeway in a procession, followed by a group of Cambodians who had hastened over from their village. At their head was an idiot, called "king of Angkor," who spends his days among the ruins, crowned with fresh flowers.[15]

The term "stupid" goes back to the very origins of the word *stupidus*, which was actually a Latin term for clown. Clowns were a subject that Graeber actually wrote about quite a lot, often in reference to indigenous Californian rituals that had mortals impersonate gods and act like "gluttons, lechers, and buffoons" with absolute, or king-like authority (see Introduction, this volume).[16] Already this shows an interesting parallel between being "great" and being odd or physically and mentally strange.

Put differently, acting like a god meant overturning ordinary assumptions about how people should act and think. Yet what Graeber did not consider was the reverse possibility: that conceptions of gods and kings might be inspired by everyday "buffoons" in our midst, who might themselves provide a source for conceptions of divinity and kingship and not the other way around. It may be that the temporary and absolute authority of clowns is less critical to understanding the situation than is their buffoonery. It could be, even, that anomalous cognition and action is at the heart of the widespread appearance of king-like persons Graeber and Sahlins observed.[17]

A failure to consider this possibility, one that would take into account how politics and disability mutually shape one another, might be due to Graeber (the avowed anarchist) having considerably more interest in capturing and critiquing authority. Fair enough. But this also accounts for why Graeber leaves aside whether (at least some) clowns are only performing for the occasion or might be acting exactly like they always do. As the quote with which I began this section indicates, "the king of Angkor," at least among some Cambodians in the past, was a village idiot with a crown of flowers. As in many places recorded throughout history and across the world, they are not just an anomalous person but a potential resource for ritual celebration with a perhaps only half-serious label of "king." The fool in this case was born to the part, they are not acting it out it would seem.

Now it could be that the indigenous groups in California that Lowie examined did not make such a distinction, between playing a fool and being one, when it came to cognitive disability (though, if so, that would also be worthy of note). By comparison, in early modern England for example, there was a somewhat commonplace distinction we seem to have inherited between "artificial" and "natural fools," which I will return to later.

Making a connection between morons and great men is partly meant to challenge the overwhelming tendency to depict history, society, and culture almost exclusively as products of "men" who are "great" because of what they accomplish and who are inherently imagined capable of greatness (which all too often just means male, white, straight, able-bodied …). "Great men," from this perspective, are nothing but pure possibility—the source of all that is creative and productive in society. In one of his chapters in *On Kings*, Graeber discusses this in the context of the Malagasy view of the king as child (about which more will be said below) which highlights the view of sovereigns-to-be as "sheer potentiality."[18] "Moron," by contrast, tends to mean the opposite: that someone is not only limited (in intelligence, talent, imagination) but, at the most extreme, inherently incapable of doing much of anything that truly matters. Here it is important to note that "moron" and related terms (fool, dummy, idiot, imbecile …) are not only terms of abuse, as many English-speakers have come to regard them, but also historical diagnoses for kinds of people who are thought too limited in ability to contribute to history, society, or culture. Morons are, in this sense, the very opposite of "great men" as popularly imagined—incapable and dependent on others, rather than leading and guiding others into new worlds of possibility or divine utopias.[19] As I will show, we can actually equally well imagine the opposite—that "morons" have far more potential than anyone.

But if there is an assumed tension between king and moron, one that more or less conforms to what "great men" and "moron" mean in everyday English (in keeping with the quote from *Game of Thrones* with which we began), then arguing that they are actually deeply connected (and that there is a lot of historical and comparative ethnographic support for this connection) might come across as distinctly odd. At the same time, if they are structural opposites of a kind, it is perhaps for this reason that madmen and kings, or the mad and the god-fearing, are so often conjoined. One thinks of the familiar sentiment that many if not all rulers are insane or deluded to think they should be the ones to rule others. Or, in the history of ideas, on the role of idiocy in Locke's treatises on government,[20] or of madness in Descartes (which went on to inspire Derrida and Foucault to quarrel with one another in the early days of post-structuralism).[21]

But this introduces a problem we have to deal with before we can get to the argument at hand: what is greatness anyway? For example, if people depict Donald Trump or Boris Johnson as foolish or as intellectually impaired, as metaphorical and literal morons in other words, does this simultaneously diminish their "greatness"? Probably not. In fact, some people may like the extent to which they think these men appear to talk and think simply and do not act better than them. Graeber himself said something to this effect after George W. Bush was elected:

> If statistics are to be believed, millions of Americans watched George Bush and John Kerry lock horns, concluded that Kerry won, and then went off and voted for Bush anyway. It was hard to escape the suspicion that, in the end, Kerry's articulate presentation, his skill with words and

arguments, had actually counted against him…. This sent liberals into spirals of despair. They could not understand why decisive leadership was equated with acting like an idiot. Neither could they understand how a man who comes from one of the most elite families in the country, who attended Andover, Yale, and Harvard, and whose signature facial expression is a self-satisfied smirk, ever convinced anyone he was a "man of the people."[22]

This can also be based on a rational calculation of sorts. Graeber went on to say that working class people can more easily imagine they could be a millionaire than a culturally effete intellectual (a human rights lawyer, a poet, a film critic). Even if the latter is possible through scholarship and higher education, it might not be ideal for them to imagine. As Leach opined with respect to Kachin politics in Highland Burma, the rational calculation can go the other way too: sometimes people can rest easier when they think their chief is a moron.[23]

In another sense, even when we insult "great men" they live on in the stories we tell ourselves about how not to behave, of models to follow and to reject, which is just greatness in another register (as in "Oz the great and terrible!"). Here greatness might not be equivalent to sheer potentiality per se, but instead serves as an influence on moral thought and imagination more broadly. To put it simply, maybe the only thing that people labeled either "great" or "terrible" have in common is that people like to talk about and learn lessons from them.

This sense of a person's "greatness" is more in line with Caroline Humphrey's interpretation of Mongolian morality. For Humphrey, it is not helpful to begin talking about moral behavior in terms of official or explicit rules, when most of what people seem to do is tell stories. People that Mongolians tell stories about are what she calls "exemplars" and "the more important arena of morality appears in the relation between persons and exemplars or precedents."[24] Other anthropologists of morality and ethics, like James Laidlaw, draw on Humphrey in order to outline a more practical and relational way of making sense of how people do and become good. *Exemplary persons* are those about whom we talk and who inform our moral imaginations by providing examples to follow … and to scorn.

For instance, some Mongolians directly draw on the unwanted possibility of creating more morons when they discuss their love lives. More precisely, stories about possible "deformed and dumb" children shape decision-making about whom to marry:

Some Mongols discourage ethnic intermarriage by invoking a local folk maxim which holds that the offspring of such marriages are usually born deformed and dumb. As one Mongol told me, "We try to hold on to them (Mongol women) in order to protect their children and thus future Mongols."[25]

In these examples, I would argue—in keeping with Humphrey—that what is happening is not so much that people are obeying a maxim ("Thou shalt not intermarry!"), but listening to and sharing stories about imagined morons (i.e. the "deformed and dumb"). These morons would serve as exemplary persons whose real and possible (or virtual) existence motivates decision-making about marriage in place of explicit rules that would punish such actions. As Sahlins writes in *On Kings*, echoing Humphrey, taboos are better seen as the stuff of social relations not moral laws:

> Of course, submission to the powers is evident in punishments for transgressions. But the same is doubly implied when the prospective rule is followed, for, more than an act of respect, to honor a taboo has essential elements of sacrifice, involving the renunciation of some normal practice or social good in favor of the higher power who authorizes it.[26]

Not intermarrying, for these Mongolians, is both about not being related to morons and continuing to relate in a positive way to divine powers-that-be.

So, my first point is this: it is useful to consider a comparative anthropology of morons as analogous to that of kings, at least in principle, since both are figures centrally involved in stories about relating and non-relating with exemplary persons (about wanting to be or become like them or unlike them). I would only add that kings and morons are also contiguous with one another, or practically connected and not only formally (or structurally) similar. This further challenges reductive and medicalized depictions of disability that many disability activists understandably resist. If those activists are less familiar with anthropology, I would suggest, it might be because we have not done a better job showing such activists the possibilities that a comparative approach can offer. But first, I want to show how anthropology can and often does do the very opposite, which is to present severe disability as purely unfortunate and something most societies would logically seek to avoid.

Divine/Sacred Kingship and Holy Fools

Better a witty fool than a foolish wit.[27]

> The ethnographic literature is full of examples of anomalous beings—
> human or otherwise—who are treated simultaneously as exalted and
> profoundly dangerous, or that alternate between the two.[28]

As anthropologists are fond of pointing out, nothing is strange if you put it in the context of the broader ethnographic record. Put differently: almost anything, any way of seeing or doing things, is possible. In a lesser-known, joint article, "Farewell to the 'Childhood of Man'" cited in note 28, Davids Wengrow and Graeber demonstrate this with reference to the discovery of burials from the Paleolithic era, filled with two things that might seem incongruous: grave goods and "physically anomalous people," that is, people who would likely be labeled "disabled" if they lived in today's Europe. They later use some of this in their popular book (*Dawn of Everything*). In both they point out that, from the perspective of the Western elites who overwhelmingly make up archaeology, this appears like a strange finding—the grave goods, rare objects of value, suggest importance and power, while the human remains suggest weakness and misfortune. But, the two Davids suggest, this is only inexplicable if you maintain a specific, and decidedly negative idea about people with anomalous bodies. That negative idea usually goes like this: If you are born with or end up with a disability, or if someone you care for or about has this happen to them, then that is tragic, maybe worse than death but certainly something no reasonable person would want for themselves. These connected ideas form part of what is known by crip theorists as "compulsory able-bodiedness."[29] In contrast, the simplest, most economical way to explain Paleolithic remains is to imagine that the people who buried these bodies and goods did not entertain such notions.

By challenging this negative appraisal of bodily anomaly, Wengrow and Graeber are siding with a core position taken up by critical disability studies over the last two decades. This has meant a shift from primarily struggling for disability rights, which specifically relates to people with disabilities, to also dismantling systemic ableism, which affects everyone.

Let's return to moral personhood, *pace* Humphrey, which is where we get back to exemplary persons and their relationship with morons.

Evidence for a functional role for morons in social life still endure in terms like "village idiot," which suggest a time when specific communities would have intellectually anomalous people whose difference was considered somehow "mental" but did not mark them for removal, elimination, or imprisonment for treatment, as it later would with a growing obsession with reasonable behavior, labor markets, and the rise of the medical gaze. Thanks to William Shakespeare, many people are familiar with the role of un-reason, of folly, as counterparts to sovereign rulers, which most often takes the form of the court jester. Unfortunately, partly owing to the historical imagery provided by Shakespeare and other early modern writers, fools are normally imaged as having been paid performers with the wit to challenge norms and, occasionally, to speak truth to power. We are back to Lowie and Graeber's example of indigenous Californian clowns—seemingly ordinary people *acting like* gluttonous, lecherous, divine buffoons.

In fact, the relationship between morons and kings goes beyond the employment of people who merely act incompetent. Going back at least to the Epic of Gilgamesh,[30] kings have partly shown their kingliness by adopting and caring for people with severe mental incompetence. Some writers consider this to have been a way to keep kings humble or aware of their own mortality and imperfection in comparison with the divine. Yet this also makes a certain amount of sense, given what Graeber and Sahlins say about kingship cross-culturally and historically. Kings, on the one hand, partly stand out because they are heavily dependent on others, who not only give them their power but literally care for and carry the sovereign, making them seem rather like children ... or like some people with disabilities. As they write, "there is at the same time a mutually constitutive relation between the king's containment and his power: the very taboos that constrain him are also what render him a transcendent metabeing."[31] Furthermore:

> Just as assertions of the absolute power of the sovereign are also, tacitly, assertions of the absolute equality of his subjects (at least in relation to him), so assertions of metahuman power are also ipso facto ways of asserting that mortal humans are—in all the most important ways—the same.[32]

In comparison with kings, everyone else is just ordinary. Everyone but morons.

There are darker ways of considering this complementarity that I detest. If kings are those typically with the power to kill anyone, then people with severe disabilities (in many examples, cross-culturally and historically) have also been described as those that anyone can kill. If kings make everyone else ordinary by comparison, it's as if morons make everyone a king. To quote Graeber again, "Whether [kings] were said to embody a god is not the issue. The point is that they act like gods—or even God—and get away with it."[33] As Edgerton pointed out over half a century ago, there is no evidence that some societies must murder severely disabled or anomalous infants more than others—due to harsher environmental conditions, for instance; but, at the same time there is abundant evidence that just about every society has people that entertain the notion.[34]

This puts kingly decisions to have a courtly fool in a different light. What better way for an actual king to reassert their exclusive monopoly over killability, and in so doing potentially demonstrate their divine beneficence, than to adopt eminently killable persons under their protection?

Whatever the validity of this proposal (and it is purely hypothetical, of course), Graeber and Sahlins make clear how the capacity for anonymous violence, meaning violence against anyone at any time for any reason, is not purely a practical exercise of power for would-be monarchs, but a symbolic act that shows them to be exemplary persons outside the ordinary rules of right and wrong, rules that otherwise keep the rest of us in line. This is where the divine king and the sacred king are worth teasing apart (as Graeber does in their book). His model resolves the tension by pointing out that being set apart as special (or sacred) is as much a solution to, as an outcome of, the divine power to kill anyone indiscriminately, as if the king is a force of nature and not an ordinary human. Like a twisted realization of Giorgio Agamben's idea of sovereign exception, divine/sacred kings are figures who show in their violent example what no one else can get away with. If they are moral exemplars, in other words, they are not showing people an example to imitate but are instead making clear where the line is that divides the fates of ordinary mortals from a more divine realm beyond good and evil. Kings would be like *amoral* exemplars. There is a way in which the moronic exemplar is similar. In fact, a case could be made that kings and severely disabled people may both be perceived as simultaneously dependent on others and free from normal moral decision-making. They are both extraordinary, both exemplars, set apart from and thereby constituting the broader moral order.

Evidence for this lies in the fact that people diagnosed with cognitive disabilities may exert a great deal of influence in social interactions, having what amounts to an outsized presence in the lives of those around them. Danilyn Rutherford describes this with respect to children in a special educational setting in the United States, all of whom have language difficulties:

> If a conversation is a game of ping pong, "defective speakers" have a habit of pocketing the ball. This is one way of thinking about sovereignty—as the power to take without returning, to turn one's back and face another world, and in doing so to compel a response.[35]

And with some kings and morons, this sense of outsized power is translated further into a divine/sacred stature, as Sahlins and Graeber make clear, giving kings a place in the cosmic pantheon. "And the more absolute their power, the greater that dependency will also tend to be."[36]

The same is found with various "holy fools," for example among Egyptian fellahin, for whom village "half-wits" grow in holy power as time goes on, may possess others, and have shrines built to them.[37] Yet other people have "dumb" gods, some of whom are also slaves, as found among Kiribati:

> Naubwebwe, on the other hand, is an old black man, evidently no relation of the beings in Matang. His look is slavish; his occupation of cleaning up rubbish on the road is that of a slave; he grins and grimaces like an idiot—or a slave, for the word rang applied to him in the context has both significations in Gilbertese; and he is dumb, which is the first mark of slavery in the estimation of the Islanders. Yet evidences of a former greatness still cling about him: his art is the wau "cat's cradle", of which he is the presiding deity, and in the changing patterns of the wau, as old men assert, an expert could portray the successive stages of creation.[38]

A slave, idiot god is about as far one can go in the direction of bringing one's deities down to size, for many people at any rate, and yet "evidences of former greatness still cling about him" and, more importantly, he is still an exemplar, still worth talking about.

The connection between cosmic divinity and idiocy is not confined to instances like these. For one thing, there are more pragmatic and clearly documented examples where kings relate to morons for more straightforward reasons. According to Edgerton, at one time the Hehe of Tanzania and the Tiv in Nigeria had chiefs who would make use of "morons" in order to deliver summons or reach out to difficult tribesmen. According to one chief, "he was used because everyone knew he was so stupid that there was no point in interrogating him about the mood of the chief."[39] But in some circumstances morons can also be exalted as if they were more powerful than they are. There are at least two versions of a popular saying among Shona of Southern Africa, documented by both Gelfand and Devlieger: "If one has a child who is an idiot, if it dances to drums, one ululates at its performance."[40] My own compulsion is to interpret this as reflecting an obligation, on the part of caregivers of morons, to appreciate their unusual behavior instead of being embarrassed by it. For example, if my son Charlie hums and stims, twiddling his fingers or mine for instance, I should "ululate" rather than feel shame and try and make him stop, to force him to fit in.

But comparison is pointless if it fails to acknowledge the alternative life-worlds that underlie these partial connections and make them possible. Aschwanden and Cooper's ethnography with the Southern Shona (the Karanga) complicates my rather secular, liberal reading.[41] Not everyone who deviates from expectations is treated the same and this has more to do with ideas about sin and punishment, spirits and God. For one thing, while "idiots" might be occasionally celebrated, if a child develops early incisors they may be dehumanized/animalized as similar to the "dirty" spirit of a crocodile and put to death for this deviation from the norm. Dirtiness is thought by these Shona to result from having resumed intercourse (a "dirty" activity for them) too soon after childbirth, a taboo the violation of which leads to sperm polluting the mother's blood and then the breast milk given to the infant. Once again, the taboo in question is a way of (not) relating, both with other persons sexually and to meta-persons, here animal spirits, coupled to the refusal to relate any further with infants suggesting their presence.

Where the "dirty" infants bearing these deformities are purportedly killed (though in no society does everyone always obey all taboos), idiots are thought to have a different origin and this reveals a more complex relationship to the divinity of sin and innocence:

[T]he Karanga call a mentally deranged person ndimwari, "he is God, do not harm him." (There is a kind of mental illness which is God's punishment for a serious crime, but we are here considering only mental illness caused by witchcraft). The Karanga say of a mentally deranged person that his head has been confused by an evil influence and that he can no longer distinguish between good and evil. Therefore, his soul is innocent of sin, and if he sins it is only his body that does so. The Karanga believe that a madman has almost reverted to the state in which his soul could return straight to God since it is without evil—like the soul of an aborted baby (also called ndimwari) which returns immediately to where it came from: to God.[42]

For these Shona, any relationship between a person and someone impaired in this way, or "mad," is not simply binary, insofar as it involves a relationship between the able-bodied person, the less able person, and divine and/or sacred meta-beings.

Human societies the world over are not only interdependent with societies of other kinds, they are also dependent for their own existence on relations with humans of other kinds. I mean the gods, ancestors, ghosts, demons, species-masters, and other such metapersons, including those inhabiting plants, animals, and natural features: in sum, the host of "spirits"—wrongly so-called; they are this-worldly and indeed have the attributes of persons—the host of whom are endowed with life-and-death powers over the human population.[43]

The moron resembles a meta-person, a species of exemplary person, as a result of this connection:

Another peculiarity of the idiot is his behaviour towards his fellow men. When they speak to him he sometimes does not reply; one never knows how he is going to react, he is entirely unpredictable. It is the same with God, the Karanga say, he does not answer us, and he is free to act as he likes. This is why they call a madman ndimwari, "he is God". Even when he commits a crime they make excuses for him by saying an evil spirit misused him. One might even suspect an identification here and, thus, a symbol. The Karanga expression ndimwari can be translated by "he is God", but they reject as impossible the suggestion that the madman really is God (Mwari chaiye). The nearest interpretation of ndimwari might be: "he is of God", or "God allows it to happen."[44]

This would seem to go further in demonstrating a contiguous link between cosmo-political otherworldly forces and morons in otherwise radically different contexts.

The point is not that morons will always be seen as powerful in this way, they might instead be considered dangerous or impure, as in need of locking up and reform as Foucault argued became the modernizing institutional imperative (though according to Graeber, following Durkheim, this would only lend further weight to their sacredness at having been set apart). Following Humphrey, morons institutionalized or hidden from view remain powerful nonetheless, not least because they often serve as what I term (a)moral exemplars about whom, the medical gaze aside, many people seem to love to tell stories, even if only to pity them or hurl abuse at others. This is perhaps very different from early modern village idiots, or contemporary Egyptian or Shona reflections, but it shows the rich and largely unexamined role of morons in cultural life.[45]

What is clear is that, no less than divine and sacred kings as explored by Sahlins and Graeber, holy fools, powerful mutes, and godly idiots have a role in the cosmopolities that some anthropologists have occasionally documented. And yet, we have had less to say about them, in general, than we have about the able-minded and "great." I had to dig through ethnographic files and texts for the examples I provided above. After all, the book does not exist where I could find them in one place: no *How Morons Think*, no *La Pensée débile*, no *Gender of the Moron* and, finally, no *On Morons*. As Tyrion Lannister says, that doesn't seem right.

Get Stupid

> Everybody, everybody, just get into it, get stupid
> Get retarded, get retarded, get retarded
> Let's get retarded (Ha), let's get retarded (In here)
> Let's get retarded (Ha), let's get retarded (In here)
> Let's get retarded (Ha), let's get retarded (In here)
> Let's get retarded (Ha), let's get retarded (In here), yeah.
>   — Black Eyed Peas[46]

Edgerton recognized half a century ago that linguistic and mental incompetence provide the most challenging form of difference to human scientists.[47] After all, if there is one form of competence they take the most for granted, as products and practitioners of formal university education, it is the value of intelligence over stupidity and words over silence.

In the back of my head, I hear an objection to this whole chapter. It goes like this: "Disability is not universal! Different people in time and space have considered different things disabling. Some societies have treated twins or left-handed people as if they had disabilities. So this comparative focus on morons is doomed from the start!" But I want to turn this criticism back on itself. Holding that "disability is not a universal category" also expresses an unresolved contradiction.

The reason some scholars are confident in asserting that "disability" (or anything at all) has no universal, cross-cultural, trans-historical meaning is that people have *competently written, spoken about*, and *translated* ideas about human difference in particular ways in distinct places and times. Any representation of alternative ideas of "disability" arose out of successful interactions between people with sufficient competence to convey ideas about "disability" across time and space. In other words, the most radically different ideas about bodies and minds anthropologists and historians provide still rely on bodies and minds capable of transmitting information about such difference in the first place. Paradoxically, challenges to the category "disability" rely on taken-for-granted conceptions of *shared ability* transcending apparent divides in cultural or historical cosmology. Either competence is truly, radically different across contexts, and therefore no translation of ideas across domains can be trusted since competence can never be gained or grasped in a shared way, or anthropology in its normal guise is essentially a neurotypical, normative enterprise.[48]

Getting back to our argument, if the modern exaltation of reason arose in part by creating and controlling people marked as "irrational" and "mad," then the social reproduction of intelligent and verbal professionals exists against a taken-for-granted background of the unintelligent and mute. Put simply, really smart folks needed and still need really dumb folks to exist, both symbolically (as their supposed structural opposite) and practically (as people to define, dehumanize, diagnose, and ruminate over).

But outside of academia, there of course are many ways of being and becoming a person between the extremes of "moron" and "king."[49] For centuries, clowns played with the reified distinction between being great and being a moron, showing how thin or non-existent the barrier is separating these as "kinds" of being and suggesting, even more radically, that they are better understood as ways anyone can be. Thanks to Shakespeare, we have an enduring glimpse into the sometimes radical role of so-called "artificial fools" in the lives of early modern elites, but he had comparatively little to say about how these performers relied for their inspiration on "natural fools." Information about this comes, instead, from Robert Armin, one of the Bard's favorite actors.[50] In Armin's *Foole upon Foole* (otherwise entitled *A Nest of Ninnies*), Shakespeare's favorite clown outlined something like a natural description of the ecology of transgressive foolishness in the Elizabethan era. Yet reading his work closely, "reveals the variety of conditions that could be denoted by the term 'natural'."[51]

Indeed, the very distinction between natural and artificial betrays a neglect of how uneven conditions of debility can harm minds just as they do bodies.[52] From this point of view, otherwise "ordinary" minds can become or be made moronic ones through hierarchical structures, kingly or otherwise. There was, for instance, a short-lived debate in the mid 1970s over whether "brain damage" could be considered a byproduct of inequality—according to well-known critic of biological race, Ashley Montagu's "sociogenic" theory—and which scholars Charles and Bettylou Valentine found theoretically one-sided and politically suspect.[53] What all seem to agree on is that being a moron is not simply a thing one is or is not, but like all ways of being exists within fields of power and difference.

Leaving that critical matter aside, it is clear that, for Armin at least, some natural fools are distinctly king-like. That is, they are not too dissimilar in their behavior from the Californian clowns with which we began:

Armin's fools, first of all, impress us with their gluttony. One maliciously eats and spoils the fresh cheeses in the dairy house and later eats a hawk, feathers and all, because he heard tell of its "goodness". Another burns his face in the oven in an attempt to get at some pies. Two of the fools are naughty enough to require whipping; two others are oblivious to the value of money; another pair make bad messengers. Three of the fools drivel from the nose and mouth. Two are jealous of artificial fools who try to take their places, and another pair are susceptible to the flattery of being addressed as gentlemen. More important, the fools are petulant and stubborn, continually involved with violence both to person and property. Their selfish and childish actions point up the risk, whatever the comic relief, in keeping a natural fool in the court of household.[54]

According to H.F. Lippincott, Armin's fools were placed in direct contrast with the witty, self-aware kind in Shakespeare's plays. Instead, like kings whose courts they might occupy, fools may stand outside ordinary measures of right and wrong like amoral exemplars, seeking only pleasure.

A more recent example of Armin's idea or Lowie's clowns is Lars von Trier's controversial 1998 film *The Idiots* about a situationist collective who cause public scenes by "spassing" as if they were natural fools. Here playing the kingly fool is a way of acting, a role to inhabit, that is potentially open to anyone.

> The group spass, or fake mental disability, taking turns acting as a minder or spasser, respectively. They do this for hours on end, both privately and very much in public. They spass in fine restaurants, biker bars, and public swimming pools, creating mayhem and acute discomfort wherever they go. They take their act on the road, going door to door selling costly but poorly constructed Chinese ornaments to their wealthy neighbors and taking guided educational tours of local businesses.[55]

The apparent lesson here, beyond its relevance to the film-making process, is that we all can be kings or exemplary persons. Over the course of the film, a new recruit joins their ranks. Not only are the group free, in other words, but *the way in which they act free* can inspire others to rethink radical freedom.

There have been critiques of *The Idiots* as ableist (just as there were of the Black Eyed Peas song with which I began this conclusion), and on the same grounds: as rudely affecting moronic behavior. But, with others, I ask to whom they are offensive? And to what end? One might consider admonitions against performing as a moron as something primarily done to comfort the sensibilities of the able-bodied and neurotypical. Change the name from "Let's Get Retarded" to "Let's Get it Started" or from "the Idiots" to "the Learning Impaired" and "we" get to go back to living within polite, bourgeois systems where the line between ordinary and deviant is clear and undeniable. Similarly, I could offend less if I did a "find and delete" and replaced every use of "moron" in this chapter with "diagnosed cognitive disability." But what would be lost when that polite comfort is gained?

In *The Idiots*, giving over to becoming a fool, becoming a moron, is an expression of freedom as much as it is about challenging the status quo.

Both narratively and in its sloppy production, the film "is about allowing oneself the freedom to be careless, to not care, which is quietly recognized as one of our culture's greatest taboos."[56] More to the point, like Graeber also did, Von Trier's cast make clear how much of the everyday culture of capitalism involves obedience to basic social constraints on proper bodily movement and proper speech. The liberal contract after all, as Durkheim and Mauss noted, is a moral and social bond. The main result of the idiot's performances in the von Trier film is that people pay for them to leave.

Disability was never a central concern for Graeber over the course of his career, but it very well could have been. As outlined most clearly in his writing on value and cosmology, Graeber was an avowed Heraclitean who repeatedly asserted that reality was subject to the inevitable forces of process and change and that, as a result, a lot of social and cultural systems are put in place to contend with this fundamental fact of life. Similarly, in disability studies it has long been recognized that ability is only ever temporary and bodily change and loss are inevitable. This reality only spurs on the ever-more-intensive commodification of bodily capital within neoliberal work discipline (the mad rush to hold on to attractiveness, energy, effort ...). And this all but ensures that nearly everyone feels like their body is flawed and failing them, a condition that Lennard Davis diagnoses as *dismodernism*, and which of course throws out the whole notion of normal to begin with.[57]

One way of calling attention to these wounds afflicted on all of us by transnational capitalism is to get retarded, to become morons, to throw into question the structure of everyday norms that guarantee the (somewhat) smooth running of bourgeois society. What makes this different from mere resistance is that flouting norms of acting and thinking is not merely a form of concrete, situationist resistance but, as any king knows, as my son knows, as Graeber knew, is also freeing and can be a whole lot of fun.

Graeber was no fan of kings or of stupidity. The latter he mostly used to criticize systems that he disagreed with, as in his Malinowski lecture on power/knowledge (later published in *Utopia of Rules*). In *Dawn of Everything* he and Wengrow take a moment to make a point about human universals, "Not only do we look the same, in many ways we act the same as well (for instance, everywhere from the Australian outback to Amazonia, rolling one's eyes is a way of saying, 'what an idiot!')."[58] Like most people, they are seemingly unaware and unbothered that this term of abuse ("idiot") has been appropriated from past labels for cognitively disabled persons.

Yet, later in the same book, they also point out that views of extreme and non-conforming individuals are far from universal or universally negative.[59] It may be that rolling eyes is quasi-universal, in other words, but what counts as unacceptable behavior varies widely. To combine their language and mine, a moron is not necessarily an idiot.

Beyond what creative uses of becoming moron can mean for social collectives and artistic projects, explorations of a shared bodily repertoire for communication and experience can also prove valuable to the lives of people diagnosed with cognitive disabilities. This also charts a course beyond the limiting—yet critical—domain of liberal disability rights discourse. As Rutherford puts it, the struggle for disability justice is also "a matter of becoming, which turns on our collective ability to open ourselves to new ways of being with one another."[60] I look up to Rutherford and admire her relationship with her disabled daughter Millie, and I've found her work helpful to take a cue from the emerging but mostly non-existent anthropology of morons I have sketched out here. I can't speak for Millie as (I think) I can Charlie. But I hope some of what I have laid out means something to others who stand out in a similar, spectacular fashion as Charlie does, as Graeber did.

Instead of someone dependent and pitiable, in truth my son is more like a royal figure. Charlie will likely never work a job, own property, suffer heartbreak or worry about the outcome of political elections or the fate of his soul. But we sure tell stories about him. I'm doing so now. Basically his job, every day, is to indulge himself, to be comfortable in his surroundings and have a good time. We do our best to support our little king in these efforts. Everyone should be so lucky as he is, as we are.

Notes

1.   On *Game of Thrones* and disability, see Katie M. Ellis, "Cripples, Bastards and Broken Things: Disability in *Game of Thrones*," *M/C Journal* 17, no.5 (2014).

2.   David Graeber and Marshall Sahlins, *On Kings* (Chicago: Hau Books, 2017).

3.   Robert Edgerton, "Mental Retardation in Non-Western Societies: Toward a Cross-Cultural Perspective on Incompetence," in *Social-Cultural Aspects of Mental Retardation*, ed. H. Carl Haywood (New York: Appleton Century Crofts, 1970), 523–559; Jani Klotz, "Sociocultural Study of Intellectual Disability: Moving Beyond Labelling and Social Constructionist Perspectives," *British Journal of Learning Disabilities* 32 (2004): 93–104; Patrick

McKearney and Tyler Zoanni, "Introduction: For an Anthropology of Cognitive Disability," *Cambridge Journal of Anthropology* 36, no. 1 (2018): 1–22.

4. McKearney and Zoanni, "Introduction," 2.

5. On the history of the invention of words like "moron" and the supposed "discovery" of deviant subjects to fit that label, see Steven Gelb, "Social Deviance and the Discovery of the Moron," *Disability, Handicap & Society* 2, no. 3 (1987): 247–258; Jay Dolmage, "Disabled Upon Arrival: The Rhetorical Construction of Disability and Race at Ellis Island," *Cultural Critique* 77 (2011): 24–69.

6. He points out that such ecological aspects also depend on whether "mind" is taken to be something internal. See Tyler Zoanni, "The Ecology of Disabled Minds in Urban Uganda," *Medical Anthropology* 40, no 2 (2012):169–181.

7. Gelb, "Social Deviance."

8. Edmund Leach, "Anthropological Aspects of Language: Animal Categories and Verbal Abuse," *Anthrozoos* 2, no. 3 (1989 [1964]): 151–165.

9. Jay Dolmage, *Academic Ableism: Disability and Higher Education* (Ann Arbor: University of Michigan Press, 2017), 37.

10. Alison Kafer, *Feminist, Queer, Crip* (Indianapolis: University of Indiana Press, 2013); Robert McCruer, *Crip Theory: Cultural Signs of Queerness and Disability* (New York: New York University Press, 2006).

11. I am doing so in order to "crip" our language for non-normative bodies and minds as some disability theorists argue, following strategies developed in queer theory.

12. McKearney and Zoanni, "Introduction," 14.

13. Klotz, "Sociocultural Study of Intellectual Disability."

14. And by "we" here I mean anthropologists and readers of anthropological texts.

15. Roland Dorgelès, *On the Mandarin Road* (New York and London: Century, 1926), 258.

16. Graeber and Sahlins, *On Kings*, 382.

17. In fact, Graeber and Wengrow come close to asserting this in their later book, where they consider that "extreme individuals" could embody radical and revolutionary potential for cultural creativity. David Graeber and David Wengrow, *The Dawn of Everything* (New York: Penguin, 2021), 98.

18. Graeber and Sahlins, *On Kings*, 337.

19. McKearney also discusses how cognitive disability challenges liberal conceptions of independence for exactly this reason. Patrick McKearney, "What Escapes Persuasion: Why Intellectual Disability Troubles 'Dependence' in Liberal Societies," *Medical Anthropology* 40, no. 2 (2021): 155–168.

20. Stacy Clifford Simplican, *The Capacity Contract: Intellectual Disability and the Question of Citizenship* (Minneapolis: University of Minnesota Press, 2015).

21. Paul Rekret, *Derrida and Foucault: Philosophy, Politics and Polemics* (London and New York: Rowman & Littlefield, 2018).

22. David Graeber, *Revolutions in Reverse* (London and New York: Minor Compositions, 2011), 121.

23. Edmund Leach, *Political Systems of Highland Burma* (New York: Berg, 2004 [1954]).

24. Caroline Humphrey, "Exemplars and Rules: Aspects of the Discourse of Moralities in Mongolia," In *The Ethnography of Moralities*, ed. Signe Howell (London: Routledge, 2007), 25.

25. William Jankowiak, *Sex, Death, and Hierarchy in a Chinese City: An Anthropological Account* (New York: Columbia University Press, 1993), 55.

26. Graeber and Sahlins, *On Kings*, 31.

27. William Shakespeare, *Twelfth Night* (New York: Penguin, 2016), 15.

28. David Wengrow and David Graeber, "Farewell to the 'Childhood of Man': Ritual, Seasonality, and the Origins of Inequality," *Journal of the Royal Anthropological Institute* 2, no. 3 (2015): 9.

29. Kafer, *Feminist, Queer, Crip*; McCruer, *Crip Theory: Cultural Signs of Queerness and Disability*.

30. Edgar Kellenberger, "Mesopotamia and Israel," in *Disability in Antiquity*, ed. Christian Laes (London and New York: Routledge, 2017).

31. Graeber and Sahlins, *On Kings*, 4.

32. Ibid., 20.

33. Ibid., 74.

34. Edgerton, "Mental Retardation."

35. Danilyn Rutherford, "The Sovereignty of Vulnerability," in *Sovereignty Unhinged*, eds. Joseph Masco and Deborah Thomas (London and Durham, NC: Duke University Press, 2023).

36. Graeber and Sahlins, *On Kings*, 249.

37. Nicholas S. Hopkins, "Spirit Mediumship In Upper Egypt," *Anthropos* 102, no 2 (2007).

38. Arthur Grimble, *Tungaru Traditions: Writings on the Atoll Culture of the Gilbert Islands* (Honolulu: University of Hawaii Press, 1989).

39. Edgerton, "Mental Retardation," 536.

40. Michael Gelfand, *Growing Up in Shona Society: From Birth to Marriage* (Gwelo, Rhodesia: Mambo Press, 1979); Patrick Devlieger, "Incompetence in America in Comparative Perspective," in *Questions of Competence: Culture, Classification and Intellectual Disability*, ed. Richard Jenkins (Cambridge: Cambridge University Press, 1998), 68.

41. Herbert Aschwanden and Ursula Cooper, *Symbols of Life: An Analysis of the Consciousness of the Karanga* (Gweru: Mambo Press, 1982).

42. Ibid., 17.

43. Graeber and Sahlins, *On Kings*, 346.

44. Aschwanden and Cooper, *Symbols of Life*, 17.

45. See Deliane Jannette Burck, *Kuoma Rupandi=(The Parts Are Dry): Ideas and Practices Concerning Disability and Rehabilitation in a Shona Ward* (Leiden: Afrika Studiecentrum, 1989).

46. Black Eyed Peas, "Let's Get Retarded," 2003. This title and these lyrics were changed to "Let's Get Started" in response to criticism of the song as ableist. I want to thank Oana Mateescu for encouraging me to develop this later part of the argument.

47. See Klotz, "Sociocultural Study of Intellectual Disability," for a review and a critique.

48. See Erin Durban, "Anthropology and Ableism," *American Anthropologist* 124, no. 4 (2021): 1–14.

49. Thanks to Luiz Costa for this insight.

50. H.F. Lippincott, "King Lear and the Fools of Robert Armin," *Shakespeare Quarterly* 26, no. 3 (1975): 245.

51. Peter Cockett, "Performing Natural Folly: The Jests of Lean Leanard and the Touchstones of Robert Armin and David Tennant," *NTQ* 22, no. 2 (2009): 144.

52. Recent attention to debility in critical disability studies is owed in large part to Jasbir Puar, *The Right to Maim: Debility, Capacity, Disability* (London and Durham, NC: Duke University Press, 2017).

53. See Charles and Bettylou Valentine, "Brain Damage and the Intellectual Defense of Inequality," *Current Anthropology* 16, no. 1 (1975): 117–150.

54. Lippincott, "King Lear and the Fools of Robert Armin," 245.

55. Tim Walters, "Reconsidering *The Idiots*: Dogme95, Lars von Trier, and the Cinema of Subversion?" *The Velvet Light Trap* 53, no. 1 (2004): 44.

56. Ibid., 42.

57. Lennard Davis, *Bending over Backwards: Essays on Disability and the Body* (New York: NYU, 2002); Nirmala Erevelles, *Disability and Difference in Global Contexts* (New York: Palgrave Macmillan, 2011). Moreover, while bodily failure might be a universal condition, in some formal Heraclitean sense, and especially exaggerated within late capitalist societies, it is still unevenly distributed as a form of misfortune or harm, afflicting hundreds of millions of Black and indigenous people of color who are debilitated by transnational capitalism, environmental devastation, and historical oppression.

58. Graeber and Wengrow *The Dawn of Everything*, 80.

59. Ibid., 102–104.

60. Danilyn Rutherford, "Proximity to Disability," *Anthropological Quarterly* 93, no. 1 (2020): 1478.

2

Birthing Possibilities

· Holly High ·

I

There is a moment in September 2020 that is preserved with strange clarity in my memory: I was sitting on the brown leather sofa at home, then in the southern highlands south of Sydney, when my phone buzzed and the screen lit up. "I just wondered if you saw that," a former student had texted, with a link to a news story. When I read the article, I had a ludicrous moment of denial. "Is this a hoax?" I shot back, slightly irritated. But my student gently pointed out that David Graeber's agent had confirmed it: Graeber was dead.

During those September days, I had been preoccupied with online teaching, beaming out lectures and tutorials from a home-office (jammed in awkwardly behind a piano in the lounge room). The pandemic was biting deep across the world, and even as teaching expanded into the online space, still my world felt reduced. COVID-19 had come to us in Australia so soon after our Black Summer, when the southeast eucalypt forests burned as they never had before. For months, with every breath, we grimly took in the incineration of millions of wild animals. Graeber once described himself as a "professional optimist."[1] He never ignored violence or injustice in his work, yet he still always saw great possibilities for we humans. I kept wondering what he would have made of these days of fire and plague. What paths out? For weeks the news of his death left me in tears at odd moments. I counted myself among David's friends, but we were not particularly close. It wasn't clear to me what, exactly, I was grieving. So, between teaching, I wrote.

My lectures and tutorials that September were for first-year students: I was introducing them to the discipline—to this "passion for difference" that I believe to be anthropology's gift[2]—by discussing something we all have in common: being born. I invited students to interview their mothers or care providers about the circumstances of the students' own births. I had been trying to teach them that listening to stories is important; that cultural context, difference, and change do exist and can be understood; and that, though cultural messaging, and norms and structures, and natures necessarily shape us, we are, nonetheless, capable of freedom. In those first weeks after David's death, I realized I wanted to write that his anthropology opened possibilities for thinking anew about birth. But my first drafts were angry. I quarreled with him for not mentioning this and not theorizing that. He never directly engaged with the anthropology of birth. Perhaps I was just passing through another stage of grief: the angry one. Or perhaps it is just that, when we value something, when it becomes a token of value for us (to use Graeber's phrasing from his 2001 book *False Coins of Our Own Dreams*), on some level we always know that we see in it something that is not there. And that something we value, that hidden dimension—which we so often misperceive as the power of valuable objects—Graeber suggested, is in fact *our own* capacity to act. That has been my experience of grief, too. The force of it—the disbelief, anger, and loss—is disorientating, but resolution can be found when the lost is understood as also somehow kept.

This chapter is the result of thinking about the anthropology of birth alongside David Graeber's anthropology. Although not usually thought of together, there is a significant kinship: both can be read as examples of activist anthropology and show the potentials (and pitfalls) of an anthropology that chooses to rebel. I argue that these two threads of the discipline can be joined in ways productive for both.

II

As a child of my time, I did not think particularly deeply about birth until the prospect of my own labor was on the horizon. In preparation for the birth, I asked my grandmother, then in her eighties, what to expect.

It was a family gathering in June 2013. We were sitting side by side at the long, polished dining table that fills almost the entire dining room of a cedar-wood farmhouse outside a town in the Great Dividing Range of New South Wales, where we'd spent many Christmas lunches. We were just a few kilometers from where she had raised her five children, at first in a shed on the land her husband had been granted after he returned from World War II. Pa never spoke about the war, except to severely ban us from pointing a gun, even a toy one, at anyone, ever. When I was an adult, I realized the land we were on had been taken from Indigenous people. My mother said that some of those first owners lived in a camp on the country there and worked odd jobs as Pa and Joan's sheep farm was established. I do know that one of the nurses that cared for Joan in her last days was a descendant of the people that had lived in that camp, but that is all I know. That is another conversation I never had with Joan.

When Joan had her first child, she told me, her father would come to visit from town. One-way, the journey took a full day by horse and cart, stopping and stepping down every few kilometers to open a gate and shut it behind him. It was not until her fourth child was born that the home they had been building—a pink, architect-designed, flat-roofed, 1950s beauty, incongruously placed on a dusty rise with a far-sighted outlook across the paddocks—was ready for the family to live in. They also acquired a car, and Joan and Pa would make the long drive into town jubilantly singing "*Qué será, será*" to the children, to distract them, my mother thought, or perhaps simply from the infectious optimism that seemed to saturate the mood of 1950s Australia. Pa died from Parkinson's Disease when I was a child. Much later, I learned that his children believed that this was likely due to his exposure to chemicals during his work on the farm. But no one spoke of this to me at the time. At his funeral, we heard that, in his dying days, he said of his life: "I married the woman I loved and put a dam in every paddock."

I was leaning toward Joan across my new and strange belly, and her smile seemed to say: no judgment that your pregnancy preceded any sort of marriage or even a plan for one. No bad words. No painful memories. Around us, the hubbub of her children, her children's children, and their partners: the joy of the crowd seemed to set a limit on what we could say. When I asked what birth was like, she laughed and told me not to think too much about it: "The doctor will give you something and you will go to sleep. When you wake up, there will be a baby. The doctor will do it all for you." I didn't press her.

Not long after, and before my first child was born, Joan died.

III

Anthropology, my profession, is my other family. By reading and (much more rarely) meeting anthropologists whose work I admire, I have found people willing to have the kind of conversations that might be too difficult in one's real family, but who still have that family-like ability to shape who you are. In pregnancy, I dug out old readings given to me when I was an undergraduate studying anthropology at the Australian National University. I remembered Robbie Davis-Floyd's 1994 article on birth in the United States: I had also given that article to my sister when she was pregnant before me, but it had not clicked for her.[3] For me, though, it provided a searing warning about the implications of the "technocratic" turn taken by biomedical approaches to birth in the twentieth century. Davis-Floyd used Arnold Van Gennep's 1909 concept of rites of passage to interpret the otherwise unnecessary interventions that riddle hospital births, like the use of wheelchairs, monitors, and bizarrely designed delivery beds. Davis-Floyd understood these as symbolic, part of a deeply sexist set of rituals that repeated the cultural messaging that women are faulty birthing machines and that technology provides the only sure means of regenerating life.

According to Van Gennep's formulation, a rite of passage is a series of rituals during which a person who is moving from one status to another undergoes first a period of separation from her previous everyday life, then a liminal stage—a threshold, neither here nor there—and finally a period of reintegration into her new role. Van Gennep included birth as a key rite of passage in his original study, arguing that both mother and child move from one status to another, as evidenced through symbols such as eating prohibitions and bans on work or religious activities.[4] Van Gennep's interpretation of rites of passage was quite conservative, though, inasmuch as he did not seek out the seeds of cultural change in his study, or even really consider the possibility of social change at all. Instead, his emphasis was on how these rites effectively reproduce existing social roles among new initiands. Victor Turner later reinterpreted the liminal stage as a potentially creative space.[5] Turner thought that the liminal stage was a time where the old certainties of life-as-it-had-been become loosened and uncertain, but when at the same time the new certainties of life-as-it-shall-now-be for the initiand in their new status have not yet coalesced. It was true, he acknowledged, that one finds all kinds of conservative symbolism in rites of passage, and that these can predispose initiands to a repetition of the established social order. But one also finds inversions of these, and also suggestions of unorthodox values and possibilities. Turner imagined the liminal stage as a kind of social limbo where one could glimpse all kinds of symbols, including the seeds of other ways of being. As I would later go on to tell my students, we will each pass through rites of passage whether we like it or not and whether we know it or not. These occur when we pass from one status to another, as when a school student becomes a university student, for instance, or when a child is born, or at retirement, and so on. If we can recognize a rite of passage for what it is, though, we do have some measure of freedom: a freedom to accept, or work with, or jam the symbols we live in these times of our lives.[6]

Thinking within this tradition, I sought out the rituals of separation, liminality, and reintegration evident around me in pregnancy. I observed the people nearest to me responding with gifts for the baby. Although I did not have a baby shower, nonetheless it seemed plain that, for many people, preparing for a birth involves the acquisition of goods. Succumbing to this pressure somewhat, my partner and I made a trip to a gigantic baby-goods store and wandered the aisles, not quite convinced of the necessity of any of it but seemingly not quite able to rid ourselves of the sense that at least some gesture was required. We ended up buying an elaborate contraption for the baby to sleep in: I was still unaware, at that time, that infant sleep is another heavily ritualized field of worry and consumerism in our milieu. These revelations were still to come.

Another ritualized element evident in my first pregnancy was worry. I tracked my budding pregnancy through daily urine strip tests, seeking confirmation through the ever-darkening purple line of whether the pregnancy was real or not. On my first consultation with a doctor about the pregnancy, I was told explicitly to worry. "It is a very inefficient process," the GP said, meaning that I would likely miscarry. She prescribed me low-dose aspirin. After a conversation with my partner, I decided not to take it. The GP prescribed an ultrasound at nine weeks to assess if the pregnancy even had a heartbeat. It did. The ultrasound technician seemed as puzzled as I was as to why the ultrasound had been necessary. At twelve weeks, my doctor prescribed a nuchal translucency test to assess risk for Down's syndrome. This again involved an ultrasound. It was quite pleasurable seeing the outline of the little future-person in my belly, but the technician went quiet and left the room to fetch the obstetrician. On arrival, with great gravity, the obstetrician reported that my son's nasal bone did not look normal. In words that are branded into my memory, she said "If you were Asian, we would not be worried. But as you are Caucasian, we would expect a different nose."

On that basis, which to me seemed entirely spurious, along with statistical formulas (largely based on my age), I was given a result of 1 in 17. This represented their assessment of the chance my son had Down's. The obstetrician requested that I consent to an invasive procedure that had a 1 in 100 chance of aborting the fetus. All my instincts told me not to do the procedure. But my partner and the obstetrician persuaded me. With such forceful cultural messaging prodding me into seeing my pregnancy through the eyes of science, my pregnancy looked risky, unsure, full of worry. I had the test. It revealed that the obstetrician's fear had been misplaced.

To this point, my pregnancy conformed to the kind of rites of passage Robbie Davis-Floyd described: the messages were that women's bodies are faulty and inadequate for efficient birthing, that my own ability to reproduce was very questionable in itself: for a successful outcome, I ought to rely on medical technology. The view of my pregnancy afforded by medical technology (such as the pregnancy test strips and the ultrasound images) was surer than my own, and to be a mother at all, and especially to be a good mother, I ought to defer to that way of seeing my pregnancy.

Yet this was not the whole story. The debacle with the nuchal translucency test was a wake-up call for us. We hired a private midwife, Sheryl, and started planning a home birth. Unfortunately, due to an early rupture of membranes with no labor at 36 weeks (which I will forever link to the unnecessary invasive procedure inflicted by the obstetrician during the nuchal translucency test), I birthed in hospital under induction at 37 weeks. Induction is notorious for sparking a "cascade of intervention" because the synthetic oxytocin used does not cross the blood-brain barrier, meaning that contractions occur without the usual accompanying benefits of feel-good hormones.[7] The contractions can easily build up too fast and too hard, creating unbearable pain and pressure on the baby. Knowing these risks, we opted for induction anyway. The hospital midwife attached a monitor to my belly to track the baby's heart rate and to look for signs of distress. I took it off. I requested a bath. The hospital midwife left to ask the obstetrician on duty if it was permissible for a woman who was being induced to birth in a bath. Sheryl went to fetch some warm water to top up the bath, in a quiet defiance that this question had even been raised. While they were both out of the room, I entered the bath and experienced a "fetus ejection reflex": the baby was born in a single spasm.[8]

It was a moment of great clarity. I want to say that it felt powerful, but not in the sense of being in control: I was completely out of control. My normal self was gone. I was overwhelmed. But something of me was in control: something not me exactly, but of me. It was a part of myself I had not encountered so consciously before. I felt that a me much more powerful than my conscious self had snatched birth back from the grips of the less-than-perfect circumstances around us and done it simply, gloriously, and rebelliously without asking anyone's permission. Sheryl came back in just after the baby's head was born: she was so sure that we were hours away from crowning that she almost tipped a steaming bucket of boiling water right in, but luckily saw the emerging baby just in time. Instead, she instructed us on how to pass the baby safely through the water, and then snapped a photo of the three of us, my partner, our baby, and me, jubilant. It was a very affirming note on which to begin my journey as a mother, and also for my partner who was commencing his new role as a father.

It seems to me that this is the key point about liminality. It is true that rites of passage can imprint new initiands with conservative meanings. All the rituals of birth that Robbie Davis-Floyd described in her 1994 article about hospital birth happened to me: the almost obsessive concerns with dilation, the bright lights, and the monitoring devices all repeating the cultural messaging that my body was a faulty birthing machine and could only be made to work through medical technology. But birth is not always reducible to the rituals constructed around it. Even in conditions of intense ritualization, such as a hospital birth, one finds seeds of other meanings.

IV

The first birth I remember attending was on an island in the Mekong River where I lived for 16 months for ethnographic fieldwork in 2002 and 2003. The village was a string of 50-odd houses on stilts, spaced out between gardens, bamboo, and coconut palms along the riverbank. The houses, which were made of teak and bamboo, faced the river, and backed onto rice fields. A gilt Buddhist temple gleamed on the higher patch of ground in the village center.

One day, I noticed a house downstream preparing a screened-off area under the house: an area, my hosts told me, for the coming birth. I walked by, curious and ever the diligent fieldworker, but too shy to intrude on what I assumed was a private event. I was pleased and surprised, then, when a lean young man, perspiring from the heat and a long walk through the dark of the evening, came to my house to invite me. He was inviting every household, using a headlamp to follow the footpaths between houses and across rice fields. Birth was one of the occasions (along with deaths, severe illnesses, marriages and feeding the dead) that required at least one member of each house to attend for an all-night vigil. By the time

I got there, though, the birth itself was over. While the woman who had just birthed rested in the screened-off space under the house drinking hot liquids and "toasting" over hot coals (really, just sitting close by or over the coals, in a ritual seclusion where heat is thought to help the body dry and close after birth), we congregated upstairs listening to music, dancing, drinking alcohol, and eating delicious morsels.

It is compulsory at such events that men gamble with playing cards. Gambling is usually illegal in Laos, but these rules are informally suspended at birth parties. Events like these are so expected that, in the case that a birth is *not* accompanied by a birth party with extensive gambling, it is generally understood to be an indication of the severe poverty and marginalization of that family. In Luang Prabang, where people are much more prosperous than in the rural village where I conducted fieldwork, these parties can go on for a month, with the regularity and length of any given guest's involvement in the party taken as a sign of their closeness to the couple who had birthed.[9]

In my field site, these events were typically referred to as *wiak* (L: labor, in the sense of work). Labor, in the sense of birth itself, is instead referred to by the direct word *cep* (L: pain). If birth labor in Australia implies the labor of faulty bodies at producing a product (much like a factory worker might labor on a production line), in Laos, the meaning of birth labor is the sociability around the birthing woman. Birth labor here is the work of revelry, the effort it takes to suspend everyday rules, and the contributions we all made by simply being there, adding to the creative, out-of-the-ordinary spark generated by gatherings. Birth was a carnival. No wonder so many women prefer to birth at home in Laos.

Since having my own children, I have paid more attention to birth in Laos. One of the characteristics of the births that I have followed in the southern provinces of Champassak and Sekong is that, even though most women broadly respect medical science, in general the preference and practice is to birth outside of medical facilities, even when doing so means that medical assistance may be too distant to access in the case of an emergency. In explaining this, women cite lack of transport, "shyness" of (and sometimes outright shaming by) medical staff, the convenience of a village birth for the friends and family who may wish to attend, and cost (even though mother-and-child health care is free in Laos). I have seen women plan a hospital birth, but when the time came, they ended up birthing in the village, saying that it never felt like the right time to go. Women also very frequently say that if they are not sick, they do not see the need for medical care. Many do not see pregnancy and birth as an illness, and when I probed them on this, I heard about the reassuring messages they received from the people closest to them. Many come to their first pregnancies having observed dozens of births firsthand: people growing up in a Laos village have often had ample opportunities to observe the births that take place there, or at least attend directly afterwards, as I mostly did. My own observation is that children are the most numerous of the attendees at a village birth in Laos. The children in Laos I have known did not grow up in ignorance and fear of birth.

In a Laos village, much cultural messaging affirms that birth is nothing to fear. And indeed, the births I knew of seemed to be usually trouble-free and over in an hour or two. All this, despite statistics suggesting that Laos has the highest maternal death rate in Southeast Asia. By contrast, in Australia the cultural messaging around birth seemed to dwell on its uncertainties (what to expect?) and dangers. The few births I had close knowledge of before having my own children seemed drawn-out and vexed, typically beset by high drama, angst, and epic time scales (by Lao standards at least). This, despite maternal deaths being considered, statistically speaking, rare in Australia. Clearly, these statistics—while no doubt indicating something true about birth—failed to capture something else: how birth is *imagined* in each context.

V

When I was pregnant for the second time, I interviewed my mother about my own birth. In a telephone call I made from my back veranda, while surrounded by piles of laundry in various stages of hanging, drying, and folding, I asked and she answered. We were sometimes halting, sometimes fluent, feeling our way around shame, reserve, and anger. I was her second child. Her first birth was in a hospital, where she had experienced what birth activists now call "obstetric violence": without her consent, she was given an unnecessary and painful episiotomy while her husband was forced to remain outside. When the pair were pregnant for a second time, she again enrolled at a hospital and went for regular check-ups. What she didn't tell these medical providers was that she had also hired two "healers," Carole and Norman, who agreed to attend her in birthing at home. Despite some misgivings about Carole and Norman's commitment to homeopathy and an anti-vaccination stance, she did birth at home. During the labor, they offered her drops of Rescue Remedy on her tongue and "Tibetan pills"—hand-rolled by lamas—said to open her birth canal.

This was the mid-1970s and my parents were then living on an MO (a multiple occupancy, a "commune," if you will) in the hinterlands around Nimbin, the center of Australia's counterculture. My father told me that, in the movement in those days, birthing at home was considered a key aspect of building community, a key affirmation of countercultural values. After I was born, my mother met weekly with other women in a "Pregnancy, birth and beyond" group in Nimbin. I grew up with the photographs taken at my own birth: my mother prone on a bed, sunlight streaming in on her glasses and her long blonde hair, me a bloody blob just visible between her legs, and around the bed, people unknown to me looking on. These were nothing like the stylized birth photography so common today. These were raw.

During our interview, some of the pauses in my mother's retelling seemed to be around shame, fear, and anger. Looking back now, she wondered: Had it been safe? Had she taken too many risks? When I was a child, she had often said that I was born with the umbilical cord around my neck, as if she was haunted by an horrific "what if" scenario of strangulation at birth. Birth specialists today no longer speak of the umbilical cord as potentially life-threatening for infants at birth, although the idea of tangled umbilical cords did have some currency in the 1980s. The idea of the umbilical cord—that link between us— choking me before my first breath seemed to have come to stand for all the reservations and compromises my mother had faced in planning her home birth in circumstances where there was so little in the way of medical support available for it, and a nightmare possibility that haunted those choices.

Nevertheless, I grew up telling people that I was born at home: I was a home birth. I had some childish sense that this difference was special, a bit like being left-handed. It was only as an adult that I realized that my story had been wrong. In fact, the birth was what people these days call a "free birth": a birth that is planned and intended to occur with no attendance by anyone qualified in biomedicine. A home birth, by contrast, is a birth that takes place at a woman's home while attended by a qualified midwife or equivalent. But such births were not an option in 1970s New South Wales. If they are an option today, it is due in large part to women like my mother. Women who rebelled.

VI

My mother continued in birth activism. When I was in high school, she was working to connect local midwives to a home birth group. The numbers were always small, the bureaucratic challenges almost over-whelming, the threat of deregistration always lurking for midwives who supported home birth. David Graeber once wrote, "to live as a rebel—in the constant awareness of the possibilities of revolutionary transforma-tion, and amongst those who dream of it—is surely the best way one can live."[10] But what is the price of rebellion? When I first met David, we were both new to the United Kingdom. In our first email exchanges, he seemed cagey, suspicious, and quickly told me that he was in "intellectual exile," after being denied a place in the United States Ivy League because of his activism. In the introduction to this volume, Josh Reno and I argue that, at least from Graeber's perspective, at least ten years of his career was spent in a kind of "wilderness," where he felt that his contributions to anthropol-ogy were undervalued, but also that his activism had cost him his career and his personal happiness. Graeber's activist sensibilities may have been a large part of the impact his work had beyond the discipline, but they also drove a wedge between him and the mainstream of anthropology, at least from his perspective, and at least for a period.

The same can be said for the activist streak in the anthropology of birth. For instance, my midwives and my mother had all read the works of anthropologist and childbirth educator Sheila Kitzinger, while I, a trained anthropologist, had not registered her work until I was pregnant myself. I am confident I am not alone in this ignorance, at least among my own generation of anthropologists: I ran pop surveys at the slow workshop behind this edited collection (discussed in the Preface to this volume) and during my talks to anthropology audiences about this chapter, and I found that by far the overwhelming majority of anthropologists also did not recognize her name. Like others in my generation, I had been schooled in the anthropology of reproduction as a matter of course,[11] but I was less familiar with the distinction between that larger field and the smaller subfield of the anthropology of birth. The anthropology of birth pre-dates the anthropology of reproduction, and although it was later folded into the anthropology of reproduction, this subfield has a stronger tradition of activism, opening possibilities for birthing women. Brigitte Jordan, Sheila Kitzinger, and Robbie Davis-Floyd are considered the founders of the anthropology of birth. Kitzinger alone wrote over 30 books over a span of 40 years. Her obituary in *The Guardian* suggests that "She could reasonably be said to have done more than anyone else to change attitudes to childbirth in the past 50 years."[12] Kitzinger's 2004 book *The New Experience of Childbirth* sold over a million copies.[13] Among her hundreds of articles are hard-to-ignore titles like her 2001 "The Great Childbirth Blackmail"[14] and the 2006 "Birth as Rape: There Must Be an End to 'Just in Case' Obstetrics."[15]

Cross-cultural comparisons have long been a part of the anthropologies of birth and midwifery.[16] Brigitte Jordan's *Birth in Four Cultures: A Crosscultural Investigation of Childbirth in Yucatan, Holland, Sweden, and the United States*, first published in 1978, is widely considered to be the founding text of both fields.[17] Carol McCormack's 1982 *Ethnography of Fertility and Birth*[18] also aimed at gathering culturally diverse details of lived experiences with the aim of improving maternal health care. Later, Sheila Kitzinger's *Ourselves as Mothers: The Universal Experience of Motherhood*[19] attempted a survey of the world's cultures of birth explicitly as a means of prompting readers to reflect critically on their own rituals and practices.

Perhaps one reason Kitzinger's work received less attention in the discipline, despite her broad popular appeal, was the way she used the ethnographic record. While Kitzinger described herself as an anthropologist and often commented on her fieldwork in Jamaica, her texts arguably were the most alive when critically describing experiences in her own society. Her cross-cultural comparisons, by contrast, were often broad-brush indications of "pre-industrial" societies as a foil to the more familiar "technological" societies.[20] At one point she commented that, "When I started studying social anthropology I soon realized that social systems are all about male power and the way in which men organize themselves so as to own, exploit, and exchange women and children."[21] This is a reading of the ethnographic record for inevitabilities, not possibilities. While this view has held significant currency in mainstream feminist anthropology, there were always other, and more hopeful, readings of the ethnographic record, such as Eleanor Burke Leacock's 1981 *Myths of Male Dominance.*[22]

In the mainstream anthropology of the 1980s and 1990s, students learned about the dangers of fast and loose comparisons and universalizing statements. In place of contrasting cultures and statements about humanity as a whole, students learned of insidiously pervasive biopower and the "-scapes" of a globalization that were taken to be inevitable fact. Influential social theory devoted itself to describing its "flows"[23] or, perhaps, the moments of "agency" found in personal consumption. George Stocking, a historian of anthropology, described a moment in the Chicago anthropology department in the 1980s–1990s in an attempt to capture this significant shift in the mood of the discipline.[24] A world map had long hung in the Chicago department, proudly displaying colored flags pinned over each of the field sites studied by students and staff, and photographs snapped of researchers in the field. These showed exotic-looking people, mostly dark-skinned, and their mostly pale ethnographers, as if to indicate that anthropology was the discipline that made comparison between "them", and between "them and us", possible. But by the end of the 1980s, this display no longer seemed proud or innocent, with one student commenting that it effectively symbolized how: "the sun never sets on the colonial empire of Chicago anthropology."[25] While early to mid-twentieth-century anthropology produced many grand syntheses and empirical generalizations, now many anthropologists devoted themselves to understanding local people on their own terms, which in practice meant years of language learning and "being there" in often small or niche field sites. These committed fieldworkers barely dared to make regional comparisons, let alone global syntheses.[26] In this context, magpie collections of examples drawn from different cultures, such as those assembled by Kitzinger, came to strike many anthropologists as naïvely decontextualizing at best, or at worst as participating in an imperialist worldview.[27]

Graeber, who went through his PhD training in the Chicago department and period that Stocking described, agreed with the need to avoid comparisons that subordinated local particularities to universal inevitabilities, but he wanted to do so in a way that maintained the link between ethnographic comparison and activism. In one of his earliest books, he pointed out that:

> While anthropologists are effectively sitting on a vast archive of human experience, of social and political experiments no one really knows about, that very body of comparative ethnography is seen [within the discipline] as something shameful … it is treated not as the common heritage of humankind, but as our dirty little secret.[28]

He noted wryly that keeping the ethnographic record as anthropology's dirty little secret was still a way of keeping the ethnographic record, keeping it to ourselves, and refusing to share it with the wider world. These criticisms are, of course, simplifications: Graeber acknowledged as much.[29] But in articulating the situation so simply, he put into words an unease that many anthropologists had felt about the de-politicizing effects of the turn to endless local contextualization. In so doing, he defended the possibility of intentional social change, even revolution, and the role of anthropology in that. And in doing so, he inspired the generation of anthropologists that would come after him, my generation.

Graeber would go on not only to defiantly practice comparative ethnography, but also to put it to work in answering questions provoked by
his activism. In the Afterword to the 2014 edition of his bestselling *Debt:
The First 5000 Years*, he noted that he had deliberately set out to write a
sprawling, scholarly work of the kind that was distinctly out of fashion
when he commenced that project.[30] His book—while unabashedly scholarly and presenting complex ethnographic material—spoke clearly to
popular concerns, such as anti-globalization, Occupy, and the 2007–8
financial crisis.

VII

Kitzinger's work arguably provides an even plainer example of the activist
potentials of comparative anthropology. Many of those who celebrated
her life after her death in 2015 argued that the revolution that Kitzinger
fought for was won in her lifetime: humanistic changes in childbirth were
achieved in many countries. Her anthropology touched millions of lives. I
birthed in a post-Kitzinger world, in a setting shaped significantly by the
kind of care Kitzinger championed. My second birth was a home birth, a
true home birth, attended by a qualified midwife, Rachele.

The build-up of contractions was slow. Five days out from the due date,
there was some cramping, blood, and gushes. Rachele encouraged us to go
about life as usual, so we did. Without my noticing it very much at first,
I found that these cramps became the tempo of my life: I could stand up
easily, but I'd wait for the cramp to finish first. If I lingered by the warmth
of the oven, it was to ease the cramp that was passing then. If I spoke, it
was because there was no cramp, and if I hummed softly, it was because
there was. Mostly I was my normal self, but when the pain came, I paused,
became more inward.

Things became more intense at about nine o'clock on the night before
our due date. Now when the pain came it would take all of my attention.
For what seemed like hours, I leaned on a chair in the dark of my bedroom
in solitude, feeling waves build and subside. It was hard work, but it felt
pleasant and possible. I loved the TENS (Transcutaneous Electrical Nerve
Stimulation) machine: a non-invasive, drug-free method of pain relief.
Who knows if these things really work? Part of the pleasure of it no doubt
was the mindless, repetitive action of turning it up at the start of each
contraction and down at the end, both done with the press of a button. It
marked the passing of each contraction and put me in charge (it was my

finger on the button!). I enjoyed the breaks between the contractions. I was entering what philosopher Orli Dahan has tentatively called "birth consciousness," which she defines as "an altered state of focus and retreat" which may feel spaceless, timeless, and nonverbal.[31] Sometimes when my partner came to check on me, I could not muster any words. At one point I gathered myself especially so I could explain to him that if I was not speaking, it wasn't because there was any problem. I was just too ecstatic. I asked him if he'd ever felt so high that he imagined entire conversations with people but when he went to speak, realized that none of it mattered because it was all beyond words? Well, that was how I felt at the time. Ridiculously happy, truly gone.

Through all this I heard Gadsby (my firstborn) crying: it was hours past his bedtime. From the bedroom I commanded: "Bring him here." Gadsby curled up in my arms as I sat on the floor in the candlelight, humming through contractions while rocking him. He looked up at me, curious but mostly sleepy. I relished letting the deliciousness of his gentle, drowsy presence, his blonde curls and angelic face, sink in, aware that this would be the last time for a while that it would be just the two of us. Gadsby slept. I laid him on the bed and rested next to him for a while. The contractions ceased, and I must have fallen asleep or into some kind of doze. Perhaps 20 minutes passed. My partner came in to check, and I got up in that way you do when you are half asleep and for some unknown reason you try to act more awake than you are. Immediately, I felt a big contraction that grabbed me before I'd even left the bed. I tried to find my rhythm there again, but it was not as easy or pleasant. The spell was broken. I tried the birth pool, but I didn't feel dreamy and content. It was harder now. I felt very alert. A catch in my breath and I was floored by the pain. I remember saying "I don't know where I am," meaning I had lost my thread, that sense of "having the finger on the button" that had carried me through the early part of the labor. Now it felt not so much that I was having labor but that labor was having me. I was being taken over, I was roaring until I was hoarse but the pain was still more than I could express. I felt "the big stretch" that I had read about, but not registered in my last birth.[32] I felt extreme pain in my lower back. But still there was no sign of the head. In a pause between contractions, I gave myself an internal pep talk:

I don't want to feel this pain anymore and there is only one way out of it: forward. Are you holding back? Are you scared? These contractions are going to keep on happening unless you go with them to the end. You need to push with everything you have got, and then this will be over. Are you scared you will break? It's fine. They will stitch you up. They will take you to the hospital to put you back together again if that is what it takes. You are not going to die from this. It is time to let go and end it.

The contraction started and I pushed. "There's the head," I said, hoping I'd catch my own baby this time. Another push. "And there's the body," I said as I felt it slide past my hand behind me, towards my partner Ed. The midwife told him to pick up the baby, and the touch of concern in her voice was enough to trigger all my adrenalin-soaked hyper-worry. I hurried to lift the baby from his hands and out of the water and into my arms. He was perfect, wonderful. We retired to our big yellow sofa and watched in amazement as he did the "birth crawl" up my chest to latch on himself for his first feed.

Rachele later told me that my contractions never took on the kind of consistency or length that would have been considered an established labor by a hospital. If I'd chosen a hospital birth, I would likely have been given synthetic oxytocin again. As it was, with my home birth, the love, respect, privacy, familiarity, and support enabled a journey that was pleasurable (at times), profound (throughout) and intricately suited for my particular needs. Looking back, I was struck by how very different my own experiences of birth had been to my grandmother's. I felt profoundly grateful for all those influences that had gifted me the chance to make the choices I did: anthropologists like Robbie Davis-Floyd and Sheila Kitzinger, and activists like my mother and my midwives.

VIII

What would a social theory of birth as possibilities look like? Graeber was a social theorist. But he was also a meta-theorist. He attempted to rethink what social theory could be. One role he saw for social theory was to:

> look at those who are creating viable alternatives, try to figure out what might be the larger implications of what they are (already) doing, and then offer those ideas back, not as prescriptions, but as contributions, possibilities—as gifts.[33]

He also identified another method:

> start out from some aspect ... that seems particularly bleak, depressing ... some failure, stumbling block ... and try to recuperate something, some hidden aspect we usually don't notice, some angle from which the same apparently desolate landscape might look entirely different.[34]

We might think of these as two paths that both lead toward social theory as possibility.

Birthing possibilities, then, would include recuperating something from the apparently desolate landscape that confronts birth today. In Australia, at least one in three women who give birth experience birth trauma.[35] One in ten develop signs of post-traumatic stress.[36] People rarely speak plainly of birth, and even more rarely spell out the details in positive terms. When I have spoken in public forums about birth, including the materials that I have shared above, it is usual for at least a couple of people in the audience to use the question time to share their own birth traumas, or even to speak of traumatic births that they have only seen depicted in Hollywood movies, as a critique of my presentation of birth as possibility: it is almost if they want to say "What right do you have to speak of births so positively—your own or anyone's—when there is so much trauma in birth?"

This trauma is real. And this trauma is cultural. Birth is, in anthropological parlance, "biocultural." Cultural meanings and physiological processes are mutually entangled in feedback loops. For instance, people approaching their first birth who have received cultural messaging about birth as trauma, perhaps through the rituals of worry that are so common during pregnancy, or perhaps through the Hollywood movies that dwell on birth trauma, may then be predisposed during labor to pull the trigger on the "cascade of interventions," one leading to the next. This stream of interventions may itself be traumatizing and perhaps life-threatening.[37] If so, these are more likely to be spoken of and easily heard, because they are affirmed by a surrounding cultural context that already frames birth as dangerous and traumatic. Yet the statistics suggest that birth does not have to be a horror show. In Australia, women on average have a 60 percent chance of undergoing an episiotomy or caesarean section,[38] while those who plan a home birth experience these at a rate of less than six percent.[39] Yet less than 1 percent of women who give birth in Australia plan a home birth.[40] More women give birth on the side of the road each year.[41] There are possibilities for better births.

A small but determined and wonderfully committed Australian birth activism scene is campaigning for continuity of care for women who birth in hospital, and for access to home birth for women who want it. A social theory of birthing possibilities would include offering back to birth activists some reflections on the larger implications of what they are doing. Graeber included hospitals among his list of "the very machinery of alienation." He described these as the:

> instruments through which the human imagination is smashed and shattered. Insurrectionary moments occur when this bureaucratic apparatus is neutralized. Doing so always seems to have the effect of throwing horizons of possibility wide open. This is only to be expected if one of the main things that apparatus normally does is to enforce extremely limited ones.[42]

By keeping open the possibility of birth outside hospitals, birth activists may (intentionally or not) be throwing open much wider horizons of possibility.

One area where birth activism and the anthropology of David Graeber already overlap is in an interest in the medieval history of Europe. For birth activists, the inspiration here is often the midwife (the "with-woman"), who had a high status in medieval times but, with the rise of possessive individualism, increasingly became associated with witchcraft, filth, and superstition.[43] Another genealogy that birth activists trace back to medieval times is to the "godsibs" (or gossips): the female friends and relatives who gathered around a woman lying-in during and after birth for talk, festivities, and companionship. At a lying-in, the patriarchal hierarchy of the household and wider society was temporarily inverted, placing "women on top."[44] Over time, however, the rituals of lying-in became associated with mere idle "gossip and tittle-tattle."[45] By the mid-eighteenth century, the word "gossip" had approached its current usage, so that Samuel Johnson could define a gossip as "One who runs about tattling like women at a lying in."[46] Here, I wish to contribute to this line of thinking in birth activism by connecting it to David Graeber's anthropology, particularly by way of Mikhail Bakhtin.

Bakhtin's analysis of François Rabelais' novels was a key inspiration for Graeber's account of manners and hierarchy in his 2007 *Possibilities*.[47]

Bakhtin argued that Rabelais' novels were popular in the Renaissance partly because they were written in a genre drawn directly from the folk culture of medieval Europe, what he calls "the language of the marketplace." This humorous and exaggerated style thrived alongside and despite the otherwise very serious tone of medieval ecclesiastical and feudal culture. It continued into the Renaissance, proving to be a fertile source not only of relief, but also for thinking about renewal, and about the changes, even "revolution" taking place during the Renaissance. Medieval towns such as Lyon, he said, would spend as much as two months a year in a state of carnival, a state Bakhtin defines as comic, playful, and sensuous. This was a folk culture of clowns and fools, but by no means trivial. It was one half of the "double aspect" of medieval culture, a contrasting but profound pair to the austere protocols and rituals of church and state. Over time, however, carnival became more constrained and retreated to private settings. Feasts, for instance, shifted from town-wide events to brief, private affairs now mostly experienced at home. The medieval period came to be thought of in terms of gothic austerity, and the laughing nature of much popular experience of that era was all but forgotten. Readers coming to Rabelais in later times thus found themselves bewildered, and strained to find meaning in his billingsgate, blazons and parodies (for instance, by reading Rabelais' extraordinary descriptions of gluttony, codpieces, and promiscuous monks only as veiled allegories for court affairs of the time). Bahktin identified Rabelais' style, and the style of the folk culture that inspired it, as "carnivalesque." Carnival forms and symbols, he argued, signaled a temporary liberation from existing rank and order, and were always found in "(m)oments of death and revival, of change and renewal."[48]

Bakhtin is not often thought of as a contributor to theorizations of birth or gender, but he often evokes birth in his attempt to describe and define the carnivalesque. Birth even appears in Bakhtin's writings a kind of master metaphor for the concept of the carnivalesque as a whole: he wrote of carnival as the "maternal womb" for the all-people through which the old would die and the new could be born. Birth is one of the bodily functions that is physically located on "the lower stratum" that was the typical focal point of carnival symbolism. In carnival culture, the lower areas of the body, especially the female body, were a common source of humor and "degradation."[49] But in carnival degradation was understood as a form of coming down to earth, an earth which was at once both the grave and the womb. The lower stratum was returned to as a source of renewal, even as it was also a source of decay and death. Birth and death were often linked in carnivalesque imagery (such as birth-giving deaths, or death-giving births), an imagery that dwelt overwhelmingly on the openings and protrusions of the body—eating, bellies, defecation, and so on—an imagery that Bahktin called "grotesque realism." He described the lower stratum as "the fruitful earth and the womb. It is always conceiving."[50]

Figure 2.1 "At the Childbed," detail from "The Severall Places Where You May Hear News," c. 1600

Source: Megan Marie Inbody, "Town/Gown Relations: The Forms and Functions of Female Gossip Communities and Networks in Early Modern Comedy" (PhD diss., Michigan State University, English, 2012), 203.

In medieval Europe, grotesque realism had a deeply positive connotation: it was the base stratum which united all people and indeed all the cosmos. Yet, over time, these images and symbols shifted in meaning, so that today these self-same bodily features and processes are at best considered private, trivial and severed from other spheres of life, or at worst as carrying only negative connotations. One of the examples Bakhtin gives of this shift is the revolution that took place in the ritual and symbolism of birth. He discusses the *Caquet de l'accouchée* ("The Cackle of the Confined Woman"), a broadsheet first published in France sometime in 1560.[51] The pamphlet was apparently quite popular, and was republished in varied editions in both Europe and England.[52] Bakhtin explains that, at the time these were published, it was usual for women and girls to continue lying-ins. These were characteristically carnivalesque, with a suspension of social conventions, ample food, and frank conversation, especially about "the material bodily lower stratum."[53] In the "Cackle," however, this old tradition was represented as shallow and meaningless, as merely one of the "severall places where you may hear news" (Figure 2.1). Bakhtin understood this shift as part of a historical process whereby the carnivalesque unity of birth and death, which had affirmed the cosmic importance of bodily processes, especially those of the lower stratum, was being sundered, leaving each holding only a rather negative meaning: their continued association with defecation and urination (other "lower stratum" elements) rendered birth and postpartum now as trivial, private, and faintly embarrassing. This, he maintained, is the contemporary meaning attached to birth.

Inspired by Bahktin's account, Graeber analyzed the shift in manners during this period arguing that, "Basic standards of how one was expected to eat, drink, sleep, excrete, make love, shifted almost completely."[54] Graeber argued that the decline in medieval carnivalesque was associated with the rise of possessive individualism that valued "avoidance" relations, as evidenced in bodies that presented themselves as closed-off and contained. He drew on C.B. MacPherson's argument that possessive individualism, evident in liberal-democratic theory from the seventeenth century through to contemporary times, assumes that one holds autonomy over one's own "person or capacities, owing nothing to society for them."[55] Graeber argued that this implicit philosophy guided not only dominant political and economic theories, but also the most intimate interactions of daily life, including common courtesies. Graeber argued that as the carnivalesque vernacular became more and more muted, if not forgotten altogether, it was displaced by an understanding of the body as the prime possession of an individual who owed nothing to anyone. Orifices, which betrayed this sense of the enclosed self by opening up to the other, were hidden from view and became a private matter. Eating, drinking, sexual life, and defecation became individual matters with narrow, trivial, and domestic connotations, "torn away from direct relation to the life of society and to the cosmic whole."[56] This shift is discernible in sentiments around birth, too: the gossip moved from her place at the lying-in to the place of a small-minded tattler of private tales. And birth, too, moved from the bawdiness of the lying-in to the closed-off world of avoidance so aptly embodied by the hospital.

Today—with the pervasive cultural influence of possessive individualism—sexuality, birth, and breastfeeding are uncomfortable reminders that, in fact: "we are not discrete beings; we emerge from other people, we merge into other people, our lives leak literally and figuratively into one another [...]."[57] With birth, one might speak of a *possessed* individual, rather than a possessive one. The pregnant woman has another within her. Insofar as a pregnant woman is able to make choices around birth and pregnancy, these are choices about if and how to make room "for the Other in her own way of being."[58]

Birth activists' campaigns for continuity of care—where a woman planning to birth at hospital could expect a stable team throughout her antenatal and postnatal care, and the right to a home birth if she so chooses—challenge possessive individualism and the rituals of avoidance that sustain it. The hospital promises bright lights, distant professionals, clean surfaces, and sterile tools. Visiting hours and numbers are limited. Birth is set apart from the day-to-day world: a potentially abstract space. As Robbie Davis-Floyd notes, most North American women—indeed, women all over the world, especially those in high-resource countries—seek out such spaces for birth.[59] Part of the appeal, I suspect, arises from today's societal discomfort with and denigration of the lower stratum, orifices, and leakages. Hospitals appeal because they offer an abstract space where bodies can be imagined through relations of avoidance, even in the extremes presented by birth. This is particularly clear in many Australian women's aspiration to have an obstetrician attend their births: a stranger who they will most likely barely know, but one of high status. The continuity-of-care model, by contrast, offers women not abstraction but familiarity and community. And the home birth offers women a birth tangled in with the comings and goings of everyday life: an inversion of the day-to-day, but not an avoidance of it. One of the larger implications of birth activism, then, is the challenge it presents to the cultural normalization of possessive individualism. Possessive individualism predisposes us to forget our continuity with each other, with the land, with the dead, and with the generations yet to come, even when our bodily experiences suggest otherwise. The need to move beyond such ways of thinking is now urgent and is a matter of survival for our own species and many others.

Birth continues to be an important rite of passage. This means that in births, cultural meanings are transmitted but can also, possibly, be transformed. Birth activism, the choices women make in planning their births, and those who work to support them in those choices, have profound importance, not only for the individuals involved but also for the possibilities of social change and for the future of humanity more broadly. Like the witches imagined by Ehrenreich and English, birth activists today hold out "the hope of change in this world."[60]

A final note is necessary here on the idea of birth choices. The idea of a choice-making individual is core to possessive individualism: a person is conceived of as the rightful possessor of their body as if it were one of their belongings. In her 1988 *Gender of the Gift*, Marilyn Strathern noted that dominant strains of Western feminism have tended to reproduce this concept of the body, defining gender justice importantly in terms of women's ownership of their own bodies.[61] One of the contradictions of birth activism is that so much of it is framed in terms of defending birthing women's abilities to make choices about their bodies, yet a woman at the alter/altar of birth has an opportunity to experience herself precisely as overcome by a force that might temporarily displace her rational, decision-making self: as possessed rather than possessive. At the same time, it is often noted that the more first-time parents plan their births, seemingly the more things go awry. The more we see birthing as something to plan and make informed choices about, the more rates of intervention rise.[62] There is something uncomfortable, then, in defining the goals of birth activism in terms of choices.

One possible way of thinking about this apparent contradiction is in terms of the kinds of choices that are actually at stake. Birth choices are not like the choices made by, say, an architect planning a building. Nor are they like the choices made by an individual who owes nothing to anyone and thinks only of their own self-interest or profit. They are certainly not like the choices made about one's possessions. Ideally, birth choices would instead be more akin to the choices made by free people. By this, I mean freedom in Graeber's sense: not freedom from obligations, but freedom to choose one's obligations and to live only under those constraints. For Graeber, "The revolution begins by asking: what sort of promises do free men and women make to one another, and how, by making them, do we begin to make another world?"[63] He noted that we barely have any experience of being free in this way. We do not live in a free society. We can only work towards making one a possibility. Even so, Graeber reminds us that we can, in the here and now, insist on living as if we were already free. Birth choices that insist on this kind of freedom have implications not only for satisfaction among new parents, but also for more expansive imaginations of the possibilities for ourselves and our place in the world.

Notes

1. David Graeber, *The Democracy Project: A History, a Crisis, a Movement* (New York: Spiegel & Grau, 2013), 237.
2. Henrietta Moore, *A Passion for Difference: Essays in Anthropology and Gender* (Cambridge: Polity Press, 1994).
3. Robbie E. Davis-Floyd, "The Rituals of American Hospital Birth," in *Conformity and Conflict: Readings in Cultural Anthropology*, ed. David McCurdy (New York: HarperCollins, 1996).
4. Arnold van Gennep, *The Rites of Passage* (London: Routledge & Kegan Paul, 1960).
5. Victor Turner, *The Ritual Process: Structure and Anti-Structure* (New York: Aldine De Gruyter, 1969).
6. I use jam here in the sense of "culture jamming," a method of using widely recognized social symbols in a way that upturn or reverse their meaning.
7. Davis-Floyd, "The Rituals of American Hospital Birth."
8. Michel Odent, *The Functions of the Orgasms: The Highways to Transcendence* (London: Pinter and Martin, 2009).
9. Charles H.P. Zuckerman, "Good Gambling: Meaning and Moral Economy in Late-Socialist Laos" (PhD diss., University of Michigan, 2018).
10. David Graeber, *Direct Action: An Ethnography* (Oakland, CA and Edinburgh: AK Press, 2009), x.
11. Faye D. Ginsburg and Rayna Rapp, *Conceiving the New World Order: The Global Politics of Reproduction* (Berkeley: University of California Press, 1995). This is the book that, by popular consensus among reproductive scholars, officially founded the anthropology of reproduction.
12. Suzie Hayman, "Sheila Kitzinger Obituary: Author and Pioneer of Natural Childbirth who Led a Crusade against its Medicalisation," *The Guardian*, April 13, 2015, https://www.theguardian.com/lifeandstyle/2015/apr/12/sheila-kitzinger (accessed May 20, 2021).
13. Sheila Kitzinger, *The New Experience of Childbirth* (London: Orion, 2004).
14. Sheila Kitzinger, "The Great Childbirth Blackmail," *Daily Mail*, June 14, 2001.
15. Sheila Kitzinger, "Birth as a Rape: There Must be an End to 'Just in Case' Obstetrics," *British Journal of Midwifery* 14, no. 9 (2006).
16. I thank Robbie Davis-Floyd (pers. comm.) for this observation and general comments.
17. Brigitte Jordan, *Birth in Four Cultures: A Crosscultural Investigation of Childbirth in Yucatan, Holland, Sweden, and the United States*, 4th edn (Long Grove, IL: Waveland Press, 1993).
18. Carol McCormack, *Ethnography of Fertility and Birth*, 2nd edn (Long Grove, IL: Waveland Press, 1994).
19. Sheila Kitzinger *Ourselves as Mothers: The Universal Experience of Motherhood* (Boston, MA: Da Capo Press, 1995).

20. I recollect one of my first anthropology lecturers, Christine Helliwell, commenting acerbically on one of my undergraduate essays in 1994 that "*all human societies use technology*." See for instance the use of such terms in Sheila Kitzinger, *Ourselves as Mothers*.

21. Ibid., 239.

22. Eleanor Burke Leacock, *Myths of Male Dominance: Collected Articles on Women Cross-Culturally* (New York and London: Monthly Review Press, 1981).

23. Ginsburg and Rapp, *Conceiving the New World Order*, 2.

24. George W. Stocking, *The Ethnographer's Magic and Other Essays in the History of Anthropology* (Madison: University of Wisconsin Press, 1992).

25. Ibid., 363.

26. Richard A. O'Connor, "Agricultural Change and Ethnic Succession in Southeast Asian States: A Case for Regional Anthropology," *Journal of Asian Studies* 54, no. 4 (1995): 968–996.

27. Sheila Kitzinger, *Rediscovering Birth* (Boston and London: Little Brown, 2000).

28. David Graeber, *Fragments of an Anarchist Anthropology* (Chicago: Prickly Paradigm Press, 2004), 96. Parentheses added.

29. Graeber, *Fragments*, 96.

30. David Graeber, *Debt: The First 5,000 Years* (Brooklyn: Melville House, 2011).

31. Orli Dahan, "The Riddle of the Extreme Ends of the Birth Experience: Birthing Consciousness and its Fragility," *Current Psychology* 42, no. 1 (January 2023): 262–272.

32. Alieta Belle and Jenny Blyth, "The big stretch: Insights about birth" (DVD) and "The big stretch: The sequel" (DVD). N.D. Birthwork.

33. Graeber, *Fragments*, 12.

34. David Graeber, *Revolutions in Reverse: Essays on Politics, Violence, Art, and Imagination* (London and New York: Minor Compositions, 2011), 4.

35. Paige L. Tsakmakis, Shahinnoor Akter, and Meghan A. Bohren, "A Qualitative Exploration of Women's and their Partners' Experiences of Birth Trauma in Australia, Utilising Critical Feminist Theory," *Women and Birth: Journal of the Australian College of Midwives* epub ahead of print (December 24, 2022), doi 10.1016/j.wombi.2022.12.004.

36. Clara-Sophie Heyne, Maria Kazmierczak, Ronnie Souday, Danny Horesh, Mijke Lambregtse-van den Berg, Tobias Weigl et al., "Prevalence and Risk Factors of Birth-Related Posttraumatic Stress among Parents: A Comparative Systematic Review and Meta-Analysis," *Clinical Psychology Review* 94 (June 2022): 102157.

37. Davis-Floyd, "The Rituals of American Hospital Birth."

38. Australian Institute of Health and Welfare, "Australia's Mothers and Babies, Summary," December 14, 2022, available at: https://www.aihw.gov.au/reports/mothers-babies/australias-mothers-babies/contents/summary (accessed April 17, 2023).

39. Miranda L. Davies-Tuck, Euan M. Wallace, Mary-Ann Davey, Vickie Veitch, and Jeremy Oats, "Planned Private Homebirth in Victoria 2000–2015: A Retrospective Cohort Study of Victorian Perinatal Data," *BMC Pregnancy and Childbirth* 18, no. 1 (September 1, 2018): 1–8.

40. Hazel Keedle, Virginia Schmied, Elaine Burns, and Hannah G. Dahlen, "Women's Reasons for, and Experiences of, Choosing a Homebirth Following a Caesarean Section," *BMC Pregnancy & Childbirth* 15, no. 1 (September 4, 2015): 1–12.

41. Australian Institute of Health and Welfare, "Australia's Mothers and Babies: Place of Birth," available at: https://www.aihw.gov.au/reports/mothers-babies/australias-mothers-babies/contents/labour-and-birth/place-of-birth (accessed March 21, 2023).

42. Graeber, *Revolutions in Reverse*, 60.

43. See for instance the classic pamphlet published by Barbara Ehrenreich and Deirdre English in 1973, "Witches, Midwives and Nurses: A History of Women Healers" (Feminist Press, CUNY), reprinted as a book in 2010: Barbara Ehrenreich and Deirdre English, *Witches, Midwives, and Nurses: A History of Women Healers* (New York: The Feminist Press, 2010).

44. Adrian Wilson, "The Ceremony of Birth and its Interpretation," in *Women as Mothers in Pre-Industrial England: Essays in Memory of Dorothy McLaren*, ed. Valerie Fildes (London and New York: Routledge, 2013), 93.

45. Mikhail Bakhtin, *Rabelais and his World*, trans. Helene Iswolsky (Bloomington: Indiana University Press, 1984), 105.

46. Quoted in Gail McMurray Gibson, "Scene and Obscene: Seeing and Performance in Medieval Childbirth," *Journal of Medieval and Early Modern Studies* 29, no.1 (1999), 11.

47. David Graeber, "Manners, Deference, and Private Property: Or, Elements for a General Theory of Hierarchy," in *Possibilities: Essays on Hierarchy, Rebellion, and Desire* (Oakland, CA and Edinburgh: AK Press, 2007), 13–56.

48. Bakhtin, *Rabelais and his World*, 9.

49. Ibid., 21.

50. Ibid., 21.

51. See Megan Marie Inbody, "Town/Gown Relations: The Forms and Functions of Female Gossip Communities and Networks in Early Modern Comedy" (PhD diss., Michigan State University, English, 2012), 203.

52. The examples Bahktin draws on were pamphlets published in 1622 and 1663 (Bakhtin, *Rabelais and his World*, 106); the example pictured in Figure 2.1 is from 1600 (Inbody, "Town/Gown Relations," 203).

53. Bakhtin, *Rabelais and his World*, 105.

54. Graeber, *Possibilities*, 14.

55. Crawford Braugh MacPherson, *The Political Theory of Possessive Individualism: Hobbes to Locke* (Oxford and New York: Oxford University Press, 1962), 3.

56. Bakhtin, *Rabelais and his World*, 321.

57. Penny van Esterik and Richard A. O'Connor, *The Dance of Nurture: Negotiating Infant Feeding* (New York and Oxford: Berghahn, 2017), 16.

58. Kalpana Ram, *Fertile Disorder: Spirit Possession and its Provocation of the Modern* (Honolulu: University of Hawai'i Press, 2013), 144.

59. Davis-Floyd, "The Rituals of American Hospital Birth."

60. Ibid., 14.

61. Marilyn Strathern, *The Gender of the Gift: Problems with Women and Problems with Society in Melanesia* (Berkeley: University of California Press, 1988).

62. Tina Miller, "'We've Bought a Tens Machine and We're Trying Aromatherapy and Hypnobirthing': Being Prepared for Labour and Birth?" *Studies in the Maternal* 13, no. 1 (2020).

63. Graeber, *Revolutions in Reverse*, 39.

3

Actually Existing Anarchist Anthropology

Holly High and Joshua Reno

David Graeber resisted the label "the Anarchist Anthropologist." At the time of his death, the tagline on his Twitter account concluded with a command: "I see anarchism as something you do not an identity so don't call me the anarchist anthropologist."[1] Perhaps the closest he came to conceding to the label was when he said, "I'm a scholar who subscribes to anarchist principles and occasionally acts on them."[2] There is a contrast here, between his willingness to identify as an anthropologist and his hedging around anarchism. The *Oxford English Dictionary* definition of an anarchist is "a person who believes that all government should be abolished," or a person who advocates anarchy.[3] It defines anarchy, in turn, as the absence of government, non-recognition of authority in any sphere, a state of disorder, chaos, political or social confusion, or as "the absolute freedom of the individual." Graeber's anarchism did not conform to any of these dictionary definitions. But he was an anarchist: he often went on the record saying as much, even if he did reject the label "the anarchist anthropologist." And he was the first anthropologist to so explicitly trace out the "fragments" of a possible but (at that time, in 2004) "non-existent" anarchist anthropology. In this chapter, we discuss his anarchism in relation to his anthropology. What did he mean by anarchism? How did it influence his anthropology? Even if he never aspired to be "the" anarchist anthropologist, we conclude, in retrospect his work did eventually come to constitute an example of actually existing anarchist anthropology.

* * *

On August 1, 2000, a 39-year-old David Graeber was attending the Republican Convention protests in downtown Philadelphia. Relatively unknown at the time, both to fellow anthropologists and to activists, he could move anonymously amid the crowds, without drawing attention to himself, making observations and occasionally scribbling in his notebook. In the voluminous tome *Direct Action: An Ethnography*, published nine years later, he presents what reads like raw fieldnotes of this occasion, apparently barely edited from the jottings he took on the day. These do not clarify if he was a participant or an observer: we must assume he was both. He refers to the protesters as "we." "We" chant while winding through the streets north of City Hall. "We" haul newspaper boxes and garbage cans onto the street to block the traffic, "we" use dumpsters as makeshift barricades, and then "we" always move on, because the black bloc swarm aims to stay mobile. But then he refers to the black bloc as "they": they are largely aged between 16 and 25. "They" stand out in the crowd, recognizable by their black outfits. Some wear black and red bandanas. "They" shut down a bus and 22 bicycle police gave pursuit, pinning down five in arrest and encircling them with a wall of bikes.

In the ensuing stand-off, David tries to call in legal support and media. He then strikes up a conversation with a woman he calls "Lucinda," an older black woman who has observed what is happening on the other side of the bike barricade and come to report back to the other protesters. Lucinda and David's conversation rambles on, and she mentions her grandchildren. David replies, "You know, I was just thinking today was something I could tell my grandchildren about someday, whereas …". "Yeah," says Lucinda, "whereas I can tell them about it right now."[4] This snippet of conversation seems to have been included in the text for multiple reasons: to record that the author had an awareness that he was living in a historic moment; to illustrate the different kinds of people and experience who came together in that inclusive "we" of the activist coalition; to note that events like this often have an open-ended, unexpected nature, with so many little details that it would be impossible to record them all; and to show that he, the anthropologist, did not know what would happen next, even if the tendency is to write about it afterwards as if it was all a foregone conclusion from the beginning.

*   *   *

Graeber did not live to have children or grandchildren, let alone tell them stories from way back when he was a young scholar who'd only recently received his PhD. He died in 2020 in Venice aged 59. Twenty years earlier, he had likely envisaged quite a different future. Back in 2000, he was two years into a tenure-track position at Yale University, known to some as the brash and brilliant protégé of Marshall Sahlins, and on the cusp of publishing his first book, *The False Coin of our Own Dreams*,[5] intended as a major contribution to anthropological theory. He could not have envisaged that he would lose his job at Yale, enter intellectual "exile" from the United States, and spend a decade in a sort of academic wilderness where not only his first book, but also his two exhaustively detailed ethnographies—*Lost People* and *Direct Action*—as well as his conceptual essays in *Fragments of an Anarchist Anthropology*, *Possibilities*, and *Constituent Imaginations*, would all receive much more hesitant receptions than he had hoped or anticipated.[6] In later years, he would comment on the difficulty of this period of his life.

With his 2011 *Debt*,[7] as we argued in the introduction to this volume, his life entered a new phase as he became a recognized public intellectual. In *Debt*, he successfully linked long-running interventions from anthropology to public debate. He later reflected that the "myth of barter" had been a constant target of anthropologists for over a century with seemingly little success. Despite ample counter-evidence, the myth of barter had persistently reappeared as the origin story for modern economics and finance (see Peebles, ch. 8 this volume). With *Debt*, this myth was seriously rattled. Serendipitously, when Graeber arrived in New York to promote *Debt*, he helped found the Occupy movement, then in its nascent stages.

His involvement with Occupy may seem far removed from the rather academic question on the veracity of the myth of original barter, but the two are interlinked. Anarchism links them. The idea that money begins out of self-interested exchange and that all individuals are responsible to pay what they owe are both grand myths that use caricatures about human nature to sustain belief in exploitative transfers of wealth and power. It was his union of classic anthropological insights (some, like the myth of barter, long-running bugbears in anthropology) with current social movements that earned him his moniker. In this sense, his work is an example of actually existing anarchist anthropology.

In *On Kings*,[8] Marshall Sahlins (Graeber's co-author on this book) drew inspiration from Edmund Leach to argue that, "what is structurally and historically effective about myth is that the people believe it is true."[9] Furthermore, Sahlins clarified that what is important about this belief is that it is used to justify action: "Stories are myths if they are used as … justifications or precedents for social action, whether secular or religious. Whether the precedent story in question was or was not true as factual history is entirely irrelevant…."[10] This echoes a very classic formulation of myth in anthropology: that myths are charters for social action.[11] In this formulation, any question of historical veracity is bracketed off, and instead the focus is on the function of the myth in observable social action.

In a sense, this classic anthropological definition of myth is the structural inverse of Graeber's definition of politics. In *Lost People*, he argued that: "Actions are political in so far as they are intended to influence the actions of others."[12] He argued that political action is recognizable by the way it attracts narration, seems to be designed to be recounted, and is successful if it is talked about.[13] He also quipped that: "Politics is that dimension of social life in which things really do become true if enough people believe them."[14] In *Pirate Enlightenment*, he writes: "political action is best defined as action that influences others at least some of whom are not present at the time—that is, that influences others by being talked about, narrated, sung, drawn, written, or otherwise represented."[15] These various formulations posit a relationship: belief, stories, and narratives on the one hand, which are the tell-tale result of political action on the other.

However, Graeber was skeptical of the Marxist tendency towards "unmasking" where what was revealed again and again was a "jaundiced picture of social reality."[16] Instead, Graeber was fascinated by the creative potentials of masks and masking (as in, for example, carnival); this was in keeping with his interest in the creative potentials of play and pleasure as fundamental to human experience and, ultimately, to politics. In fact, he commented that what was so interesting about Lévi-Strauss's structuralism, including the structural analysis of myth, was the playful possibilities it opened up (see also Edwards, ch. 6 this volume).[17] Through structuralism and myth-busting, he did not seek answers: he sought new possibilities. For him, opening up possibilities for new thought was an important political act, because he wrote—by his own account—in a time and place when there seemed to be a real limit on saying anything new at all, insofar as "the war on imagination" had triumphed. He argued that under neoliberalism, "it is plain to everyone that capitalism doesn't work, but it is almost impossible for anyone to imagine anything else. The war against the imagination is the only one the capitalists have actually managed to win."[18] Graeber defined alienation as a kind of violence, but one that occurs not only physically but also on the level of the imagination: in an alienated existence, one imagines that one has no influence over the structures and conditions that frame one's own life.[19] He also viewed violence as resulting in a fracturing and splintering of imagination.[20]

Reflecting on events at the anti-globalization protests (which he described in *Direct Action*), Graeber noted that while police violence was an important part of the picture, violence also existed on the level of the imagination:

> there was a level of symbolic, even mythological warfare on top of the actual warfare. The anarchists would create silly looking giant puppets and appear with turbans and belly dancers to make the police response seem crazed and disproportionate. The cops would respond by trying to convince the public that the puppets might really contain bombs or hydrochloric acid to throw in their faces.[21]

He speculates that it was only when police were armed with such outlandish images that they were capable of the violence witnessed at the World Trade Organization protests. He also argued that this twisted imagination (that a playful giant puppet actually conceals a giant weapon) is typical of the structure of imagination of the political right. For the right, he commented, there is a "political ontology of violence, where being realistic means taking into account the forces of destruction," which are perceived as the underlying reality of everything, everywhere.[22] The left, meanwhile, is rooted in "a political ontology of the imagination" that affirms the creative potential of human imagination.[23] Graeber intimated that both of these ontologies display the ignorance typical of the privileged, in that both assume that the world is something that is essentially created (through overwhelming force in the case of the right, and through mere imagination in the case of the left). Thus, the oft-repeated quote attributed to Graeber, that "the ultimate, hidden truth of the world is that it is something that we make, and could just as easily make differently."[24] When this quotation is read in context, it is clear that this is a position he is attributing to the left, but not a position he was seriously adopting as his own argument.[25] While Graeber often reaffirmed the liberatory capacities of human imaginations, he was also fond of pointing out that violence—physical, structural, and ideological—is a profound underlying lived experience.

*   *   *

Graeber frequently pointed to his parents as influences on his politics: they were "1930s radicals."[26] His father fought with the International

Brigades in Spain, with the ambulance corps based just outside Barcelona. His mother was the lead in a radical musical about workers, called *Pins n Needles*.[27] It was a household full of books and ideas. His parents did not identify themselves as anarchists, but he describes how they never conveyed a sense that the idea of anarchism was ludicrous or easily dismissed. This sense of serious possibility was reaffirmed when he travelled to Madagascar for fieldwork at a time when the state had, for all practical purposes, ceased to function in the towns where he lived. People managed their own affairs largely through consensus decision-making (see Ralph, ch. 7 this volume).

Although he was interested in anarchism, the scene he could access in 1980s New York was dominated by what he describes as "squabbling egomaniacs."[28] In an interview with *Village Voice* after he was ousted from Yale, he claimed, "I've been an anarchist since I was 16.... I tried to get involved in radical politics in the '80s and '90s but the mainstream groups were extremely hierarchical and the anarchists insufferable."[29] His first real involvement with a self-consciously anarchist movement came at the beginning of the new millennium—the global justice movement in Philadelphia alluded to above. These experiences arguably had more influence on his self-identification as an anarchist than any anarchist text. By contrast, Noam Chomsky, as a 13-year-old schoolboy in the 1940s, discovered anarchism in New York City's Fourth Avenue second-hand bookstores, news-stand debates, and anarchist journals.[30]

For Graeber, anarchism was primarily an approach to practice, not a body of doctrine.[31] He thought of anarchism as a moral project, not an intellectual one.[32] He noted that debates in anarchist movements are typically not about points of arcane theory but about how to organize and facilitate processes in the here-and-now to bring about non-alienated experiences—both as an end in themselves and as a pathway to radical alternatives for society as a whole.[33] Although he did once provide a citation analysis of Vaneigem (noting how often he was cited in contrast to Baudrillard),[34] and described a polemical piece by Hakim Bey as offering an interesting new angle for anthropologists,[35] in general he argued that "I'm not a scholar of anarchism in any sense."[36] This was not a statement evaluating the limits of his own abilities or expertise per se, so much as a reflection on what makes the political movement distinct. He noted wryly that while different branches of Marxists tended to take the name of some Great Man (Trotskyites, Gramscians), various branches of anarchism tend to be named after how they understand processes (Anarcho-Syndicalists,

Anarcho-Communists, Individualists).[37] Anarchism, for Graeber, was
more of a process than a doctrine.

In his scholarly work, Graeber made several attempts to define anarchism. Anarchism, as he wrote in *Direct Action*, is:

> a political movement that aims to bring about a genuinely free society
> ... where humans only enter those kinds of relations with one another
> that would not have to be enforced by the constant threat of violence.[38]

That is, his anarchism was not one of "absolute freedom of the individual" (as in the *Oxford English Dictionary* definition) but rather one where
people are engaged in voluntary relations and obligations. He theorized
human freedom not as absolute but as the ability to choose our obligations, and live only under those constraints. As he quipped: "it's not a
promise if you can't break it: this was one of my great realizations when I
was writing *Debt*."[39] In this formulation, his anarchism is not so much anti-
state; it insists rather on placing the state as only one of many potential
actors in the governance of human affairs. In fact, he thought the state was
quite a parochial concept likely in the process of unravelling.[40] The state,
he said, was perhaps less helpful (comparatively speaking) as a category
for thinking about authority throughout human history than, for example,
kingship.[41] The concept of the state rests on a binding together of sovereignty, administrative organization, and a competitive political field, and
he picks these apart in his work, showing that it is actually very difficult
to find examples in the ethnographic record, historical sources, or prehistory where these have come together as the concept of a state suggests.[42]

In another attempt at definition, he put it this way:

> I am an anarchist. The anarchist problem remains how to bring that
> sort of experience, and the imaginative power that lies behind it, into
> the daily lives of those outside the small, autonomous bubbles we
> anarchists have already created.... [one of] creative, non-alienated
> experience.[43]

In this formulation, he understands anarchism as a direct experience of
the freedom—of the imagination and action—that comes when the contradictions and ridiculousness of any given ideological arrangement or
cosmology become apparent. Anarchist moments—epiphanies, as it were,
of one's freedom, and of the potential creativity always has to exceed any

given set of orthodoxies and norms—are already here, all around us, and the work of anarchism is to expand these and allow more people to recognize and access them. This is again in keeping with the idea, mentioned earlier, that Graeber was inspired not so much by anarchist theory as anarchist practice, or even direct experiences of insurrectionary moments.

These various attempts to explain his anarchism, along with his repeated explanations of how and why he came to anarchism, suggest that he was responding to questions raised about his anarchism. In one recent podcast, anarchist theorist John Zerzan says angrily of Graeber "the man's a fraud! Where is his anarchism?"[44] Graeber himself notes that, in the coverage of the World Trade Organization protests, when the media mentioned "anarchists", this word was invariably prefaced with adjectives such as "self-professed" or "self-proclaimed," as if to question the plausibility of anyone's claim to truly be an anarchist. Likewise, the coverage after Graeber's death also often tagged him in such terms (see for instance, the *Washington Post*'s description of him as "an anthropologist and self-proclaimed anarchist").[45]

By comparison, Graeber's self-identification as an anthropologist seems much less problematic. He rarely explained himself on this point. His writings give little clue about what originally drew him to the discipline (when he was directly asked why he came to anthropology, he sometimes mentioned a hobby he had as a 12-year-old translating Mayan scripts). In the absence of a story about how and why Graeber became an anthropologist, the impulse was occasionally to assume that he must have always been one, "my entire life" as he put it.[46] Even though he spent much of his career feeling rejected and unrecognized by the discipline, it seems his identity as one never really was in doubt. By contrast, his identity as an anarchist drew significant speculation.

* * *

Although David Graeber did not identify himself as an anarchist anthropologist, his body of work does seem to be an appropriate case study for considering what an actually existing anarchist anthropology might look like. His 2004 *Fragments of an Anarchist Anthropology* will likely live on as the most important attempt yet to link these two categories and commitments together. In that book he argued that "an anarchist anthropology doesn't really exist. There are only fragments."[47] He had made a similar point about value theory in his first book: that anthropologists had carried on as if a coherent anthropological theory of value existed when there wasn't one.[48] In both cases, he aimed to assemble the fragments—on value and anarchist anthropology, respectively—into a meta-theory capable of the broadest possible application. In fact, his theory of value directly reflected his growing anarchist principles; in *The False Coin of our Own Dreams* he argued that in valuing the things and people that we do, we are in fact expressing our own free, creative capacities. But these were his first two books, and they appeared relatively early in his career. Does anything in the large volume of writing he left us with subsequently comprise an existing anarchist anthropology?

At first glance, it is striking how many of the prescriptions he laid out in *Fragments* for a potential future anarchist anthropology he went on to develop in his later work. For instance, Graeber outlined what he saw as the three most important directions in anarchism at the time of writing: the anti-globalization movement, the struggle against work, and democracy.[49] He went on to write an ethnography of the first,[50] and a popular salvo about each of the other two.[51] Among the topics he identified in *Fragments* as appropriate for an anarchist anthropology were a new theory of the state, a theory of political happiness (what he later called political pleasure), and the dimensions of non-alienated experience.[52] These formed the backbone of some of his most important contributions in the years that followed. *Fragments* proposed that anthropologists can find inspiration for conceptual work in the ideas and practices of activists. He went on, in much of his intellectual work, to elaborate on the anti-globalization movement's use of "play" as a practice, and the Occupy movement's practice of "care."[53] *Fragments* can be read as a sort of recipe for his career that was to come, a program foreshadowing the general shape of the contributions he would go on to make. Graeber's anthropology seems to have grown to fit his own description of what an anarchist anthropology would look like. He did this, it is worth repeating, despite spending half of that career feeling as if no one was particularly interested in what he was up to.

In summary, Graeber's anthropology was "anarchist" in the sense that he used his observation of actually existing anarchist practice and thought as an inspiration in his thought, writing, and activism. He found anarchist inspiration all around him, whether in the de facto non-state space of post-austerity Madagascar, in the meetings and actions of the explicitly anarchist Direct Action Network, in the ethnographic and prehistoric record that evidences thousands of very real acephalous societies, in the fragments of already existing anthropological affinities with anarchism, and the everyday experience of non-alienated experience that exists in pockets even in societies dominated by markets and states. He took these fragments of evidence, observation, and experience as the basis for the construction of anthropological concepts and theories, which he hoped would help people to think about their own lives in ways that may never have occurred to them before. With his earnest attempt to write clearly and engagingly, and to publish widely, he offered these inspirations back—to activists, to scholars, and to the public in general—as gifts and possibilities. He offered these in the hope and faith that, by broadening the conversation, conceptual work could influence matters of public importance. Below, we illustrate how his anarchism influenced his approach to anthropology by taking as an example his involvement with the journal *HAU*.

* * *

Given that Graeber perceived himself to be writing against a very powerful war on imagination, it is understandable that he would be particularly open to opportunities aimed at generating and disseminating novel ideas. This is how one might understand his involvement with the journal *HAU: The Journal of Ethnographic Theory*. He did not mention this journal in his scholarly works, but it was prominent in the final decade of his life.

The journal was launched in 2011, with Graeber as "editor-at-large" and with an introduction co-authored by Graeber and the journal's driving force, Giovanni da Col.[54]

The journal promised to revolutionize anthropological publishing, offering gold standard Open Access free to both readers and contributors, courtesy of the voluntary labor of reviewers and editorial staff. In doing so, it likened academic labor and publications to "gifts" (this was part of the thinking behind the name of the journal, a Māori word much discussed in the anthropology of the gift, as discussed by Stewart elsewhere and in ch. 4, this volume.)[55] The journal also promised to revolutionize anthropology by returning the discipline to its original promise as a source of "ethnographic theory"—as da Col and Graeber put it[56]—or the generation of novel concepts from the analysis of the ethnographic record.

Graeber once wrote that activist groups often emerge from one person's vision, but eventually come to a point of "peasant insurrection," where that one person is asked to step aside so that the movement can continue in a more participatory manner, "and, if the collective doesn't dissolve in bitter recriminations, it becomes a genuinely democratic group."[57] Something along these lines appears to have occurred at *HAU*, but instead of evolution into a genuinely democratic group, da Col refused to step aside. Complaints about da Col (abusive language, unreasonable demands, threats, and even a physical attack) were circulating as early as 2012, and were acted on by individual anthropology departments, but there was no clear process whereby these could be dealt with by the journal itself.[58] Donations had been raised in the initial uprush of enthusiasm to support the journal, but donors became concerned when financial reports were delayed. Audited accounts were at first non-existent and, when they finally appeared, the detailed report was not available to the public or even to financial donors. In addition to questions swirling around da Col's alleged mismanagement and unethical behavior, some critics used the attention *HAU* was drawing to call for renewed disciplinary commitments to decolonization and anti-racism. There were fears, for example, that ethnographic theorizing would only serve to justify renewed enthusiasm for appropriating cultural knowledge and meaning for mostly privileged, Western and white academic audiences. Of course, this was not at all in keeping with what David Graeber argued passionately for over his whole career.

Complaints circulated on email, at conferences and via the "whisper network." Graeber worked behind the scenes to seek a resolution, and—when that appeared impossible—to support those who wished to speak out. He publicly distanced himself from the journal in 2017. This created a breakthrough: what had been a matter of private, even secret, concern, burst into an open conversation. The Twitter hashtag @HAUtalk became not only a way of airing concerns with HAU but also an influential platform for rethinking the ethics of anthropology. An article appeared in the anti-PC soapbox *Quillette* criticizing Graeber for his move and the subsequent public outcry.[59] A report more sympathetic to Graeber was run in *The Chronicle of Higher Education* just weeks before his death.[60] At the time, Graeber's personal website (davidgraeberindustries.com) featured an apology for his initial support of the journal and any harm that might have caused, first posted in 2018. His willingness to speak out was in contrast to many of the luminaries who had initially supported the journal, but who fell silent when it became clear that some kind of public and principled action was due.

Graeber ultimately took an admirable stand against *HAU*. But the debacle also hinted at some of the shortcomings that might be perceived in his work overall. For instance, the very title of the journal is an appropriation of a Māori concept, but the journal brushed aside concerns about the politics of such ethnographic prospecting in Indigenous thought. This was characteristic of the relationship between politics, anthropology, and ethnography evident in Graeber's early work: in seeking to make the ethnographic record available for those wanting to imagine political alternatives, his early work tended to downplay the politics of ethnography itself. In his posthumously published works however (particularly *Dawn of Everything* and *Pirate Enlightenment*) engaging with decolonizing intellectual history became a key theme of his work (as we argued in the Introduction to this volume.)

@HAUTalk also highlighted the pervasive sexism of the discipline. This was something that Graeber sought to expose, but again this was most prominent only in his later and posthumous works. In *Dawn of Everything*, Graeber and Wengrow admit that the kind of myth-work they accomplish there, including the creation of long, sprawling scholarly books, is an act that is regularly indulged in by men but effectively barred to women.[61] When Marija Gimbutas had published similarly ambitious work (on the possibility of a "Great Goddess" religion prevalent throughout "Old Europe" from the Upper Palaeolithic through to around 3000 BC), she had been dismissed by many. Graeber favorably cited feminist work: his book on value was arguably made possible because of the work of feminist economist Diane Elson (specifically her influential interpretation on "the value theory of labor"[62] which helped inspire the once-structuralist Terence Turner to become a Marxian), and the approach of his book with Sahlins was inspired (they say themselves) in part by Mary Helms' *Ulysses' Sail*.[63] Yet neither Elson nor Helms have arguably received anything equal to the attention that Graeber has for their related ideas. We predict the same will be true of Gimbutas, despite the popularity of *Dawn of Everything*.

Graeber pointed out in his late work the relative neglect of contributions made to the history of ideas by women, Indigenous thinkers, Black scholars, and everyday people, but invariably, when he did co-author a major book, it was with a white man occupying a privileged nook of the academy. Perhaps we could think of his engagement with feminist, decolonized, antiracist and Indigenous thought as among the "doors left open" in his work. And these are perhaps doors he would have gone through had he lived longer. Certainly, speaking as feminist anthropologists ourselves, we find ample inspiration for thinking anew about feminist issues in Graeber's work.[64]

HAU was notorious for playing prestige games. At its launch, an almost laughably long list of endorsements from heavy-hitters was circulated.

Graeber's own work, in a much milder form, could also be said to play prestige games. For all his self-styling as an oddball and misfit (a feature we mentioned in the introduction), he held a quite privileged place in the discipline: he was a Chicago PhD and held positions at some of the world's leading departments. His years in the wilderness did not involve unemployment and precariat employment. Thinking about *HAU* alongside his posthumous *Pirate Enlightenment*, it occurs to us that there is a pirate-like tension in Graeber's work between this apparent privilege and his self-styling as an outcast.

Perhaps we could think of his engagement with *HAU* as an attempt to found a Libertalia—the fabled pirate utopia that Graeber discusses in *Pirate Enlightenment*—for anthropologists. The first bombastic missives from *HAU*—which caused such a sensation (excitement, horror, disgust, interest) in the metropolitan centers of anthropology—share more than a passing resemblance with the exaggerated stories told by the pirates in Graeber's account, who set themselves up as mock kings, sending emissaries from Madagascar to the courts of Europe claiming to be a new kingdom. They told tall tales designed to impress outsiders, while among themselves the real aim was quite different: to survive and, he speculates, to create the possibilities for a new, more democratic way of being. His point in part is that these pirates, as marginal as they were in reality, in fact did influence conversations in Europe and must be viewed as part of the Enlightenment. If Graeber sought to be a "big man" of anthropology, a winner in the prestige game of academic recognition, perhaps it was more after the fashion of these mock kings.

*   *   *

Graeber often wrote in his scholarly work with the certainty of neither an insider nor an outsider.[65] He was at his most winning and eloquent as an ethnographer when he presented himself as an awkward but observant outsider. One of the most memorable images, for us, of him as a fieldworker is from *Lost People*: Graeber is smoking a cigarette by an apparently abandoned ancestral tomb early on in his fieldwork, not sure about anything, but especially in that moment not sure about what to do with his cigarette butt. Was it OK to leave it by this tomb? Moments later, he meets the woman who would be his key informant, and who guides him on this and other Malagasy matters, large and small. This is also the Graeber that we see in that moment in *Direct Action* where he chats with

Lucinda: he is not quite sure what is happening. But more than anything he seems grateful to have an unexpected conversation with her.

From our point of view, his writing was duller and harder to read when he seemed to be wanting to claim a privileged perspective as an insider of an anarchist movement. In *Direct Action*, there is an uncomfortable scene where Graeber pulls on a black balaclava and, dressed entirely in black, runs with the black bloc through Quebec streets. In these passages, Graeber seems to assert that, in these moments at least, he really was part of the pack. Some readers (us included) may find these passages cringe-inducing, but they are consistent with Graeber's defense of the destruction of property as a legitimate form of protest.[66] In the scene we have in mind in *Direct Action*, after hours of hit-and-run strikes on property, a bloc'er turns to him and says that no one in the bloc recognizes him, and tells him to find his own affinity group.[67] The mood abruptly changes from feeling like the author (and by extension, the reader) is "running with the pack" to feeling lost and disorientated. As a writerly tactic, this abruptness throws back onto the reader whatever expectations or reactions that image of Graeber running with the black bloc might have provoked. In *Direct Action*, he claims an insider status but also quite openly disavows the notion that any one person can have a privileged insider perspective of any given action: there are only fragments.

David Graeber apparently felt comfortable with such ambiguities. Josh protested alongside him in the "student protests" in London, challenging the proposed increase in university fees in the fall of 2010 (see Chari, this volume). After Josh had to leave the march early to go do childcare, David came to his office the next day with a gift: a fragment of glass from the smashed windows at Tory HQ, which was both a present and sign of his own (possible) role in the destruction. Was he merely observing what others did? Was he involved in smashing that window? He did not say and Josh did not ask. And that was entirely in keeping with Graeber at his best. His anarchism was not one of totalizing wholes (you are either in or you are out). Rather, it was an anarchism of fragments, direct experiences, and possibilities.

Notes

All URLs last accessed March 6, 2023.

1.   David Graeber, "Here's a Thought re #hautalk – Why Not Take the Occasion to Ask What is Going on in Our Own Departments?"

Twitter, June 17, 2018, available at: https://twitter.com/davidgraeber/status/1008309270188843008.

2. David Graeber, Mehdi Belhaj Kacem, Nika Dubrovsky, and Assia Turquier-Zauberman, *Anarchy—In a Manner of Speaking* (Belgium, France and Luxemburg: Diaphenes, 2020).

3. Lesley Brown, *The New Shorter Oxford English Dictionary* (Toronto: ECW Press, 1997), 73.

4. David Graeber, *Direct Action: An Ethnography* (Oakland, CA and Edinburgh: AK Press, 2009), 411.

5. David Graeber, *Toward an Anthropological Theory of Value: The False Coin of Our Own Dreams* (New York: Palgrave, 2001).

6. David Graeber, *Lost People: Magic and the Legacy of Slavery in Madagascar* (Bloomington: Indiana University Press, 2007); Graeber, *Direct Action*; David Graeber, *Fragments of an Anarchist Anthropology* (Chicago: Prickly Paradigm Press, distributed by University of Chicago Press, 2004).

7. David Graeber, *Debt: The First 5,000 Years* (Brooklyn: Melville House, 2011), 94.

8. David Graeber and Marshall Sahlins, *On Kings* (Chicago, IL: HAU Books).

9. Ibid., 214.

10. Ibid.

11. Michael W. Young, *Malinowski: Odyssey of an Anthropologist 1884–1920* (New Haven and London: Yale University Press, 2004), 523.

12. Graeber, *Lost People*, 214.

13. Ibid., 130.

14. Graeber, *Debt*, 94.

15. David Graeber, *Pirate Enlightenment, or the Real Libertalia* (New York: Farrar, Straus and Giroux, 2023), 149.

16. Graeber, *Toward an Anthropological Theory of Value*, 35.

17. Graeber and Sahlins, *On Kings*, 77.

18. David Graeber, *Revolutions in Reverse* (London and New York: Minor Compositions, 2011), 112.

19. Stevphen Shukaitis, David Graeber, with Erika Biddle (eds.), *Constituent Imagination: Militant Investigations, Collective Theorization* (Oakland, CA and Edinburgh: AK Press, 2007), 32.

20. Graeber, *Revolutions in Reverse*, 112.

21. Graeber et al., *Anarchy*, 312.

22. Graeber, *Revolutions in Reverse*, 42.

23. Ibid.

24. David Graeber, *The Utopia of Rules: On Technology, Stupidity, and the Secret Joys of Bureaucracy* (Brooklyn and London: Melville House, 2015), 54; see also Graeber, *Direct Action*, 512–514; and *Revolution in Reverse*, 42.

25. Graeber, *The Utopia of Rules*, 54.

26. David Graeber, *Possibilities: Essays on Hierarchy, Rebellion, and Desire* (Oakland, CA and Edinburgh: AK Press, 2007), 6.

27. Ibid.

28. Ibid.

29. Nick Mamatas, "Take It from the Top," *Village Voice*, May 31, 2005, available at: https://www.villagevoice.com/2005/05/31/take-it-from-the-top/

30. Robert Franklin Barksy, *Noam Chomsky: A Life of Dissent* (Toronto: ECW Press, 1997).

31. Graeber, *Fragments*.

32. Graeber, *Possibilities*, 211.

33. Graeber, *Direct Action*, 214.

34. Stevphen Shukaitis and David Graeber, "Introduction," in *Constituent Imagination*, eds. Shukaitis and Graeber with Biddle, 22.

35. David Graeber, "Culture as Creative Refusal," *Cambridge Journal of Anthropology*, 31, no. 2 (2012), 1–19.

36. Graeber et al., *Anarchy*.

37. Graeber, *Fragments*, 4.

38. Graeber, *Direct Action*, 187.

39. Graeber et al., *Anarchy*, 117.

40. Ibid.

41. Graeber and Sahlins, *On Kings*.

42. Ibid.; David Graeber and David Wengrow, *The Dawn of Everything* (Great Britain: Allen Lane, 2022).

43. Graeber, *Possibilities*, 410.

44. John Zerzan, "New Books in Anthropology Podcast," March 4, 2022, https://newbooksnetwork.com/when-we-are-human.

45. Matt Schudel, "David Graeber, Scholar, Anarchist and Intellectual Leader of Occupy Wall Street, Dies at 59," *The Washington Post*, September 5, 2020, available at: https://www.washingtonpost.com/local/obituaries/david-graeber-scholar-anarchist-and-intellectual-leader-of-occupy-wall-street-dies-at-59/2020/09/05/df66b16e-eeb9-11ea-99a1-71343d03bc29_story.html

46. David Graeber, "From Maya Enthusiast to Occupy Activist: Allegra Meets David Graeber," *Allegra Lab*, June 2014, https://allegralaboratory.net/from-maya-enthusiast-to-occupy-activist-allegra-meets-david-graeber/

47. Graeber, *Fragments*, 38.

48. David Graeber, *Toward an Anthropological Theory of Value*, 22.

49. Graeber, *Fragments*, 77–94.

50. Graeber, *Direct Action*.

51. Graeber, *Bullshit Jobs*; David Graeber, *The Democracy Project: A History, a Crisis, a Movement* (New York: Spiegel & Grau, 2013).

52. Graeber, *Fragments*, 65–76.

53. Graeber, *Direct Action*, 20, 221.

54. In the interests of disclosure: Holly was also involved at the launch stage, offering advice and editorial support. She resigned in 2012. Giovanni Da Col and David Graeber, "Foreword: The Return of Ethnographic Theory," *HAU: Journal of Ethnographic Theory* 1, no. 1 (2011).

55. See Georgina Stewart, "The 'Hau' of Research: Mauss Meets Kaupapa Māori," *Journal of World Philosophies* (Summer 2017).

56. Da Col and Graeber, "Foreword."

57. Graeber, *Direct Action*, 20.

58. Sarah Green documented her frustrated efforts, from her position on *HAU*'s External Advisory Board, to implement a transparent process, see: https://allegralaboratory.net/hautalk-the-tyranny-of-structurelessness-and-no-end-in-sight/

59. Clare Lehman, "How David Graeber Cancelled a Colleague," *Quillette*, September 9, 2019, available at: https://quillette.com/2019/09/09/the-anarchist-and-the-anthropology-journal/

60. Jess Singal, "How One Prominent Journal Went Very Wrong," *Chronicle of Higher Education*, October 5, 2020, available at: https://www.chronicle.com/article/how-one-prominent-journal-went-very-wrong

61. Graeber and Wengrow, *Dawn of Everything*, 218.

62. Diane Elson, "The Value Theory of Labour," in *Value: The Representation of Labour in Capitalism*, ed. Diane Elson (London: CSE Books, 1979).

63. Mary Helms, *Ulysses' Sail: An Ethnographic Odyssey of Power, Knowledge and Geographic Distance* (Princeton, NJ: Princeton University Press, 1988).

64. See for example High (ch. 2, this volume); Josh Reno with Britt Halvorson, "The Gendering of Theory in Anthropology since 2000: Ontology, Semiotics and Feminism," *Current Anthropology* 64, no. 4.

65. See Faye V. Harrison, *Outsider Within: Reworking Anthropology in the Global Age* (Urbana, IL: University of Illinois Press, 2008).

66. This is a major theme of *Direct Action*, but see also David Graeber 2007 "On the Phenomenology of Giant Puppets: Broken Windows, Imaginary Jars of Urine, and the Cosmological Role of the Police in American Culture," available at the time of writing from davidgraeber.org.

67. Graeber, *Direct Action*, 176–181.

4

Ka Mate, Ka Ora: On Truth, Lies, and Knowing the Difference

Georgina Tuari Stewart

Introduction: Life in the Symbolic Zone

In 2006 David Graeber gave the Malinowski Memorial Lecture, which he later published as "Dead Zones of the Imagination: On Violence, Bureaucracy, and Interpretive Labor."[1] Graeber noted that the key ideas about power and ignorance in his article were already "commonplace" in feminist literature, about which he was "entirely oblivious" when he first wrote the article, using his own experience as an example of the power/*ignorance* nexus he delineated (though not in these words) in his article. Referring to such blindness as "lopsided structures of the imagination" that become embedded in society, Graeber asks:

> whether our theoretical work is ultimately directed at undoing or dismantling some of the effects of these lopsided structures of imagi-nation, or whether—as can so easily happen when even our best ideas come to be backed up by bureaucratically administered violence—we end up reinforcing them.[2]

Graeber's article fits into a twenty-first-century "ignorance tradition," coined "agnotology," that claims to study ignorance in the same way as epistemology studies knowledge.[3] The inherently Western knowledge base of education has untruth embedded so deeply it is almost entirely invisible. This was pointed out in two famous books from half a century ago, *Knowledge and Control* by Michael Young and *Deschooling Society* by Ivan Illich.[4] While Young's critique centered on the teaching curriculum, Illich critiqued the institutionalization of education as schooling, in terms similar to those of Graeber. Within my own local context, my arguments follow a similar path to those of Illich, tracing how these untruths work as agnoses, or forms of managed social ignorance, to deliver human beings via education to the global war/profit machine.

Graeber calls "areas of violent simplification" those "boring, humdrum, yet omnipresent forms of structural violence" that impact on daily life. Graeber gives *bureaucracy* and *social theory* as two important examples of social systems or ways of thinking that enable and promote simplistic interpretations of everyday human life and interpersonal interactions. This description also fits compulsory state schooling in modern Western nations, in which both bureaucracy and social theory play key roles. Schooling is a favorite political football in a country like Aotearoa New Zealand that prides itself (or used to, anyway) on providing state education as a "level playing field" on which, according to the egalitarian dream, each individual can achieve their potential if they work hard and make good choices.[5]

Aotearoa New Zealand is closely culturally connected to, though physically distant from, centers of global culture such as the United States. One difference between the two is that the interethnic dynamic operates on an exceedingly subtle level in New Zealand. Given the growing visibility of Māori in media and public spaces, it may seem to an outsider that Māori are a valued or even privileged part of national society. The disproportionate numbers of Māori caught up on the wrong side of the nation's prisons, hospitals, and homeless shelters, however, suggests the opposite. Propaganda or "thought weapons" regarding Māori and national histories were deliberately taught in schools for many years and are still firmly embedded in dominant discourses of national identity.[6] Pākehā or White Kiwi identity and its quirks, even as mild as the tendency until the 1960s to think of England as "home," can best be understood by noticing how such devices supported Pākehā to identify as being *not*-Māori.

In Aotearoa New Zealand, education is widely regarded as a benefit and a force for good in people's lives. Even—or especially—within communities whose educational achievement statistics are significantly lower than national norms, adults tend to share this belief in the power of schooling to improve the lives of their children. After 35+ years of neoliberal education and social policy, the main aim of education has become generally equated with economic advantage; education is now valued mainly in terms of access to "good jobs" and the accompanying personal benefits.[7] Regardless of other changes, belief in the beneficial power of "a good education" is stronger than ever. This "immaculate conception" ideology allows education "to maintain and at the same time hide" its real nature and what drives it.[8]

But education "has no ontological status independent of agentic factors": it is a social process and discourse, not a natural phenomenon.[9] That means education "is 'always already' political" and thus can be relied on to distribute its benefits unequally, favoring those who are already advantaged. For groups who are socioeconomically disadvantaged, including Māori in Aotearoa New Zealand, education is even more politically complicit and damaging to social psychology in its normativity. There is a widespread view portrayed in public media, and also among the teaching profession, that Māori people have equal chances as non-Māori (or, better, the notion of "Māori privilege" has appeal in some political quarters) but make "bad choices" that end up consigning them to lives of poverty. The effects of the colonial bases of contemporary social systems are ignored. Education is held over Māori students, families, and communities as both carrot and stick; despite the odds stacked against them, Māori students who fail are said to have parents who "don't value" education, or are pathologized in some way. The agnosis at the heart of current education policy is to ignore the reliable link between family wealth and educational success, which involves other untruths, such as the pedagogical fantasy of measurable and predictable learning. To analyze how power operates unseen in Māori education entails paying attention to the larger power relations that link education to violence and the subjugation of personal autonomy, ultimately to war, in our contemporary "democratic" globalized nation-states. Hence the Māori part of the chapter title, taken from the words of the famous haka (war dance), means "life or death."[10]

The stories Māori people tell about their family histories often feature the relationship with schooling.[11] In my own family on my father's side, my people have been "going to school" for only one or two generations above me. Like many such families, there were 17 children, born over a period of about 20 years. Aged 90+ my aunt (my father's oldest sister, born in 1919) recounted snippets about how, in the 1920s, she and all the Māori children living in the valley would walk a few miles around the unformed coastal road each day to and from school, with only a few being rich enough to ride horses, but how the little ones would hold onto the horses' tails to help them up the hills. For all those Māori children, going to school meant learning English and being inducted into Pākehā/Western ways. My dad said they were "given the supplejack" by the teachers if they were heard speaking a word or two in Māori in the playground, despite it being their home language, because speaking in Māori was deemed "swearing." Most, like my father, were pulled out once they could fulfill a useful economic purpose. My dad resented for life being unceremoniously removed from school aged 13 to look after the team of horses his father was using to build, on contract, a driveable road around to the next bay—the same route his eldest sister, my aunt, had walked a decade earlier.

Schooling has been an important part of the process by which Māori have been marginalized in our/their own land. The basic rationale for Britain to displace Aotearoa and create New Zealand, taking the lands and sovereignty of my ancestors, was the "declining rate of profit" in the United Kingdom and the consequent need to export excess people so as to protect the economic advantage of the already-wealthy.[12] Later, in the 1980s, the same need to maintain profit was served by exporting manufacturing to poorer countries lacking unions or social welfare systems.

In any country, favorite social truth-myths have a longevity in the national imaginary that far exceeds their shelf-life as policy drivers. The "Kiwi way" of giving everyone a "fair go" is one such idea in Aotearoa New Zealand, still used in a "State of the Nation" political speech in 2007.[13] Schooling is an important plank of that "fair go" aspect of national identity. The "fair go" idea can be considered one of Pākehā culture's most cherished "areas of violent simplification." Such an idea supports a "lopsided structure" or blindness in the national imaginary, an agnosis whose unspoken purpose is to enable socioeconomic policies that favor the already-wealthy at the expense of the impoverished sectors of society.

We already know that the benefits of school are unevenly distributed, so that they tend to reinforce existing wealth and social power relationships.[14] Education policy in Aotearoa New Zealand remains fixed on "equity" as policy driver, which focuses on working towards fairer distribution of the benefits of education. But both school success *and* school failure are part of one machine called education, which serves the purposes of capitalism according to the underlying logic of war, as the next section explains in more detail. Western education systems such as the state schooling system of Aotearoa New Zealand serve the complete *opposite* of the dream of social justice through education. Education systems are working as effectively as ever to produce the requisite set of subjectivities, winners *and* losers (but mostly losers); individual citizens who are credulous consumers of advertising and commodified forms of culture, fodder for the profit machine and blind to the larger workings of their social conditions.

Graeber reminds us that the implicit structural violence of our peaceful countries, including Aotearoa New Zealand, is always underwritten by the threat of physical violence. "Racism, sexism, poverty, these cannot exist except in an environment defined by the ultimate threat of actual physical force."[15] All forms of power, including symbolic power, inevitably link into this underlying structure of violence, in the sense of the power to hurt and kill other humans. If, as academics, we fall prey to agnosis and forget or ignore the reality of physical violence that underwrites our society, we cannot fully analyze how power works in our schools and other social institutions. In that case our academic labor becomes complicit in supporting the profit/war machine that drives capitalism. We would then fulfill Graeber's prophecy, reinforcing the lopsided structures of imagination that fuel structures of violence of all kinds.

I have been studying the interface between science and Māori knowledge for 50+ years; as a 10-year-old I spoke about Māori astronomy and appeared in the local newspaper.[16] Today, as a Māori scholar in a mainstream university, I hold a paradoxically doubled position as both expert in, and critic of, Māori education policy. The gift/responsibility of my Indigenous Māori identity is a perspective that actively "others" the dominant Euro-American global culture. The criticality of my analysis depends on this doubled identity; an insider/outsider view of both local *and* global culture/knowledge/power.

This Māori attention and critique of the dominant culture is a form of aroha (the nearest Māori word to "love").[17] For a Māori scholar to study the Western Other is an act of love: dedicating time and energy to research that looks through more than one set of cultural lenses. The gift of the Māori/Indigenous critique is that it holds up a mirror to the West, to bring into view what monoculturalism hides from its people. In this way, Kaupapa Māori and Māori Philosophy are Māori-centered approaches for studying Māori-Pākehā educational relationships, which distinguish themselves from colonizing educational research and its methodologies.[18]

Last summer I enjoyed a "beach crawl" with my sister, visiting a different beach each day along the stretch of coast to which we belong, in Māori terms. Sitting on the sand on our folding chairs at one of those beaches, looking back at the gentle grassy hills rising up from the foreshore towards the public road, my sister told me the story of how our uncle and another local elder had made a deal some decades ago, signing over the entire beachfront to a wealthy Pākehā, now living the dream, the mansion and helipad hidden from public view up the private access road beyond the locked gate. By many means, including shady deals, owner-ship and occupation of Māori lands is continuously chipped away from the descendants of the original owners. As Indigenous peoples, Māori and our lands are raw materials for the profit machine; our post-European history in this way reminiscent of the "enclosures" movement with which capi-talism began in England, as explained in the next section. An important disclaimer is that I am *not* writing comprehensively about "capitalism" in this chapter, nor even from an economics perspective, but rather am inter-ested in capitalism's big ideas, essence, or philosophy.

War, Capitalism, and Education

Capitalism can be described in many ways, but in simple terms it acts like a "concentrating mechanism" for money, that transfers monetary wealth from the less wealthy to the more wealthy. Monetary wealth is an anony-mous form of power extracted from primary sources, namely human labor and natural resources. Through the concentrating mechanisms of capital-ism, power over natural resources *and* over the quality of most people's lives is becoming increasingly privatized—concentrated in the hands of fewer and fewer people. So how did all this begin?

Standard accounts of capitalism usually begin with the "English Enclo-sure movement (circa 1400–1800)," meaning, in simple terms, building fences and transferring lands that formerly had been "the commons" into private ownership—a process of "wrenching" non-wealthy people away from the land.[19] The "multitude" of ordinary English people moved from living and working on the land to waged work in the mills and factories, and the industrial age arrived. This historic socioeconomic shift catalyzed traumatic psychological/philosophical changes for the people concerned, with the reinscribing of subjectivity and the invention of the "individual" of liberal humanism. This disconnection from the land and nature, and the adoption of a modernist "atomistic" notion of the human being are key steps by which, among others, Western culture breaks from its original, Indigenous subjectivities of the old cultures of Europe and Great Britain. This process was recapitulated in Aotearoa New Zealand by the Māori urbanization process in the post-World War II (WWII) period, whereby the Māori population transformed in 20 years from mostly rural to mostly urban.

Cliff Falk labels capitalism as "unique" in releasing personal identity from place, by replacing work on the land with work for wages in the "rise of money."[20] In the academy, within social science disciplines like anthropology, and applied fields such as education that draw on those disciplines, Western culture has been taken as the norm against which "other" cultures are appraised; from that perspective, Indigenous cultures are characterized as "place-based," but Falk's sketch of the onset of capitalism shows how it is actually the Western culture that is the odd one out ("unique") in this regard. Today's globally dominant Western culture ruled by "the market" is the end result of this de-territorialization (and re-territorialization, in repeated cycles) of subjectivity that begins with "the rise of money" signaling the birth of capitalism and modernity.

The rise of money as the standard measure of value transformed Western understandings not only of subjectivity but also intersubjectivity, as explored by Marcel Mauss in his 1925 book *The Gift*, which initiated a wide-ranging, ongoing debate about the nature of a gift, and the difference between gifts and economic transactions.[21] This debate, including the treatment of the Māori example of "the hau of the gift," was lucidly sketched by David Graeber in a chapter of his book *Toward an Anthropological Theory of Value: The False Coin of Our Own Dreams*.[22] Mauss analyzed primary anthropological data on gifting practices in non-Western societies, exposing the concept of the gift as "the hidden face of modernity" because one can always find reasons for saying that gifts "are not really gifts at all."[23] This paradox has been built into Western social theory, which speaks "of social ties without using the words that are associated with them in daily life: surrender, forgiveness, renunciation, love, respect, dignity, redemption, salvation, redress, compassion, everything that is at the heart of relationships between people."[24]

Whether a transaction tends towards gift or commodity depends on whether the relationship between donor and recipient is considered to be permanent—what Graeber called "open reciprocity"—or delimited (i.e. "closed reciprocity") denoting a transactional relationship, where transactions are subject to "careful accounting" and incur legal debt.[25] The binary in Western thinking points to the *lie* at the heart of global economic theory, an illusionary binary:

between freedom and obligation [which] is, like that between interest and generosity, largely an illusion thrown up by the market, whose anonymity makes it possible to ignore the fact that we rely on other people for just about everything.[26]

The gift objects discussed by Mauss (including "taonga" in Māori traditions) carry "traces" of their former owners and histories, but money is generic and resistant to history. It is the "inhuman" nature of the market that allows us to believe we can satisfy our needs and wants without considering the needs and wants of those with whom we engage in so doing. It seems reasonable to suggest that this disconnection via the market from the "others" with whom we engage in carrying on our economic activities lies behind the acceptance in Western culture of the otherwise implausible "unlimited greed" hypothesis as defining the default ethical position of market actors, dubbed "*Homo economicus*."

Falk traces how capitalism "proceeds by decoding representation altogether" and is "inherently unmeaningful":

> Capitalism destroys the Transcendental Signified wherever it finds it, replacing the stable signification of despotic society with the irresolute signifying system demanded by the logic of the capitalist system. Under capitalism, the focus of desire moves from the regus (monarch) or deus (God)—as was the case in precapitalist societies—to abstracted wealth (money).[27]

Falk argues that education as a social institution, far from its "beneficient" reputation, is in fact "an interested technology of subjective formation, as the primary means to realize the de- and re-territorialization process."[28] In education in Aotearoa New Zealand, this point is particularly relevant to Māori people, for whom education has been extremely important, and even more ideological, as in deceitful, with its real nature being hidden behind a shiny surface, than for students from mainstream, that is, Pākehā/White backgrounds. Falk pursues his argument that education is therefore essential to the pursuit of violence against citizens, ultimately to war, drawing a convincing chain of links between war and education, as summarized in the next section of this chapter ('Education, Psychology, Technology, War').

Falk's point of departure is that education is viewed "as a force for unilateral good" and "as indiscriminately beneficial, as a good in its own right." These descriptors overstate how well education is viewed today, particularly among academic commentators, because (among other things) the deleterious effects of decades of neoliberal policy on national provision of education are more apparent now, compared with fifteen or more years ago, when Falk wrote his chapter. But Falk's comment that capitalism "destroys the Transcendental Signified" goes to the heart of the classic essay by C.S. Lewis, *The Abolition of Man*, which uses the word *"Tao"* to refer to the transcendental concept.[29] While Falk focuses on the consequences for education of the outgrowth of capitalism, Lewis was interested in the effects of the rise of the bureaucratic forms of modernity, and the consequent loss of the *Tao* (as he phrased it), on British culture, people, and education.

Lewis considers what today remains an urgent question for humanity's future, namely, the progress of applied science, which he noted was then-commonly expressed by the phrase "Man's conquest of Nature."[30] "Man" with a capital "M" is Lewis's word for what is now called humanity or humankind, in seeking to purge language of its sexist "trace." Lewis consistently refers to Nature as a proper noun, in keeping with the older convention. Also dated is the verbal form "conquest of" to depict the advance of science, now sounding impossibly coy, evoking the old metaphors of Nature as feminine and Science as masculine, with all the patriarchal undertones of Western modernity. Literally speaking, conquest is a military verb meaning to win in war. The existential question—the temper of the times, or spirit of the age—has flipped in the seven decades since Lewis wrote: today the concern is no longer about humanity "winning" against nature, but whether nature can survive against the human onslaught. Current plans by the global elite for interplanetary colonization would seem to suggest they hold a pessimistic view on this question.

The dead-end dilemma of Western philosophy arises from "the fatal serialism of the modern imagination—the image of infinite unilinear progression which so haunts our minds."[31] Lewis's words evoke not only the teleology that blinkers much of White scholarship, but also the reductionism, presentism, and quantification of the economistic social theories that influence contemporary education systems.

> Because we have to use numbers so much we tend to think of every process as if it must be like the numeral series, where every step, to all eternity, is the same kind of step as the one before…. There are progressions in which the last step is *sui generis*—incommensurable with the others—and in which to go the whole way is to undo all the labour of your previous journey. To reduce the *Tao* to a mere natural product is a step of that kind.[32]

Two key differences pertain to the *sui generis* last step, which Lewis hypothesized would involve the emergence of a group he called "the Conditioners."[33] First, these planners would have access to unprecedented levels of power, comprising the sum total of all the technological power accumulated by humanity until that point in time; and, second, the last step involves, for the Conditioners, stepping outside and complete emancipation from the *Tao*: "Values are now mere natural phenomena."[34] In arguing that the Conditioners would have thus "sold" their humanity for the power of maximum knowledge, Lewis coins the word "posthuman" possibly de novo:

> Man's conquest of himself means simply the rule of the Conditioners over the conditioned human material, the world of post-humanity which, some knowingly and some unknowingly, nearly all men in all nations are at present labouring to produce.[35]

Lewis was not arguing for one particular version of "a doctrine of values" but for the need for people to retain values at all, understanding "values" in the sense of an ethos or meta-narrative by which to live, which arises from a sense of (Indigenous) identity, and from which derive central values and principles for right behavior in the world. That Lewis took the Chinese word "*tao*" as his keyword for this essay, and that he appended a list of examples from a wide range of world philosophies, indicate his effort to think reflexively, cross-culturally and critically from and about his own (Anglican, analytical philosophical) perspective. He concluded that the modern, scientific worldview tries to "have it both ways" and that a "dogmatic belief in objective value is necessary."

> Either we are rational spirit obliged for ever to obey the absolute values of the *Tao*, or else we are mere nature to be kneaded and cut into new shapes for the pleasures of masters who must, by hypothesis, have no motive but their own "natural" impulses.[36]

Lewis imagines "a regenerate science" of the future, evoking the commonly expressed hopes that Western science and philosophy can learn from engaging with Indigenous knowledge, including Mātauranga Māori.[37] "When it explained it would not explain away. When it spoke of the parts it would remember the whole."[38] Lewis recognized the significance of "education and propaganda based on a perfect applied psychology" in the changes he saw taking place around him, and combined logic with imagination to argue those tendencies through to their final conclusions, making a lasting contribution to philosophy of education.[39]

Education, Psychology, Technology, War

Over time, Western systems of education became increasingly industrialized, from the later stages of the Industrial Revolution onwards. Education, including compulsory state schooling, formed part of the imperial power machine in the era of European expansionism, of which the contemporary nation-state of Aotearoa New Zealand is a product.

War and education became increasingly entangled during the twentieth century; increases in military spending invariably led to the expansion of education systems, while knowledge production has been an active front of modern warfare "to the point where *the research university itself proved to be the greatest war weapon ever invented*."[40] That statement must give any university academic pause for thought. "The mutually determining relationships between knowledge production, education, empire, and war have been generally evident in every industrially developed jurisdiction for at least a century."[41] Yet most academic theory—social theory including Marxism, or economic theory, which sees war as an "aberration"—cannot account for the relationship.

Falk traces three major links between education and war:[42]

1. mutual benefit: military spending leads to expansion of education systems, which in turn furnish more powerful war weapons;
2. the application of psychology to propaganda and advertising, and education for the production of subjectivity and subjects more susceptible to propaganda;
3. digital technologies and the ongoing development of artificial intelligence, which threatens to make education redundant.

The National Academy of Sciences (NAS) was "set up in 1863 under United States President Lincoln to harness science to the Union war effort," which recalls what Lewis termed "some people exercising the power of nature over other people."[43] NAS was responsible for the "well-funded overhaul of high school science and mathematics" in the 1960s in the United States and parts of Canada. Today it is accepted that science and mathematics (STEM—Science, Technology, Engineering, and

Mathematics) education is essential for any country to maintain its "international competitiveness"—a phrase generally taken to mean economic competitiveness—but the same logic extends to all forms of international competition, ultimately including war.

The exponential growth in destructive power of war weapons in the twentieth century coincided with unprecedented growth of every type of educational and research institute. Most analyses note the influence of military spending on material technologies, but rarely include "technologies of 'invisible materiality' like propaganda, political and economic theory, and educational psychology."[44] Education is the prime social institution for influencing the production of subjectivity, which is essential to the postindustrial economy (the "knowledge economy"). Subjectivity itself is the primary source of wealth in the "luxurious postindustrial jurisdictions like Canada and Sweden." Education enters the twenty-first century "as the *primary* driving force in the world economy."[45]

A major application of psychology knowledge has been to propaganda, which in simple terms is the manipulation of subjectivity, that is, of human thought, motivation, and desire. Psychological operations (psyops) are a "favored military strategy" and, from WWI onwards, these operations were "scientized (academized)" for military purposes and used both to "demoralize the enemy" and to "control domestic populations" in promoting the war effort "at home."[46] The civil or commercial application of military knowledge of propaganda as a "waging of psychic warfare" was renamed "advertising" in the late 1920s. Propaganda is a form of education in its own right; and the educated people within any society are the most susceptible to propaganda, since it works by manipulation of symbolic systems, so is dependent on literacy. These remarks recall how daily life in a Western country like Aotearoa New Zealand is saturated with advertising; and how "advertising campaigns" are often today's answer to social concerns.

Experimental psychology was applied first to warfare, in the development of the IQ test for the United States army in WWI, then to education, notably with the post-WWII testing movement, and including "military technologies" such as learning theory and instructional design.[47] "Educational technology, instructional technology (design, programming), and educational psychology are so tightly related as to make them almost inseparable."[48] Education and psychology are thoroughly entangled with the military, hence with war.

Falk points to the development for military aims of the digital world—ICT, the internet and the infrastructure of the information age: "Life as we know it is an offshoot of post-WWII United States weapons research and development."[49] Falk considers the rapid advances in artificial intelligence (AI) and robotics, with obvious advantages for "waging contemporary warfare whether military, ideological, or economic."[50] Falk predicts such machines could replace masses of educated people who are currently employed "in every area of the private and public sectors, in banking, industry, education, government, and the military. These thinking systems could technologically replace that last redoubt of humanism, the educated human being."[51]

The logic of war that drives capitalism, in other words, will eventually make education completely obsolete. Falk's train of thought converges with that of Lewis: the future of humankind is at stake. The posthuman idea so popular today was predicted by Lewis in 1943 to result from "stepping outside the Tao."

No Flying Cars?

In a second essay published in the same year as "Dead Zones," Graeber noted the "broken promise" of science and technology for the post-WWII generations, asking what happened to the "flying cars" he and his peers were encouraged as children to anticipate owning when they grew up.[52] Graeber covers similar ground as Falk in making the points, first, that technological advances were in fact slowing by the 1950s and 1960s, even as the "awesome space race" made innovation appear to speed up; and, second, that United States' spending on science and technology has always served military goals.[53]

Graeber recalls that "end of work arguments were popular in the late seventies and early eighties."[54] But instead of the imagined "robot factories," mass production for Western consumption was shifted to wherever widespread poverty and international development agreements meant that labor could be obtained cheaply enough to maintain and increase the monetary profits delivered to private, corporate shareholders/owners. Much as propaganda machines of media and advertising may seek to blind us to the facts, those living in the wealthy West, in "Europe, North America and Japan [have] an uneasy awareness that the post-work civilization was a giant fraud."[55]

Our carefully engineered high-tech sneakers were not being produced by intelligent cyborgs or self-replicating molecular nanotechnology; they were being made on the equivalent of old-fashioned Singer sewing machines, by the daughters of Mexican and Indonesian farmers who, as the result of WTO [World Trade Organization] or NAFTA [North American Free Trade Agreement]–sponsored trade deals, had been ousted from their ancestral lands.[56]

Graeber compares the "astounding dreams" and peaceful aims of the Soviet leadership, up until the 1980s, with the military aims of the United States:

> for instance, the [Soviet] attempt to solve the world hunger problem by harvesting lakes and oceans with an edible bacteria called spirulina, or to solve the world energy problem by launching hundreds of gigantic solar-power platforms into orbit and beaming the electricity back to earth.[57]

Graeber characterizes the Soviet approach to technology as "poetic" as opposed to the "bureaucratic" approaches born in the West, and overgrowing all global culture.

> From this perspective, all those mad Soviet plans—even if never realized—marked the climax of poetic technologies. What we have now is the reverse. It's not that vision, creativity, and mad fantasies are no longer encouraged, but that most remain free-floating; there's no longer even the pretense that they could ever take form or flesh. The greatest and most powerful nation that has ever existed has spent the last decades telling its citizens they can no longer contemplate fantastic collective enterprises, even if—as the environmental crisis demands— the fate of the earth depends on it.[58]

But here Graeber ignores a more obvious binary: the Soviet dreams were for everyone, while Western dreams were of "private" visions of wealth, luxury, and freedom. The 'Jetsons' version of everybody owning a flying Mini was a fantasy, but today, a tiny percent of the population do have "flying cars" called "private jets/helicopters." That childhood promise came true by about 2000 for the elite upper crust in which Andrew met

Donald. In a globalized economy, such uber-wealthy individuals can be thought of as "global owners."

As Māori/Indigenous academics, if we look *away* from these links between power, profit, and cross-cultural relationships between Māori and Pākehā, we end up *participating* in the "lopsided structures of imagination" that support the bureaucratic structures of violence, which, in turn, protect our own privileged university positions. This complicity is clear in the expectations placed on Māori academics to make everything comfortable for their non-Māori colleagues, while taking responsibility for ensuring their department becomes culturally compliant—the terminology keeps changing, but the underlying condition of White normativity remains in place.[59] Employer institutions, it must be noted, are much less interested in having their Māori scholars point out the ignorance and propaganda that underpin dominant Eurocentric systems, including university systems.

Conclusion: Earth to the West

What I am calling "global owners" correspond to Lewis's predicted class of "the Conditioners." Though the name sounds quaint today, his description of them as operating "at their own whim" is disturbingly reminiscent of the behavior of the uber-wealthy global owner class of today. That Western culture and education thinks it can find redemption in Indigenous philosophy is a sign that "the West has stepped outside the Tao" (using these terms while remaining aware of the inherent risk of reification and caricature) and was likely already starting to do so when Lewis wrote his essay in 1943. The history and spirit of capitalism seems to lead up to that *sui generis* step, which, conceivably, could take a generation or more to complete, and involve only a tiny subset of the human population.

The versions of globalized Western culture represented by the lives and achievements of these powerful individuals, with so much capital at their disposal they effectively are global owners, are quite extreme and do seem to have moved beyond a sense of what it means to be human—a phase Lewis aptly dubbed "posthumanity." It has been left to the billionaires, for example, to drive space exploration, seemingly to escape a ruined terrestrial ecosystem. Standard terms such as "the environmental crisis" reflect the way in which science-influenced thought reduces nature to a glorified resource bank. The *Gaia* concept of the living Earth aligns well with Papatūānuku, the Māori concept of the Earth Mother.[60] The Indigenous cultures of the world are diverse, but only the Western culture seems to have rushed towards taking that step beyond. If, as Graeber notes, the future survival of the Earth depends on "fantastic collective enterprises" to try to tackle the environmental crisis, the extreme individualism of globalized culture is possibly where the problems begin, and a good place to start to address them.

Indigenous cultures, including Māori, insofar as they retain a working base of cognitive, material, and human resources, remain closer to operating "within the Tao" than globalized Western culture, which, at its extreme, has stepped outside a humane framework. Perhaps this is why the liminal space invoked by cross-cultural educational relationships is a humbling, awe-inspiring experience, even for those who walk comfortably in both cultures.[61] The purpose of an Indigenous politics such as Kaupapa Māori is to stay in touch with the interests of the Earth (Papatūānuku or Gaia) against the implacable logic of late capitalism that concentrates wealth and power in the hands of a tiny number of individual humans, putting at risk the planet ark and all its inhabitants.

Notes

1. David Graeber, "Dead Zones of the Imagination: On Violence, Bureaucracy, and Interpretive Labor," *HAU: Journal of Ethnographic Theory* 2, no. 2 (2012): 105–128.
2. Ibid., 123.
3. Robert Proctor, "Agnotology: A Missing Term to Describe the Cultural Production of Ignorance (and Its Study)," in *Agnotology: The Making and Unmaking of Ignorance*, ed. Robert Proctor and Londa L. Schiebinger (Stanford, CA: Stanford University Press, 2008), 1–33.
4. Michael Young, *Knowledge and Control: New Directions for the Sociology of Education* (London: Collier-Macmillan, 1971); Ivan Illich, *Deschooling Society* (London, New York: Calder & Boyars, 1971).
5. David Pearson, *A Dream Deferred: The Origins of Ethnic Conflict in New Zealand* (Wellington, NZ: Allen & Unwin, 1990).
6. Georgina Tuari Stewart, "Truth-Myths of New Zealand," *Asian Journal of Philosophy* 2, no. 1 (2023): 5.
7. Patrick Fitzsimons, Michael Peters, and Peter Roberts, "Economics and the Educational Policy Process in New Zealand," *New Zealand Journal of Educational Studies* 34, no. 1 (1999): 35–44.
8. Cliff Falk, "Education and War: Primary Constituents of the Contemporary World-System," in *Education, Globalization, and the State in the Age of Terrorism*, ed. Michael Peters (Boulder, CO and London: Paradigm, 2005), 201–237.
9. Falk, "Education and War," 204.

10. Tihema Baker, "Ka Mate, Ka Ora," *New Zealand Geographic*, 2023, available at: https://www.nzgeo.com/stories/ka-mate-ka-ora/ (accessed May 26, 2023).

11. Arapera Blank, "One Two Three Four Five," in *The Māori People in the 1960s*, ed. Erik Schwimmer (Auckland, NZ: Longman Paul, 1968), 84–96; Kimai Tocker, "Living and Learning as Māori: Language Stories from Three Generations," *Australian Journal of Indigenous Education* 46, no.1 (2017): 115–125.

12. David Novitz and Bill Willmott (eds.), *Culture and Identity in New Zealand* (Wellington, NZ: GP Books, 1989).

13. New Zealand National Party, "Key: The Kiwi Way: A Fair Go for All," *Scoop*, January 30, 2007, https://www.scoop.co.nz/stories/PA0701/S00197.htm (accessed May 26, 2023).

14. Philip Brown, Hugh Lauder, and David Ashton, *The Global Auction: The Broken Promises of Education, Jobs, and Incomes* (New York: Oxford University Press, 2010).

15. Graeber, "Dead Zones," 113.

16. Auckland Star, "Starry-Eyed Mum and Her Daughter," *Auckland Star* newspaper (Auckland, NZ), May 17, 1971, 15.

17. Māori words are not italicized in this chapter because te reo Māori is an official national language of New Zealand, so cannot be considered foreign. In any case, more and more Māori words are being adopted into New Zealand English, so any decisions about which Māori words should be italicized are likely to become outdated.

18. Georgina Tuari Stewart, Māori *Philosophy: Indigenous Thinking from Aotearoa* (London: Bloomsbury, 2021); Te Kawehau Hoskins and Alison Jones (eds.), *Critical Conversations in Kaupapa* Māori (Wellington, NZ: Huia Publishers), 2017; Linda Tuhiwam Smith, *Decolonizing Methodologies: Research and Indigenous Peoples*, 3rd edn (London and New York: Bloomsbury, 2021).

19. Falk, "Education and War," 206.

20. Ibid., 207.

21. Marcel Mauss, *The Gift: The Form and Reason for Exchange in Archaic Societies*, trans. Wilfred D. Halls (New York: Norton, 1990, 1925).

22. David Graeber, *Toward an Anthropological Theory of Value: The False Coin of Our Own Dreams* (New York: Palgrave Macmillan, 2001).

23. Ibid., 161.

24. Ibid.

25. David Graeber, *Debt: The First 5,000 Years* (New York: Melville House, 2011).

26. Graeber, *Toward an Anthropological Theory of Value*, 221.

27. Falk, "Education and War," 208.

28. Ibid., 209.

29. Clive Staples Lewis, *The Abolition of Man: Or, Reflections on Education with Special Reference to the Teaching of English in the Upper Forms of Schools* (London: Geoffrey Bles Ltd, 1967 [1943]).

30. Ibid., 39.

31. Ibid., 54.

32. Ibid. 54–5, emphases in original.

33. Ibid., 44.

34. Ibid., 43.

35. Ibid., 51–2.

36. Ibid., 50.

37. Dan Hikuroa, "Mātauranga Māori—the Ūkaipō of Knowledge in New Zealand," *Journal of the Royal Society of New Zealand* 47, no. 1 (2017): 5–10; Carl Mika and Michael Peters, "Blind, or Keenly Self-Regarding? The Dilemma of Western Philosophy," *Educational Philosophy and Theory* 47, no. 11 (2015).

38. Lewis, *Abolition of Man*, 54.

39. Steven R. Loomis and Jacob P. Rodriguez, *C.S. Lewis: A Philosophy of Education* (New York: Palgrave Macmillan, 2009).

40. Falk, "Education and War," 210, emphasis in original.

41. Ibid., 221.

42. Ibid.

43. Ibid., 212.

44. Ibid., 211.

45. Ibid., 214, emphasis in original.

46. Ibid., 221.

47. Stephen Jay Gould, *The Mismeasure of Man*, revised and expanded edn (London: Penguin, 1997).

48. Falk, "Education and War," 225.

49. Ibid., 227.

50. Ibid., 229.

51. Ibid., 229.

52. David Graeber, "Of Flying Cars and the Declining Rate of Profit," *Baffler*, no. 19. (2012): 66–84, available at: https://thebaffler.com/salvos/of-flying-cars-and-the-declining-rate-of-profit (accessed May 26, 2023).

53. Ibid., 73.

54. Ibid., 69.

55. Ibid., 69.

56. Ibid., 73.

57. Ibid., 74.

58. Ibid., 82.

59. Georgina Tuari Stewart, "A Typology of Pākehā 'Whiteness' in Education," *Review of Education, Pedagogy, and Cultural Studies* 42, no. 4 (2020): 296–310.

60. James E. Lovelock, *Gaia: A New Look at Life on Earth* (Oxford: Oxford University Press, 1987).

61. Alison Jones, "Cross-Cultural Pedagogy and the Passion for Ignorance," *Feminism & Psychology* 11, no. 3 (2001): 279–92.

5

Actualizing the Public University: For Debt-Free, Antiracist, Accessible, Quality Higher Education

Sharad Chari

Introduction: State Disinvestment and the Folly of the 'Public Ivy'

I came to the University of California at Berkeley (UC Berkeley) in 1987 as a wide-eyed undergraduate, dazzled by bookshops, cafes, vestiges of counterculture, and student politics on Sproul Plaza. I was an aspiring moron (Reno, ch. 1 this volume), determined to find the most exemplary or anomalous experience of any kind, and with absolutely no interest in imagining a professional or marketable future. It must be said, fees were about $1,400 a year and rents were not yet exorbitant; I bartered one month for an old TV and lived rent-free for months in a home with a leaking roof. Lucky to have supportive parents and odd jobs, I had something close to a charmed undergraduate experience.

My family had emigrated from India to California scarcely five years earlier. Our migration was part of the phenomenon of upper caste, middle-class flight from struggles to democratize access to higher education in India which my people had benefited from unduly. Without the financial means to secure college admissions through "donations," or the certainty that their children would get into the best universities through their own merits, my parents wisely decided on international relocation, despite the cost to their professional and personal lives. My mother remembers vividly being reassured by a staff member at the United States Consulate in Chennai that California was the right place for us, because the California Master Plan for Higher Education, with its linked tiers of Community Colleges, Cal State Universities and the University of California system would offer a route to college for us one way or another. A career public school teacher herself, my mother recalls this as the beginning of her lifetime commitment to high-quality public education, something she defended in a variety of ways, including fighting a deeply entrenched system of racial tracking that sent Black and Latinx students to vocational paths and only white and Asian students to the Master Plan's promise of quality higher education.

Fast forward two decades, and I am back as a tenured faculty member at UC Berkeley, to find a place almost diametrically transformed from the one I had inhabited 35 years back. Tuition and fees for California residents had tripled by the time I was a graduate student at Berkeley in the 1990s and are now ten times what they were when I was an undergraduate. And this doesn't begin to account for the rising costs of commodified means of life, including housing prices grossly inflated by the inequality machine that is the San Francisco Bay Area tech boom. Alongside skyrocketing costs, the share of state investment in Berkeley's operating budget plummeted from 47 percent in 1991 to 11 percent in 2011. State disinvestment and increasing privatization has been a defining feature of so-called "public Ivies," a category that includes the universities of Michigan, North Carolina at Chapel Hill, Virginia, University of California Los Angeles (UCLA), and UC Berkeley. Table 5.1 compares tuition and fees with endowment-to-enrollment ratios in these universities, against bastions of privilege Harvard and Stanford, and also University of California Merced, which, like University of California Riverside, focuses on under-represented Black and Latinx undergraduates with much smaller endowments.

Table 5.1   Comparing "public Ivy" fees and endowment-to-undergraduate-enrollment ratios[1]

Name	In-state tuition and fees	Out-of-state tuition and fees	Undergraduate enrollment	Endowment	Endowment: undergraduate enrollment ratio
UCLA	13,268	43,022	31,636	5,389,297,000	170,353
UC Berkeley	14,361	44,115	30,980	4,798,851,000	154,902
Michigan	16,178	53,232	31,329	12,476,874,000	398,253
Virginia	19,698	53,666	17,311	7,255,701,000	419,138
North Carolina	19,399	36,776	19,399	3,712,117,000	191,356
Harvard	55,587	55,587	5,222	40,575,027,000	7,770,016
Stanford	56,169	56,169	6,336	28,948,000,000	4,568,813
UC Merced	13,565	43,319	8,276	55,474,000	6,702

The top and bottom rows of Table 5.1 show the University of California system stretched between two poles. On the one hand, the wealthier research universities aspire to join the Ivy League in the reproduction of unearned privilege through the asset economy, but in fact their endowment-to-undergraduate-student ratios pale in comparison to the Ivies.[2] On the other hand, campuses that focus on undergraduate education serve Latinx students (39.4 percent of the state in 2019, greater than the non-Latinx white population at 36.5 percent) under constraints of high fees, smaller endowments, and limited state support. How did this divergence come about?

Just a bit more than six decades past, veteran University of California President and Chancellor of UC Berkeley, Clark Kerr, adversary of the radicals of the Free Speech Movement, famously quipped that his main challenges as an administrator were to organize sex for the students, athletics for the alumni, and parking for the faculty. As University of California President, Kerr had been key to the survey team that formulated the California Master Plan for Higher Education in 1960.[3] In congressional testimony in 1999, Kerr lays out the survey team's objective through the Master Plan, which was to push the state to commit to a process of investment in public higher education across the three tiers of junior colleges (later California Community Colleges), California State Colleges, and the University of California, to meet the massive growth in numbers of "baby boomers" arriving at the university over the decade of the 1950s.[4] The aim, to paraphrase Kerr, was that every high school graduate resident or otherwise qualified young person would be ensured a place in the multi-tiered system of quality public higher education, with the possibility of transferring between the tiers to end up as a University of California graduate. Quality and access were fundamental to this vision of public higher education, with general support from the State of California and from the electorate at a time in which public beneficiaries were predominantly white, male, and Californian.[5]

Two important pieces of legislation mediated the confluence of state disinvestment and the erosion of this vision of accessible, quality public higher education. Both pieces of legislation emerged from organized reaction in defense of racialized and gendered class privilege, in which the Republican Party and right-wing think tanks planned disinvestment of all things in the public good; and they did so precisely as a counter-offensive in a "war of position" against radical antiracist movements of the 1960s and 1970s inside/outside the University of California that fought to expand the university's "public" from heritage recipients of (unnamed-white) affirmative action.

First, a tax revolt through a popular ballot initiative, Proposition 13 of 1978, capped property taxes at 1 percent of a property's assessed value, fixed the assessed value at the original purchase price, and allowed the assessed value to change by only 2 percent each year while actual home prices skyrocketed. Proposition 13 entrenched the class power of California homeowners, allowing them to become part of the "asset economy" that could transfer racialized, patriarchal class privilege intergenerationally. This intergenerational reproduction of class was effectively subsidized by working-class denizens of the state increasingly reliant on debt and insecure tenancy, particularly in the wake of the property boom in places like the San Francisco Bay Area. Proposition 13 also undermined the state fiscus, driving down state revenue for public education and other public goods dramatically; the exception, for a while, was the building of prisons across the "Golden State," which Ruthie Gilmore has argued was a product of a different re-articulation of surplus land, labor, capital, and state capacity.[6] Dollar for dollar, state priorities shifted from public higher education to prison building. With a two-thirds majority required to overturn it, Proposition 13 has been difficult to dislodge.

Second, Proposition 209 of 1996 co-opted the language of antidiscrimination from antiracist movements that sought to widen the purview of the California Master Plan by preventing race, gender, and other kinds of discrimination in public employment, education, and contracting. These two pieces of legislation, and the political currents behind their enactment through ballot initiatives, as well as their continued enshrinement, have been part of the way in which California's ballot initiatives effectively defeated a rich regional history of antiracist and civil rights activism.[7]

As a UC Berkeley graduate student in the 1990s, I witnessed the failure of student political mobilization to foresee and prevent the backlash that Proposition 209 represented. The numbers of Black and Latinx undergraduates on campus dropped, though Latinx numbers would later rise again in the 2000s. The effects of this demographic shift in student politics and associational life on campus in the 1990s was striking. Work with an undergraduate People of Color (POC) magazine called *Diatribe* opened my eyes to radical perspectives from Chicanx/ Latinx students with connections to radical mobilization from California's cities to the agrarian Central Valley. That moment ended. Ironically, my mother had been working as a public high school teacher in Los Angeles at this time to try to break the pernicious system of racial tracking of Black and Chicanx/ Latinx students away from the University of California. The efforts of antiracist teachers like her seemed to have been coming to fruition, only to be undercut by Proposition 209.

The graph shown in Figure 5.1, from UC Berkeley's Diversity and Inclusion office, shows that while the numbers of eligible California high school graduates from "Under-represented Minorities" (Black, Chicanx/Latinx, Native American and Alaskan Native) was rising, Proposition 209 helped actively undermine the founding principles of the California Master Plan for Higher Education.

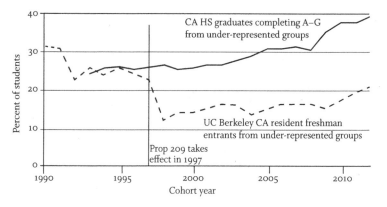

Figure 5.1   Drop in under-represented minorities (Black, Latinx, Indigenous) since Proposition 209

Source: US Berkeley Division of Equity and Inclusion, diversity.berkeley.edu/sites/default/files/diversity-snapshot-web-final.pdf

Since the late twentieth century, the UCLA and UC Berkeley Foundations have been repurposed to hunt for private philanthropic funding. While some members of these campuses try to investigate the strings that this funding comes with that might further undermine "the public mission," campuses have also invested more deeply in amenities meant to attract fee-paying students, particularly those paying expensive non-resident fees; they invest in stadia, gyms and sports arenas; and they forge new public–private partnerships to build off-campus student housing, often but not always at absurdist market or above market rates (while writing this, UC Berkeley committed to housing 1,000 students at sub-market rates, and began building a major project to house transfer students at sub-market rates.) For most working- and middle-class denizens of the state, access to these public universities requires getting deeper into debt. Aspiring young people without stable familial support, as well as formerly incarcerated and non-traditional students, face special programs that target success for the few, while many are forced into periods of hunger, homelessness, and mental ill-health. One survey commissioned by Berkeley in 2017 found that 10 percent of its undergraduate, graduate, and postgraduate respondents reported having been homeless for some period of time.[8] These are just some indicators of a broader process through which the University of California seems to have shifted from an instrument of class mobility to one of class differentiation.

There is a global context to consider, and a progressive way to approach international students increasingly sought after for their non-resident tuition; after all, this tuition is built on the labor of working households elsewhere in the world. Data from the 2018 *World Inequality Report* represent how slices of the world in income deciles, or 10 percent chunks of income groups, have seen their real incomes change in the heyday of neoliberal reform and globalization of capital, between 1980 and 2016. The "Elephant Curve" graph from the *World Inequality Report* is useful as a way of visualizing some key shifts, in Figure 5.2.

On the right, the graph shows that the global 1 percent have captured 27 percent of income growth between 1980 and 2016, exponentially steeper for the global 0.1 percent, and ridiculously so for the plutocrats of the

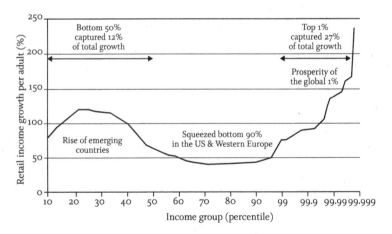

Figure 5.2   The "Elephant Curve" of global inequality and growth, 1980–2016

Source: Facundo Alvaredo, Lucas Chancel, Thomas Piketty, Emmanuel Saez, and Gabriel Zucman (eds.), *World Inequality Report* (Cambridge, MA: Belknap Press of Harvard University Press, 2018).

global 0.001 percent (the 1 percent of the 1 percent of the 1 percent.) The dip in the middle represents the squeezed bottom 90 percent in the United States and Western Europe, including the traditional "publics" reliant on public education who can only continue to do so through deeper levels of personal debt. These classes include the white populations who have overwhelmingly supported the political means through which plutocrats have effectively transferred public wealth to private coffers. Significantly, the bulge on the left shows the lowest 50 percent of income groups in the world who have garnered 12 percent of total global income growth, primarily in the fast capitalisms of East Asia. These working- and middle-class households in East Asia, much poorer than their counterparts in the North, have been able to cobble together the means to send some of their children abroad. These are precisely the international fee-paying students whose income gains the "public Ivies" sought to capture in their privatized response to state disinvestment. Often, the decisions to pay high fees in dollars, also through personal debt, are the result of the calculated gamble that these are investments in familial futures in the casinos that are East Asia's fast capitalisms. I raise this because antiracist diagnosis of the rising significance of East Asian fee-paying students ought not reiterate a xeno-racist response.

The consequence of the search for tuition and fees, and donor funds, to take the place of dwindling state investment has meant that the antiracist possibilities of the California Master Plan's hope for providing accessible, quality public higher education have seemingly been left by the wayside. How might we refuse the terms of the current compact, and the very idea of "the public Ivy," which entrenches the asset-based reproduction of racial and class privilege, and how might we instead reclaim the political hope of the relatively recent past?

Graeberian Provocations

Speaking at Occupy Wall Street in 2011, Gayatri Spivak remarked that twenty years before, when people referred to "the university," they meant the faculty; now when they say "the university," they mean the administration. Elaborating on Spivak's statement, David Graeber remarks that "universities are no longer corporations in the medieval sense; they are corporations in the capitalist sense, bureaucratic institutions organized around the pursuit of profit," in other words, "a nightmare fusion of the worst elements of state bureaucracy and market logic."[9] While pronouncing the university organized around "the pursuit of knowledge and understanding as a value in itself" effectively dead, Graeber notes that market-driven universities see no contradiction in harsher and more violent use of police to quell dissent.

This diagnosis is of course consistent with the history of liberalism and its reliance on violence, particularly in the United States, as Chandan Reddy and others have argued.[10] And yet, Graeber also notes that the university seeks to draw within its ambit various kinds of autonomous cultural production, from the arts to investigative journalism. Is this just a cover, a way of postponing the funeral of the university as the site of creativity and critique? Whose body would be buried at the funeral of the public university; should it not be that of a bloated administration? Graeber concludes his argument by calling for a prefigurative politics built on the kind of confidence and pleasure in the pursuit of knowledge that comes easily to some; this may have been what I aspired to as a youthful would-be-moron. Might this sensibility, Graeber asks, be the seedbed for the prefigurative practice of a different university?

Graeber modeled the refusenik intellectual in the ruins of the neo-feudal-neoliberal university through his own unique trajectory as a working-class intellectual rightly disdainful of the crass materialism that has taken over the contemporary university. I am also persuaded by his focus on sites of play in autonomous cultural production, as a call for widening access to that which was the preserve of aristocrats (or their third sons!). From the perspective of the foolhardy yearnings of elite public universities like UC Berkeley and UCLA to become "public Ivies," there is no question that innovation can only be guaranteed by fostering sites of serious play. What this means for the collective politics of reclaiming the California Master Plan as an instrument of antiracist class mobility, indeed reparation, and of the need to pressure the state to find the fiscal and ideological means for this task, is that the public university has to be made to fulfill its democratic mandate. While it is very difficult to determine the varieties of public response to the long aftermath of the current pandemic and the annual fires that beset the western United States, we must imagine the formation of new alliances linking antiracist and labor movements with mobilization around student debt, homelessness, and precarity. Spaces of activist-intellectual creativity and play are also required to bring these necessary political alliances into being. Graeber's refusenik position pushes us to imagine what it might mean to actualize the public university—and not just the elite ones—through activist-intellectual labor across the land-scape of public higher education.

Hence, with a steady periodicity, also posthumously, Graeber's work continues to try to shift the foundational terms of debate across topics, to help us see other possibilities than the status quo, including ones he did not pursue. Consider the "short version" of Graeber's "Turning Modes of Production Inside Out: Or, Why Capitalism is a Transformation of Slavery."[11] Here, Graeber grapples with his relationship to Marxism, beginning with the provocation that "mode of production" is an undeveloped concept in Marxist theory, usually posed in state-centric terms, and that debates about the history of capitalism turn on whether "capitalism" ought to be defined through the existence of capital accumulation or the prevalence of wage labor. Ultimately, he argues, the choice of definition is ideological: "one can define 'capitalism' as broadly or narrowly as one likes. It would be easy enough to play the same trick with terms like socialism, commu-nism or fascism."[12]

He then reconstructs "mode of production" through a set of proposi-tions, the first of which is that we ought to conceive of this concept not just as the production of material objects, but also of people and social rela-tions. Graeber would agree that Marx had argued that only the fetishized view of capitalism saw social relations between people in the mystified form of relations between things, rather than as social relations between things and people. One aspect of Antonio Gramsci's reworking of Marx's thought was focused on clarifying a dynamic conception of personhood; and we could trace this line of thought on a dynamic conception of per-sonhood in a figure like Stuart Hall. Setting aside how novel Graeber's first proposition is for the Marxist tradition, it remains useful for rethinking specific institutions such as the University of California as part of a mode of production not just of employable and marketable fee-paying widgets, but also of forms of sociality that might enhance or diminish the capaci-ties of people to be responsible, critical denizens of California and of the planet. These are diametrically opposed possibilities, however, which must be thought dialectically, and the question is when they provoke concrete struggles that might tip the university towards life-enhancing possibilities.

Second, Graeber argues that "the real stakes of human existence … always have to do with human ends and human relations," while these stakes are dissimulated by the treatment of humans "as if they were mere automatons competing over abstractions like 'wealth' or 'power.'"[13] This point ought to be foundational to the public university today as well, recast thus: the real stakes of the public university should have to do with expanding the space for reflection and actualization of human–environment mutuality rather than the reduction of human endeavor to competition over abstractions. The privatization of the public university is precisely driven towards the expansion of competitive human endeavor over abstractions like economic growth, resilience, or diversity, without adequate reflection on how these abstractions are wielded to the detriment of the public university, and its capacity to defend and enhance human–environment mutuality. Campus debates during the COVID-19 pandemic were instructive, as the administration never could quite admit that its considerations on the return to in-person teaching have had to do with the abstractions circling around the profitability of the university as a corporation.

Third, continuing on a reconstruction of "mode of production" also of people and social relations, Graeber proposes that "very simple forms of social relation most typical of long-distance relations between people who do not know much about each other are continually introjected within ... societies to simplify social relations that need not be that way"; by this, he explains that simplified forms of action, principally violence, stand in for deeper understanding in a more intricately relational form of social interaction, and that "the existence of structural violence—social hierarchies backed up by a systematic threat of force—almost invariably creates forms of ignorance internally."[14] This is an important insight that is extremely pertinent to what we see at the University of California and elsewhere. As the *universitas*, or wholeness of the university, is increasingly hierarchized into an array of classes which have no actual understanding of each other's conditions of work let alone their psychic lives, they are actually in a condition of structured ignorance. This production of ignorance is what Robert Proctor and Londa Schiebinger propose ought to be a new field of study they call "agnotology," the study of ignorance not as lack of information but as the outcome produced by political struggle.[15] This is exactly what Graeber suggests of the molecular workings of our contemporary mode of production, that what we call "structural violence" is made through the "introjection" of these simplified and often violent forms of action.

When we recast the widespread indifference to one another across classes of employees as the production of an agnotological condition, it is clear that some people can afford not to worry about others. On the one hand is a class of administrators that Michael Burawoy calls "spiralists," who spiral in from outside the university, have no deep investment in its life-worlds and who create "signature projects" to maintain their own spiraling class mobility; Burawoy notes that the number of senior managers at Berkeley increased five-fold in the 20 years before 2014, while faculty numbers were stagnant and student enrollment increased 20 percent.[16] "Spiralists indulge in conspicuous investment," argues Burawoy, "signature projects that enhance their reputation to facilitate moving on while saddling the university in debt." But spiralism is premised precisely on agnotology. The point is not to inspire liberal guilt among the senior administration, but to remind us that the university is also a place of sociality in which other classes are for various reasons tied to place. On the other end of the spectrum of faculty, adjunct lecturers battle to survive, graduate students from non-wealthy and non-traditional backgrounds join them in multifaceted insecurity and precarity. The violence inherent in this system is seen as natural and immutable, rather than accentuated by a mode of social interaction that relies on everyday indifference about how our co-workers survive.

Fourth, emerging from the last proposition, Graeber suggests that "it is possible to see industrial capitalism as an introjected form of the slave mode of production, with a structurally analogous relation between workplace and domestic sphere."[17] Graeber does not explicate his use of the psychoanalytic category "introjection," even though the term recurs with some frequency in these arguments, and yet it provokes us to consider that capitalism's mystified forms might draw their phantasmic support from lapsed, peripheral, or dormant modes of production. Keeping this in mind, consider Graeber's argument that capitalism does not work just in pursuit of capital accumulation, nor just to subjugate working classes, but also to maintain the "systematic distinction between homes and workplaces, between domestic and economic spheres" in order to separate the production of people from the production of commodities.[18] Importantly, the domestic sphere does not produce people *as* commodities. Graeber then turns to a Marxist conception of slavery as a mode of production reliant on appropriating the production of people, and this takes him to a comparison of shared characteristics of slavery and capitalism: the separation of production and social reproduction of labor, the exchange of "human powers" (a wider term than labor power) for money, "social death" (the severing of all other social ties), the financialized relation that produces abstract labor ("sheer power of creation, to do anything at all"), and the ideology of freedom that accompanies these arrangements.[19] All these elements, Graeber argues, are evident at different spatiotemporal scales in both the trans-Atlantic slave trade and in contemporary capitalism, producing endless catastrophe in the former and "endless mind-numbing drudgery" in the latter.[20] Graeber does not propose a historicist line of argument. He points to widespread evidence that transitions to capitalism relied on a variety of forms of "abstract labour" including from various kinds of forced labor. Capitalism has been highly non-linear in its labor regimes, and ways of articulating the production of commodities and people (workplaces and households, economic and domestic spheres), but the argument about capitalism as "introjected" by slavery or forced labor seems to be about rendering structural violence banal in workplaces and in households.

Consider this in relation to Wendy Brown's insight that the defunding of public higher education at a time of rising antiracist and antiauthoritarian campus activism was designed by the early neoliberals around Ronald Reagan as Governor of California to discipline students by driving them back into the patriarchal sphere of the family, whose private wealth (or debt) they would have to rely on for access to the public university.[21] This argument is premised on what Graeber points us to, the dialectical relationship between public and private spheres, the university as both a growth machine and a regime of discipline, but also one that could rely on the family when the police are insufficient to tame "unruly" students. The defunding of the public university is related not just to the production of better automatons—famously decried in Mario Savio's speech during the Free Speech Movement—but also, perhaps increasingly in the time of the COVID-19 pandemic, the production of people as dependent subjects of patriarchal power, as some aspire to marketable skills in order to pay off college debt, to achieve a modicum of autonomy.

Finally, and inconclusively but still provocatively, Graeber cautions that "capitalism's unlimited demand for growth and profit is related to the transcendent abstraction of the corporate form," and that "when these transcendent forms encounter 'material' reality, their demands are absolute."[22] Here, the question is what kinds of material encounter with reality will matter to the transcendent form of the university that seeks the mirage of the "public Ivy," reliant on private sources of capital, resistant to demanding from the state a larger share than a meager 11 percent, and inured to the lived sufferings of students, adjunct lecturers, and other precarious workers. In its long process of negotiation with UC-AFT, the union representing non-senate faculty and librarians at the University of California, the university relied on corporate labor bargaining, showing itself to be ruthless in refusing the very basic guarantees of job security and career pathways, while wage increments always lag behind inflation. UC-AFT's steady and creative organizing tactics led to a major win in 2021. In the material encounter with a growing army of indebted students, the university maintains that its "public mission" is best served if students, as customers, pay the true cost of their premium education, worthy of the brand. What kinds of encounters with material suffering will matter enough for the veneer of the liberal public university to fall off, to reveal the intensified burdens placed on low-income, under-represented minority families and students?

Towards the Post-Bullshit Public University

In his magnum opus, or one of them, Graeber argues that debt is the relation between groups who "cannot yet walk away from each other, because they are not yet equal," and he adds that they exist in relation, "in the shadows of eventual equality."[23] This is a precise provocation for progressive academics in the debt-ridden public university. Debt forgiveness is not unusual, Graeber argues; it has been foundational to the sacred at various places and times, not least in the idea of the "jubilee." The Anglican rewriting of the biblical line "forgive us our trespasses as we forgive those who trespass against us" in the time of ascendant private property, he reminds us, conceals widespread consensus in other places and times for periodic debt forgiveness in the interests of actual, concrete relations between people and their lived environments.

As I have mentioned, one of the most outlandish forms of "production of people" in the neoliberal public university has been the class of "spiralist" university administrators who speak as "the university," defenders of its "public mission," even if state investment goes to zero, as former UC Berkeley Chancellor Nicholas Dirks put it. But should we be looking for enlightened administrators who see themselves as public servants, invested in respect for all the university's constituencies, and for the new demands of our planetary crisis?

Once again, Graeber helps us shift perspective, to look anew at what we know. In his 2018 *Bullshit Jobs*, he writes against the view in capitalist societies, accentuated in our time, that we are worth the amount we are paid, rather than how beneficial to others and to the planet our work might actually be:

If someone had designed a work regime perfectly suited to maintaining the power of finance capital, it's hard to see how he or she could have done a better job. Real, productive workers are relentlessly squeezed and exploited. The remainder are divided between a terrorized stratum of the universally reviled unemployed and a larger stratum who are basically paid to do nothing, in positions designed to make them identify with the perspectives and sensibilities of the ruling class (managers, administrators, etc.)—and particularly its financial avatars—but, at the same time, fostering a simmering resentment against anyone whose work has clear and undeniable social value.[24]

What if the majority of denizens of the public university agreed on the final death of the "public Ivy," taking back from administrators a narrow, financialized and ultimately revanchist approach to the privatized university hiding behind the veneer of a "public mission"? We would join the movement for a debt-free university that renews its promise of equal access to quality public higher education. This "post-bullshit" university would have a sign at the entrance that reads "No thanks, Spiralists," cutting off what Graeber calls "managerial feudalism," and redistributing resources towards making the university a more egalitarian, playful, and engaged critical space. In the face of pandemics and climate disasters, such a university might shift focus to the production of people and knowledge committed to our mutual survival. Graeber concludes *Bullshit Jobs* with the example of a universal basic income grant as a means of delinking work from compensation; this would also be a way of reversing the neoliberal devolution of the production of people to the patriarchal domestic sphere, and to households increasingly stretched in secure access to land, labor, and money. The University of California prides itself on its vast access to public land; stolen land though it is, access to land has been a motor of the university's growth machine for a century and a half.[25] Might the university begin to commit to use its command of public land, its relationship to people as the dominant public employer, as well as its command of money, toward an actually mutual future? The only university worth not being a refusenik in is the actual public university to come.

Notes

1. "Best University Rankings," *US News and World Report*, available at: www.usnews.com/best-colleges/rankings/national-universities; "UC

Endowments as of 2020," in the UCOP Annual Endowment Report, 2019–2020, available at: https://www.ucop.edu/investment-office/investment-reports/annual-reports/annual-endowment-report-fy-2019-2020.pdf; Michigan, Virginia and North Carolina in National Association of College and University Business Officers (2021), "US and Canadian Institutions Listed by Fiscal Year 2020 Endowment Market Value and Change in Endowment Market Value from FY19 to FY20," downloadable at www.nacubo.org (websites in this note accessed September 1, 2021).

2. Lisa Adkins, Melinda Cooper, and Martijn Konings, *The Asset Economy: Property Ownership and the New Logic of Inequality* (Cambridge: Polity Press, 2020).

3. University of California, "Master Plan for Higher Education," 1, available at: https://regents.universityofcalifornia.edu/regmeet/july02/302attach1.pdf (accessed October 7, 2022).

4. Clark Kerr, *The Uses of the University* (Cambridge, MA and London: Harvard University Press, 2001).

5. Wendy Brown, "Wendy Brown: In Defense of Higher Education," interview by Sharad Chari, ucbfa.org, September 2, 2021, audio 38:53, available at: https://charir.podbean.com/e/wendy-brown-in-defense-of-public-higher-education/ (accessed June 9, 2023). This interview informs much of the chapter.

6. Ruth Wilson Gilmore, *Golden Gulag: Prisons, Surplus, Crisis, and Opposition in Globalizing California* (Berkeley and Los Angeles: University of California Press, 2007).

7. Daniel Martinez HoSang, *Racial Propositions: Ballot Initiatives and the Making of Postwar California* (Berkeley and Los Angeles: University of California Press, 2010); Sharad Chari interview with Colleen Lye and Chris Newfield, forthcoming at ucbfa.org; Christopher Newfield, *The Great Mistake: How We Wrecked Public Universities and How We Can Fix Them* (Baltimore, MD: Johns Hopkins University Press, 2016).

8. University of California Berkeley, *Housing Master Plan Task Force Report*, 2017, available at: https://housing.berkeley.edu/sites/default/files/pdf/HousingSurvey_03022018.pdf (accessed October 7, 2022).

9. David Graeber, "Anthropology and the Rise of the Professional-Managerial Class," *Hau: Journal of Ethnographic Theory* 4, no. 3 (2014): 78–88.

10. Chandan Reddy, *Freedom with Violence: Race, Sexuality, and the US State* (Durham, NC: Duke University Press, 2011).

11. David Graeber, "Turning Modes of Production Inside Out: Or, Why Capitalism is a Transformation of Slavery," in *Possibilities: Essays on Hierarchy, Rebellion, and Desire* (Oakland, CA, and Edinburgh: AK Press, 2007), 85–112.

12. Ibid., 93.

13. Ibid., 96.

14. Ibid., 101–2.

15. Robert Proctor and Londer Schiebinger, *Agnotology: The Making and Unmaking of Ignorance* (Stanford, CA: Stanford University Press, 2008).

16. Michael Burawoy, "The Neoliberal University: Ascent of the Spiralists," *Critical Sociology* 42, nos 7–8 (2016): 941–2.

17. Graeber, "Modes of Production," 102.

18. Ibid., 103.

19. Ibid., 105.

20. Ibid., 106.

21. Brown, "Wendy Brown: In Defense of Higher Education," interview by Sharad Chari.

22. Graeber, "Modes of Production," 107.

23. David Graeber, *Debt: The First 5,000 Years* (Brooklyn: Melville House, 2011), 122.

24. David Graeber, *Bullshit Jobs: A Theory* (New York: Simon & Schuster, 2018), xxi–xxii.

25. The alternative that we currently face is perfectly diagnosed in Davarian Baldwin, *In the Shadow of the Ivory Tower: How Universities are Plundering our Cities* (New York: Bold Type Books, 2021).

6

Reading Graeber, Leach, and a Revolution in Myanmar

Michael Edwards

I would never have expected Ruth to join the revolution. But then so much of what's happened in Myanmar in recent years has been somehow unexpected, from the coup itself, in the early hours of February 1, 2021, to the scale of the popular reaction. Friends who expressed little interest in politics or protest during my fieldwork, only a few years earlier, were in the streets, rallying against the dictatorship in the face of what became an unthinkably violent crackdown. Striking has been the role of young women—women like Ruth, a Christian born in the Chin Hills, who works at a Pentecostal church in Yangon where I did much of my research.

As the uprising grew through February, Ruth's posts filled my Facebook feed: selfies in COVID-19 face masks amid the swelling crowds around the Sule Pagoda; memes mocking the generals behind the coup; advice for fellow protesters on what to do in the event of tear gas or rubber bullets; photographs of bloodied bodies of victims wounded by security forces. One thing that wasn't surprising was the brutality of the crackdown. As it intensified in late February and early March, Ruth's posts started to show her wearing not just a face mask, but also a helmet and goggles. By the time I was doing final revisions on this essay, in early October 2022, 2,338 had been killed in the crackdown and 12,576 were in detention.[1]

As Pentecostals, believers like Ruth were also praying—for the downfall of dictatorship and for the restoration of democracy, or at least for the restoration of the imperfect political arrangement, between the National League for Democracy and the generals, in place since Myanmar entered a period of apparent reform around 2011. One video streamed via Facebook Live had about twenty members of Ruth's church engaged in a session of collective prayer, dancing to the beat of a traditional Chin drum, and asking God to protect Myanmar and those leaders who had, the previous November, secured a landslide in the second general elections since the formal end of military rule. While such prayers were common-place during my fieldwork, this one resonated with the revolution then building momentum in the streets: put to the rhythm of a familiar call-and-response protest chant made famous in the 1988 uprising, the prayer replaced the usual rejoinder "*do ayei! do ayei!*" ("Our cause! Our cause!") with "Amen! Amen!"

*   *   *

What drew these Christians so fully into the revolution through their protest and prayer? There's been much said about how a decade's experi-ence of a more open public sphere makes return to military rule impossible to countenance, especially for young people.[2] Many have also remarked on how this moment has transcended lines of difference that have long animated Myanmar's politics, with Chin Christians and even Rohingya Muslims manning barricades alongside majority Burman Buddhists.[3] But maybe part of an answer also lies in the imagination.

I say this, in part, because of another question I've had, watching Myan-mar's Spring Revolution unfolding from afar over social media: What would David Graeber make of this?

Graeber never wrote about Myanmar, but he was, of course, deeply interested, intellectually and practically, in the question of revolution. This interest, which emerged both from his anthropology and his activism—insofar as the two could be separated in his case—led him, in the last few years of his life, to support the democratic experiment then under way in Rojava in northern Syria. "I support the revolution in Rojava," Graeber wrote, "because I would like to see the revolutionaries win."[4] For him, the question of revolution was intimately tied up with the question of imagi-nation, something which both animated his approach to anthropology and was also an object of the analysis it generated.

In one essay, he distinguished a "transcendent" form of imagination, the terrain of fiction and make-believe, of "imaginary creatures, imag-inary places ... imaginary friends," from an "immanent" form, one not "static and free-floating, but entirely caught up in projects of action that aim to have real effects on the material world, and as such, [are] always changing and adapting."[5] It was the latter, for Graeber, that had revolution-ary potential. In the essay, he contrasts an "ontology of violence," where "being realistic means taking into account the forces of destruction," with an "ontology of the imagination," grounded in the idea, to invoke his oft quoted formulation, that "the ultimate, hidden truth of the world is that it is something that we make, and could just as easily make differently."

While Graeber never wrote about Myanmar, had he not died in September 2020, that might not have remained true for long.

A few years before he died, he agreed to write the foreword to a new edition of Edmund Leach's *Political Systems of Highland Burma*.[6] The foreword was never finished, so we can't now know what Graeber would have written. We can't know how he would have engaged with Raymond Firth's original, laudatory foreword, which praises the book as a "superb piece of craftmanship"; or with Leach's introductory note to the 1964 reprint, which restates his rejection of the equilibrium assumptions of his structural-functionalist colleagues. We can't know how he would have dealt with Leach's later reappraisal of the book, when he acknowledged that he had somewhat essentialized *gumsa* and *gumlao*, the Kachin categories famously at the heart of his analysis. We can't know exactly how Graeber would have situated the book in relation to debates in anthropological theory in the decades since, or how he would have dealt with critiques that have been directed toward it, including from Kachin scholars, and amid growing calls to meaningfully decolonize the study of Myanmar.[7]

What we do know is that Graeber was a fan. "Edmund Leach," he once wrote, "may have been the man who most inspired me to take up an anthropological career." He went to describe Leach as "a model of intellectual freedom."[8] Elsewhere he referred to Leach as an anthropologist who "always managed to come up with something brilliant and startling by largely ignoring where you were supposed to start and what you were supposed to say."[9] References to Leach appear across Graeber's body of work. These include citations of work by the younger Leach and by the older Leach following his so-called "conversion" to structuralism—a break which, as Chris Fuller and Jonathan Parry argue, has been overdrawn:

> Not only are there striking continuities in the sort of questions Leach asked of data, and the sort of answers he offered, but more importantly he kept faith throughout his career with one broad vision of the anthropological enterprise.[10]

If the same might also be said of Graeber, it is not the only way in which the two men were similar. Both thought across relatively long stretches of historical time: 140 years in the case of Leach's study of the oscillations in Kachin political systems; millennia in the case of Graeber's work on debt and his collaborations with the archaeologist David Wengrow. Both were also prolific and lucid writers, eager to engage audiences beyond anthropology—including, incidentally, via the BBC, which broadcast Leach's Reith Lectures in 1967 and Graeber's 12-part series on debt in 2016. What James Laidlaw and Stephen Hugh-Jones write about Leach could perhaps just as easily be said of Graeber, that "the lessons of anthropological inquiry were relevant to the everyday moral and political questions that were being debated all around him."[11] Both were interested in the micro and macro forces that impacted the production of knowledge in anthropology, and both reflected on how their own biographies and—albeit very different—insider/outsider positions in the discipline shaped the work they produced.[12]

There are, however, few references to *Political Systems* in Graeber's corpus, which raises another question: What would he have written in this foreword?

It's impossible to give a confident answer. Graeber was far too creative for that. But he was also, like Leach, fairly consistent in the kinds of questions he asked of ethnography, and in his advocacy for a certain vision for a comparative anthropology, one tethered to a politics of possibility. Central to this vision, again, was the place of imagination. So, I don't think it's going too far out on a limb to suggest that imagination might have been a central theme of the foreword. For what are the political categories of *gumsa* and *gumlao* analysed by Leach if not products of the "immanent" mode of imagination that interested Graeber?

One reference that appears at least twice in Graeber's body of work—in his early ethnographic monograph *Lost People* and in his later book on bureaucracy *The Utopia of Rules*—is to a point Leach made in his short 1982 treatise simply titled *Social Anthropology*.[13] There Leach suggests that the distinction between humans and non-humans is not that the former have a soul, but that they are able to conceive—or imagine—that they have one, and thus, that it's imagination, not reason, that sets humans apart.[14]

If imagination is, according to Leach and Graeber, a general and constitutive feature of the human condition, it's also one thrown into relief at certain moments, such as moments of revolution. "When one tries to bring an imagined society into being," Graeber wrote, "one is engaging in revolution".[15] It's maybe not too much of a stretch, then, to also imagine that if he'd lived long enough to write his foreword to *Political Systems*,

Graeber would have attended to the revolution now under way in the valleys and the highlands that feature in Leach's book: a revolution whose participants, like Ruth, imagine not just a political system in Myanmar with the military no longer in charge, but a society radically transformed in myriad other ways.

This chapter is an exercise in reading—reading the revolution alongside the foreword that Graeber never wrote. To imagine how Graeber might have approached today's revolution in his foreword, to conjure a text which doesn't exist, is to pursue a speculative reading, but one I think he would support, as allergic as he sometimes was to anthropology's navel-gazing tendencies. That this kind of imaginative work is possible, this filling in of the gaps—even across apparent chasms of time, space, and cultural difference—is what made anthropology conceivable in his view. Leach makes a similar point in his introduction to *Political Systems* when he declares upfront that approximate interpretation of foreign verbal and non-verbal statements is always possible, and that "without it all the activities of anthropologists becoming meaningless."

*   *   *

It's unlikely that Leach and Graeber ever met. Leach died in 1989, the year Graeber started his PhD fieldwork in Madagascar. *Political Systems* was published seven years before Graeber was born in 1961. But there are indirect connections between the two. In the 1980s Leach spoke of being drawn to the work of Marshall Sahlins, Graeber's advisor, especially to Sahlins' effort in *Islands of History* to grapple with the emic categories through which historical change and continuity are experienced. Leach claimed that his analysis of Kachin verbal categories in *Political Systems* was his own fumbling attempt at something similar. During his period at Cambridge, Stanley Tambiah, Leach's friend and colleague, supervised Maurice Bloch, who would go on to become one of Graeber's main interlocutors about Madagascar. There are likely other threads that would have interested Leach and Graeber; like many anthropologists, both were obsessed with the matter of intellectual genealogy.

Genealogies are also, famously, a topic of conversation among highland groups in Southeast Asia, including the Kachin. In Leach's study, the depth of recounted genealogies varies across Kachin society, between commoners, whose genealogies can be relatively short, consisting of up to five generations at most, and chiefs, who in the interests of securing their legitimacy, recount extremely long genealogies of over forty generations going back to the creator.[16] In all cases, however, Leach tells us that such genealogies ought to be regarded as "fictional," and thus, in tune with a central argument of his book, that, in acting "as if" they were true, people in search of power and status exploit a productive gap between the ideal and the real.

Genealogies are also important to the populations that live to the west of the Kachin in the Chin Hills that today border India. It is from here that most of my Christian interlocutors hail. Many, like Ruth, were born in or around the town of Tedim, in the northern part of the Chin Hills. This was an area where the Buddhism of the lowland Burmese kingdoms had made few inroads. American Baptist missionaries arrived around the turn of the twentieth century. Their success, as in other upland regions, was in contrast with the indifference with which the gospel was greeted by valley populations, who remained resolutely Buddhist. Foreign missionaries remained active in the Chin Hills until they were expelled in 1966 by the military junta that seized power four years earlier. In the early 1970s, a charismatic revival swept through the northern part of the Chin Hills, prompting an exodus from mainline Baptist churches to new smaller Pentecostal churches with an emphasis on healing, prophecy, and other gifts of the Holy Spirit.

In the early 2000s, large numbers of Christians from the Chin Hills began to migrate down to Yangon, many in search of jobs, including in construction or in the garment factories springing up on the city's peri-urban fringe. Others came in search of better phone and money transfer connections to family members who were increasingly moving abroad on refugee visas. Upon arriving in Yangon, many established new Pentecostal churches, often in small apartments across the city. These churches took an active interest in evangelizing to the predominantly Buddhist communities in whose midst they now stood. Indeed, in the absence of foreign missionaries, many at these churches claimed that the Chin had a special responsibility for sharing the gospel with Buddhists, contributing to the salvation of Myanmar in both a spiritual and political sense.

Things began to change around 2011, with the growing number of foreign missionaries who arrived amid Myanmar's democratic opening—alongside tourists, development professionals, and anthropologists. In any event, the upshot is that the evangelism that churches such as Ruth's pursue is not just an encounter between Buddhism and Christianity, but also between the highlands and the lowlands, between people from Myanmar's cultural and geographic periphery and those from its centre. To study this evangelism is therefore to pick up a thread where the anthropologist F.K. Lehman left off, whose work on Chin-Burman interactions Leach praises in his 1964 introductory note to *Political Systems*.

In Lehman's *The Structure of Chin Society*, published one year earlier, he pursues a similar line of inquiry to Leach, exploring encounters between the lowlands and highlands and, in a move that Leach claimed validated his own argument, shows the limited utility of the bounded tribe as a unit of difference in anthropological analysis.[17] Chin conversion to Christianity, for Lehman, needed to be understood as a product not just of the encounter between locals and missionaries, but also the relation between the highlands and lowlands, and as a Chin attempt to secure equal status with Burmans without becoming Buddhist. "One of the important political functions of Christianity for the Chin," he writes, "has been to serve as a symbol of their being a part of a larger world of civilization via the churches and their missions."[18]

* * *

I didn't travel to Myanmar with plans to study Christianity. I was drawn instead to the question of how people experienced a public sphere thought to be emerging from the shadows of five decades of censorship and surveillance. I was particularly interested in how the democratic transition unfolded through the medium of sound. Which new voices were making themselves heard in public and through what media? It so happened that some of the most audible voices I heard—on streets and buses and trains—were those of Christian evangelists. Ruth worked at one independent Pentecostal church known in Christian circles for its commitment to evangelism. Housed across the top two floors of an apartment building in Yangon, roughly two thirds of its 80 staff were employed as evangelists. Ruth was responsible for running the church's media output, which included conducting interviews with the evangelists about their work, which she then posted online. The senior pastor founded the church upon moving down to Yangon from the Chin Hills, after God told him that it would play a key role in Myanmar's transformation from a Buddhist into a Christian nation.

I noted above that Leach and Graeber shared a belief in an anthropology premised on translatability and the possibility of communication across difference, even in the face of significant barriers. Such a conviction was also shared by Pentecostals at churches such as Ruth's.[19] Indeed, like many Christians elsewhere, they spent a great deal of time acting on this belief in their pursuit of evangelism. Following 2011, as the country began to emerge from 50 years of military rule, these efforts intensified. Taking advantage of a tentatively more open public sphere, Christians began to preach more energetically than they had in decades.

The main period of my fieldwork, from 2014 to 2016, was a time of particularly spirited activity. Distributing gospel tracts on footpaths, using megaphones to preach on public transport, holding outdoor tent revival meetings in the shadow of Buddhist pagodas: these were activities few Christians would have dared pursue only a few years earlier. Such activities, it was felt, would help fuel the spiritual awakening these believers held to be under way. This was a time, they said, when God was saving Myanmar, and doing so in a dual sense: on the one hand, rescuing the country from decades of military rule, and on the other, offering its population, roughly 90 percent Buddhist, ultimate salvation through Jesus Christ. "God's hand is on Myanmar," was the frequent refrain.

When Myanmar entered its period of reform, the changes—which also included the release of political prisoners, the liberalization of the economy, and the holding of relatively free elections—were read as signs that this other, more profound, more unlikely, transformation was also under way. In this Pentecostal reading of Myanmar's transition, the "real change" that the National League for Democracy (NLD) promised voters in its landmark election win a few years later indexed a rupture occurring at the level of national politics and at the level of individual Buddhist souls alike. One particularly auspicious sign was the appointment, in April 2016, of a Chin Christian, Henry van Thio, as one of two vice presidents in the NLD party's new civilian government.

But even before the 2021 coup, there was mounting evidence that the rupture might not be forthcoming. Surging costs of living alongside a growing sense that economic liberalization might benefit only a small group of well-connected cronies; new forms of censorship impinging on what was supposed to be an open public sphere; an ascendant Buddhist nationalism rendering increasingly precarious the position of religious minorities and playing out most horrifically in the Rohingya genocide— these were signs that Myanmar's transition was stalled, if not "backsliding," to invoke a term used by evangelists and analysts alike. There was also no evidence that people were newly interested in Jesus. "It's more difficult for a Burman to become a Christian than it is to extract a tooth from a tiger's mouth," wrote Adoniram Judson, the pioneering American Baptist missionary who arrived in Rangoon in 1813.

The transition appeared to have changed little on this front. Evangelism here seemed on paper to be a deeply ineffective activity.[20] Yet, my questions about the effectiveness of evangelism usually went nowhere. They were mostly met with the reply that "God works in his own time," an understanding of the relationship between human and divine agency that undergirded their approach to evangelism and much else besides. Christians in Myanmar could capitalize on new "democratic" opportunities to share the good news with Buddhists, but only God could touch their hearts, and it was up to him when and how that was done. Signs of apparent political and personal backsliding, then, did not mean that God's hand was no longer on Myanmar. Nor did they stop believers from doggedly sharing the gospel, working with him to fuel a rupture they held to be already under way.

We could put this down to a matter of conviction or belief. These are the terms through which anthropologists have tended to approach the religious commitments that people sustain in the face of potentially destabilizing evidence. But what happens if we approach such commitments not through the lens of conviction or belief, but through the prism of the imagination? What might that reveal, not just about the work of evangelism but also of revolution, and about possible continuities between the two?

*   *   *

I think it's fair to say that imagination has not been a key term in the anthropology of Christianity. There are probably several reasons. It might be that imagination does not feature prominently as an emic term, in contrast, say, to belief. This is certainly true of the Pentecostals with whom I work. But then this hasn't stopped other terms from gaining serious analytical traction. Think, for instance, of one I used just now: rupture. Joel Robbins recently reminded us that the Urapmin don't themselves use this term, though they live their Christian faith in a way that emphasizes a break that conversion makes with tradition.[21] This hasn't stopped the term being enormously productive in and beyond the subfield, even if, as Naomi Haynes has recently written, debates around it are starting to run out of new things to tell us.[22] Her own alternative model of Christian time—"the expansive present"—is similarly an etic term, not one used by the Pentecostals in Zambia with whom she works.

I will return to the question of rupture below. But perhaps another reason why imagination has not featured prominently in the anthropology of Christianity has to do with the term's common association with the fantastical, with how what is usually conjured when we talk of imagination is what Graeber calls its "transcendent" mode: that domain, recall, of "imaginary creatures, imaginary places ... imaginary friends."[23] It might be out of respect, then, that anthropologists have chosen to speak in terms of belief rather than imagination. Perhaps "imagination" impinges on our methodological agnosticism in a way "belief" somehow does not. One term that anthropologists of Christianity have used, and often, is "imaginary"—as in, "the Pentecostal imaginary." However, the imaginary, in this usage, as David Sneath, Martin Holbraad, and Morten Pedersen suggest, often comes to stand simply for culture, "seen as it is as a holistic horizon of meanings."[24]

But if imagination has not featured much in the anthropology of Christianity, it also seems that Christianity has not been much discussed in the anthropology of the imagination. Robbins, a decade ago, while noting an uptick in anthropological work on imagination, also suggests that imagination has been somewhat overlooked in the discipline.[25] He puts this down to a tendency to locate imagination in the space of individual psychology, and to the difficulties that the field has in dealing with genuine processes of change—what he elsewhere influentially calls "continuity thinking." Imagination, for Robbins, promises to be a useful topic insofar as it allows anthropologists to study one way through which "newness enters the world."[26] It's interesting, I think, that Christianity gets only a fleeting reference from Robbins here. This perhaps reflects a broader trend in anthropological work on imagination to sideline Christianity, and religion more generally.[27] Sneath, Holbraad, and Pedersen similarly do not mention such topics in their call for anthropologists to attend to "technologies of the imagination," nor does Graeber in his discussion of the "transcendent" and "immanent" modes of the imagination. He is careful not to lump religion in with his "transcendent" mode; though he does mention the Kingdom of Prester John, alongside Narnia, as an example of the "imaginary places" that constitute it. But nor does Graeber mention it with reference to the immanent mode, that one "entirely caught up in projects of action that aim to have real effects on the material world."

The reasons Christianity has been sidelined in discussions of the imagination might be the inverse of the reasons the imagination is sidelined in discussions of Christianity. It might be that Christian thought is regarded as too constrained, too pre-given, for imagination, with the unbounded sense of freedom it evokes, to be considered an appropriate term. If imagination sits uncomfortably with efforts by some anthropologists to take Christians seriously, perhaps Christianity impinges on the imagination in a way that other scholars find uncomfortable. I don't think this applies to any of the anthropologists cited just now; their understandings of both religion and imagination are too sophisticated for that to be the case. Importantly, for all of them, the imagination is not quite so unbounded, so untethered, as it might first appear. It is, for Robbins, "a culturally defined realm of play and experiment," albeit one relatively more free than other realms.[28] For Sneath, Holbraad, and Pedersen, it is the material and social conditions—"the technologies"—from which imagination emerges, in an underdetermined form, that warrants study.

But consider a line from a work that Robbins cites as an example of the uptick in work on the imagination, Vincent Crapanzano's *Imaginative Horizons*. Crapanzano remarks that he came to the topic of imagination not through his fieldwork with Christians, but in reaction to that experience. He writes, "What I missed was the wonder of imagination, something the Christian Fundamentalists with whom I'd been working would certainly have considered depraved …"[29] The denomination matters here, and it might be that the literalist Christians Crapanzano studied are an especially unimaginative group, at least in the terms he prizes. But one wonders if this doesn't reflect a more general attitude, and, in turn, what insights might be gained from bringing Christianity and imagination into the same orbit. This isn't an original proposition. Maurice Bloch goes so far to suggest that religion itself is an evolutionary product of the capacity to imagine other worlds, and that this capacity is not just integral to human sociality, but what distinguishes humans from other animals.[30] And this gets us back to Edmund Leach.

*   *   *

It had been a while since I had thought properly about Leach's work. The coup on February 1, 2021 did not initially change that. It took about a week for large-scale protests to get going. The first couple of days after the coup were somewhat quiet. Healthcare workers and teachers were among the first to go on strike. Garment factory workers followed soon after. Each evening people in Yangon and other cities took to balconies and street corners to bang pots and pans, driving away, in a cacophonous wave, the evil represented by the coup. As the civil disobedience movement took shape, more and more people took to the streets. By the middle of February, tens of thousands of protesters were assembling each day in Hledan, a busy commercial district close to Yangon University.

Ruth was among them. We had been in touch since the hours following the coup. She sent photos and videos of the swelling crowds. In one photo her white-sneakered foot stamps on a poster of the face of Min Aung Hlaing, the general behind the coup, that had been taped to the pavement for protesters to walk over. In another she holds up a placard with the words #justiceformyanmar alongside an image of Aung San Suu Kyi, the imprisoned NLD leader. "Young people will not be turning back," she wrote in one message.

A series of photos posted to Facebook on February 20, Chin National Day, showed Ruth and others from the church joining the protests wearing the traditional black, red, and green scarfs associated with the part of the Chin Hills where she was born. One of the most striking things to have come out of the revolution has been the emergence of multi-ethnic solidarity in opposition to a common oppressor. The spokesperson for the parallel government established by the elected parliamentarians deposed by the coup has been a prominent Chin Christian doctor, Dr Sasa. At some points, protest signs featuring his face seemed to eclipse those featuring Aung San Suu Kyi's. In late February Ruth posted an old photo of her with Dr Sasa, with the caption, "May the Lord bless you and use you for our nation and His kingdom." Like the appointment of the Chin vice president in 2016, Dr Sasa's role has been particularly important to Chin Christians, accustomed, like other religious and ethnic minorities, to being treated like second-class citizens, if citizens at all, by a state whose leadership has been dominated by Burman Buddhists.

There is a vast anthropological literature on ethnicity in Burma, often in dialogue with Leach's work on the Kachin. If one was looking for its central finding, it might have to do with the plasticity of ethnic categories. Lehman, in a 1967 essay in which he builds on Leach's work, proposes that ethnic categories in Burma ought to be approached as "roles" that can be adopted or discarded depending on the kind of interaction in which one is engaged.[31] He also suggests that cultural and social systems are best thought of as "models," of which people make "selective use ... to guide their real-life situations," and that these models "generate meaningful interpretations to situations and things."[32] Leach famously opens *Political*

Systems with the case of an individual who appears to have moved flexibly between "Kachin" and "Shan" ethnic categories.

The arguments that Leach's book goes on to make are so well known to anthropologists that they hardly need repeating. His dynamic analysis of oscillations between political categories—the hierarchical *"gumsa"* and the egalitarian *"gumlao"*—is deployed to attack the equilibrium assumptions of his structural-functionalist colleagues, and the allied tendency to treat ethnic groups or tribes as bounded units. Like Lehman, for Leach social systems do not correspond to reality. Instead, they are models, used by the anthropologist and those they study to "impose upon the facts a figment of thought."[33] These models find their clearest expression in myth and ritual, which present social orders in their ideal forms, making "explicit what is otherwise fiction."[34] In Leach's classic formulation, myth and ritual conjure this ideal order by acting "as if" it did really exist. Thus presented, these orders come to serve as a "charter for social action" for actors.[35] Leach also emphasizes that such a model does not float freely from the messy world of social facts; it "can never have an autonomy of its own."[36]

I asked earlier if it might be possible to see the models of *"gumsa"* and *"gumlao"* thus presented as products of the "immanent" mode of imagination that interested Graeber, that mode "caught up in projects of action that aim to have real effects on the material world." For Leach's critics, the problem is that both his models and the facts on which his analysis is based are, in important ways, figments of his own imagination. One of the best-known of these critics is David Nugent, who in the early 1980s charged that, for all of Leach's emphasis on historical change, he had missed the forest for the trees by ignoring the wider economic forces that shaped the transformations in Kachin political systems during the 140-year period he studied.[37] Chief among these were changes in opium trade in the second half of the nineteenth century, which upended the economic basis for the more hierarchical Kachin system and led to a shift toward more egalitarian arrangements. Leach did ultimately acknowledge that he had overlooked these larger historical forces in the original analysis.[38] But in his famously bellicose response to Nugent—incidentally titled "Imaginary Kachins"—he accuses him of engaging in "fantasy" through falsification and omission of facts.[39]

It's especially noteworthy, then, that other more recent criticisms, including those by Kachin scholars, home in on Leach's confession, toward the end of the book, that he is "frequently bored by the facts."[40]

This attitude, his critics charge, had disastrous effects. "[O]ne might with justification," write François Robbine and Mandy Sadan, "accuse Leach of reducing the Kachin sphere to a kind of intellectual laboratory without any expression in reality because of the way in which he moulded his case study to a theory, rather than the other way round."[41] Notwithstanding Leach's commitment to an anthropology premised on the translatability of foreign terms and concepts, much of this criticism turns on Leach's mistranslations of the verbal categories at the heart of his analysis.[42] It is also that the meanings of these terms changed over time. *Gumlao*, Sadan writes, refers today less to a political system—in either a real or fictive sense—than to a process of revolution, a meaning shaped by the Kachin experience of being locked in armed struggle against the Myanmar military for much of the country's independence.[43]

I'm sure Graeber would have dealt with these criticisms in his foreword, but I'm less sure what he would have said about them, or how his own view of the relationship between facts and theory would have shaped his assessment. Leach would later write that while he was "often exasperated by the obsessive empiricism" of some of his colleagues in British anthropology, he "never came close to sharing Lévi-Strauss's view that theory is the only thing that matters, and that if the ethnography does not fit, it can simply be discarded."[44]

In a sense, what Fuller and Parry write about Leach's attitude to theory could also be said of Graeber: that it was "first and foremost the comparative, generalizing analysis of ethnographic data for the light it would throw on 'us' as well as 'them'."[45] Recent years have seen a push to problematize these two companion terms, "us" and "them," which Fuller and Parry, it must be said, do place in scare quotes—an effort to unsettle, as Nayanika Mathur and Liana Chua put it, "the real and imagined 'we's' that are often coterminous with a "vague image of 'Western' society as a homogenized foil to depictions of 'otherness'." [46]

Their shared interest in human similarities meant that Leach and Graeber questioned this binary throughout their careers. Graeber, in multiple places, did so through a sustained effort to highlight how ethnographic curiosity is a more general feature of societies across space and time, and thus worked to reveal the hollowness of the anthropological "we."[47] There is something of Leach in Graeber's specific kind of comparative commitment, something which comes through clearly in his exchange with Eduardo Viveiros de Castro. "We appear to be in the

presence of two quite different conceptions of what anthropology is ultimately about," Graeber writes.

> Are we unsettling our categories so as (1) to better understand the
> "radical alterity" of a specific group of people (whoever "we" are here
> taken to be); or (2) to show that in certain ways, at least, such alterity
> was not quite as radical as we thought, and we can put those apparently
> exotic concepts to work to reexamine our own everyday assumptions
> and to say something new about human beings in general?[48]

Graeber was unequivocal that he sat in the second camp.

Pointing to similarities in comparative method, or in their view of
the relationship between theory and ethnography, is not to suggest that
Graeber would have given Leach a pass when it came to factual inaccura-
cies in his Kachin material. I also suspect something else he would have
subjected to critique is the individualizing dimension in Leach's analysis,
the argument, an inheritance from Malinowski, that it is individuals'
self-interest and the pursuit of status that compels them to exploit incon-
sistencies between the ideal and the real, which, in turn, drives change at
a wider social level. In his otherwise laudatory foreword, Firth's scepticism
on this point also comes through, in his remark that "in other ethnographic fields it would seem that valuations of a moral or religious order
enter and jostle the power and status-seeking elements."[49]

However, my main hunch is that Graeber would have devoted much
of the foreword to what Leach tells us about the "as if"—the otherwise
conjured, or imagined, in ritual and myth; an otherwise, recall, that is
tethered to social reality and action, one that "never has an autonomy of its
own." Thus, Leach's objection to claims by Ernest Gellner and others that
his book is erroneously "idealist."[50] Again, I say this because of echoes with
the "immanent" mode of the imagination that drew Graeber's attention
throughout his anthropology, even when he was not using that specific
term. One place where the idea finds its clearest expression, I think, is
in the foreword Graeber wrote to another book, *The Chimera Principle* by
Carlo Severi, which deals with the relationship between ritual objects, on
the one hand, and memory and the imagination, on the other. Graeber
praises the book for showing that "imagination is a social phenomenon,
dialogic even, but crucially one that typically works itself out through
the mediation of objects that are ... to some degree unfinished, teasingly

schematic in such a way as to, almost perforce, mobilize the imaginative powers of the recipient to fill in the blanks."[51]

He goes on to suggest that what Severi shows for the relationship between people and objects has broader implications for the relationship between people themselves. And the focus here on "technologies" of the imagination, broadly conceived, expresses Graeber's interest in that form of the imagination rooted in social reality—the one that is "defined" or "located" in Robbins' terms.[52] It is also one that, when communicated in the subjunctive mood of myth or ritual, might, to use a word of which Graeber was fond, "prefigure" realities to come. I think it's likely, then, that it is this element in *Political Systems* that Graeber would have homed in on in his foreword, particularly if he had been writing it in the year following his death, watching the revolution in Myanmar unfold.

*   *   *

The brutality of the crackdown intensified through March. The protesters, including Ruth, continued to assemble in the streets. By late February, Ruth and I had shifted our conversation from Facebook Messenger to Signal because of the safer encryption that app offered. Stories were circulating of police randomly stopping people to check their phones for anti-coup material. Still, Ruth continued to post on Facebook, using a Virtual Private Network app to access the site in the face of the junta's effort to block it, and, periodically, the internet altogether. The content became more graphic. In early March she posted a widely circulated video of three paramedics being beaten by security forces. Videos of shootings and photos of funerals followed daily. Posts were often accompanied by the popular slogan, "The revolution must succeed." In one photo, on March 14, she stands behind a makeshift barricade of sandbags, bamboo, and corrugated iron assembled by protesters in her neighborhood in downtown Yangon. "Our neighborhood," reads the Burmese-language caption.

I was reminded of a conversation Ruth and I had in Yangon in 2017. Ruth had just returned from a year living in Singapore, where she had been attending Bible school. Her church in Yangon had covered her tuition. We met at Junction City shopping mall, which had just opened, to much fanfare. There were pop concerts and dance performances in its atriums, glistening water features, and a seemingly endless expanse of air-conditioned space through which people could stroll on the polished floors and soak up the atmosphere. The mall had been an enormous building site for much of my fieldwork, part of the construction boom that accompanied Myanmar's "transition." Built by Shwe Taung Group, a construction company whose chairman is widely considered to be a crony who got rich by laundering drug money, the mall was decidedly slicker than others in Yangon.

"It really is like Singapore," Ruth said upon entering the mall. We had a look around, browsing the shop windows of global fashion brands before somehow securing a table at Bread Talk, a hugely popular Singaporean multinational bakery café. Over smoothies, she told me about her time in Singapore. But the conversation soon turned to what she considered the fundamental differences between Singapore and Myanmar. Where Singapore was open, Myanmar remained somehow closed—politically and spiritually—even at this moment of apparent transition. The consequence was that there had not yet been the surge in conversions that believers anticipated, notwithstanding the signs that it was on its way, signs that included the new Singapore-style shopping mall in which we sat. Buddhists were not yet coming to Christ.

For Myanmar Pentecostals, the figures of Singapore and South Korea loomed large in how they contemplated the spread of the gospel globally—as modern Asian countries whose economic success and political stability were directly related to the success Christianity has had in both of them. Still, none of this meant that God's hand was no longer on Myanmar, or that an "awakening" was not already under way. Pentecostals like Ruth continued to share the gospel, to act "as if" they lived in a world where Buddhists would soon accept Jesus as their saviour. It is not that the facts bored them too, but perhaps that the imagination downplayed the relevance of certain facts and foregrounded the significance of others. And in this sense, maybe they were already engaging in a form of revolution.

Such a claim is far from out of place in the anthropology of Christianity. Consider the attention paid to the temporal frame of the "already/not-yet" in which some Christians dwell: "a time split in twain through the event, a cleaving of the present moment into past and future … [in which] things are either redeemed or are in need of redemption."[53] It resonates too with what anthropologists have shown about how Pentecostalism in particular works to overlay political and religious soteriologies in various settings, a grafting that propagates such phenomena as the prayer/protest that I mentioned at the top of this chapter. Other forms of Christianity have also been shown to afford this possibility. Caroline Humphrey, for example, shows how the schismatic impulse of Orthodox Christianity can be thought of as the "moral-social basis" for the Russian Revolution, particularly if "revolution is understood not simply as a political event but also as the forging of new and 'true' meaning." [54] Imagination features in Humphrey's discussion. Indeed, she opens her article by noting that, "The anthropology of Christianity ... has pointed to the centrality of temporal ruptures in Christian imagination."[55] But again, this is not quite in the sense that I've been considering it here; that is, to return to Robbins, as a way through which newness enters the world. The denomination matters here too, and Humphrey is explicit that the Orthodox emphasis on continuity prizes "what is held to be the old and original," even if, "when enacted in the present as a deliberate spiritual stance, [that] becomes new in the sense that it partakes of a newly defined messianic time."

Still, where Christianity and revolution have been brought together, it is often via a discussion of the Pauline event, read through the philosophy of Badiou and Agamben, in which Paul's conversion comes to foreshadow the possibility of a revolutionary break.[56] This resonates with the definition we get in a recent book on the anthropology of revolution: "[U]nlike more gradual and piecemeal forms of political action, revolutions set themselves up as projects of total and radical transformation, expressed characteristically as a desire to bring about a 'different world'—sometimes an altogether 'new' one."[57]

This strikes me as an apt description of what Ruth and others have been doing, in proselytism and protest, and also somehow not. What the Pauline emphasis sidelines perhaps are the everyday prefigurative, immanent, acts—distributing gospel tracts, preaching to indifferent audiences on trains, joining demonstrations—that work to usher that new world into being by acting "as if" it already existed—acting, here, "as if" Myanmar is already saved; "acting," as Graeber often put it, "as if one is already free."

*   *   *

So, when Ruth joined the revolution, maybe I shouldn't have been surprised. Maybe that was a failure of my own imagination. Perhaps her Christianity was a "technology" for her revolutionary imagination all along. There will be multiple overlapping technologies of the imagination generating the current waves of revolutionary action in Myanmar. I have focused here on those aspects that might be relevant to some of the people I know there. I've approached their role in unfolding events with a question lingering in my mind: What would Graeber make of this? Or rather, I've approached it through a speculative reading of the foreword to Leach's book that I imagine Graeber might have written if he had lived long enough to write it.

Doing so has shifted my analytical vocabulary somewhat, from "belief" and "rupture" to "imagination" and "revolution". This is not itself a radical break, but perhaps more of a continuum, and a move possibly congruent with what being part of the revolution has meant for Ruth and some others in Myanmar. In the time since I first drafted this chapter, Myanmar's revolution has shifted and evolved amid a military assault that has grown especially vicious in Chin State and other ethnic areas. The revolution is still unfolding, as is Graeber's legacy.

"Every real society is a process in time," Leach famously writes in the introduction to *Political Systems*. The structural-functionalist "equilibrium" assumptions that he challenged were in part, he suggested, a product of the conditions of fieldwork and the way it got written up: "We get studies of Trobriand society, Tikopia society, Nuer society, *not* 'Trobriand society in 1914', 'Tikopia society in 1929', 'Nuer society in 1935'." "The authors write as though the Trobrianders, the Tikopia, the Nuer, are as they are, now and forever."[58] Tambiah suggests that there is much in Leach that resonates with—prefigures, perhaps—Johannes Fabian's critique of the "denial of coevalness," which, he claimed, undergirded anthropological analysis.[59] There's a certain irony, then, that many of the critiques of the book focus on Leach's elision of the historical circumstances in which his study occurred. It's also worth noting that, in the 1964 introductory note to the book, Leach has nothing to say about the coup that took place in Burma in 1962, or about the Kachin uprising against the central state which had started one year earlier.[60] These are details on which Graeber would have likely remarked, especially if his appraisal of another major figure in British anthropology, E.E. Evans-Pritchard, is anything to go by.[61]

It's quite possible—likely, even—that Graeber's foreword would have gone in a different direction to what I've imagined. It's possible that he would have made much more of the charges of idealism, the ways in which Leach's attempts to connect the ideal to the real are patchy at best, the ways in which a gap between the imagination—as "theory" or "model"—and social facts remains, such that the imagination that comes through in Leach is perhaps more transcendent than immanent. It's also possible that he would have made much more, as others have, of the place of status-seeking individual action in Leach's analysis, action stemming, perhaps, not from an "ontology of the imagination," but from an "ontology of violence"—an ontology, recall, that foregrounds force and power—and an ontology, incidentally, in which Min Aung Hlaing and others behind the coup and subsequent crackdown also seem to be rooted.[62]

"Stick to the facts of the case and exercise your imagination," is how Leach concluded his essay "Rethinking Anthropology."[63] The line is classic Leach in its directness. Yet, we've seen here how the relationship between the two—facts and the imagination—can be a little bit more complicated, including for Leach himself. It's not been my intention to recruit him into the anthropology of Christianity—nor Graeber for that matter. But in reading the foreword that Graeber never wrote, reading a text that doesn't exist, I've offered a partial reading of the revolution in Myanmar. There are, no doubt, other reasons for Graeber's admiration of Leach, present perhaps in Graeber's invocation of a certain ideal of an anthropologist at the end of his article, "Anthropology and the Rise of the Professional-Managerial Class": an aristocratic ideal which recognizes that what "drew us to this line of work was mainly a sense of fun, that playing with ideas is a form of pleasure in itself"—an ideal that, importantly for Graeber, should be open to everyone.[64]

There are also echoes, relatedly, in the style of argument, a style that might be thought of as "revolutionary," not in the Pauline sense of rupture, but in the sense of turning something around, or upside down, a meaning perhaps better captured in the Burmese word for revolution, *taw lan ye*, with its sense of reversing, or turning things inside out, even if one completely disagrees with the final analysis. There are important differences and discontinuities, too, political and otherwise. Where Leach, as Laidlaw and Hugh-Jones write, "seems to have proceeded not from any consistent political opinion," Graeber's immersion in anarchist practice animates much of his anthropology, including his interest in prefiguration.[65]

But another similarity is that Graeber and Leach were not just prolific writers, but also prolific readers. Anna Grimshaw recounts that being supervised by Leach involved a "a great deal of reading the classic ethnographies in preparation for writing my own."[66] Geertz's famous answer to the question, "what is it that the ethnographer does?", is that they write. Yes, but they also read. Sneath, Holbraad, and Pedersen ask whether it might be possible to see ethnography as a "technology of the anthropologist's analytical imagination."[67] Leach, of course, claimed to have written up his Kachin analysis in the absence of fieldnotes, famously lost amid the chaos of war. Notwithstanding what is said about the power of Leach's photographic memory, we might also ask: What kind of imagination did *that* entail?

There's been much written about the place of the imagination in the writing of anthropology, but less, I think, about the role of imagination in its reading. If "all ethnography is fiction,"as Leach claimed in one of his final public lectures in 1986, and even if it isn't, what kind of imaginative faculties are brought to be bear in its reading?[68] For many Christians, reading and the imagination naturally come together—in how believers, via scripture, imagine themselves in conversation with God;[69] or in how they imagine themselves living out the very narratives from the Bible passages they study.[70] What modes of imaginative reading do anthropologists pursue, through gaps, from afar, of Facebook posts, of classic monographs, and of texts that don't really exist? In his foreword to Severi's book, Graeber pushes against the "utopian ideal" of a text produced by a "single, unique" genius. Instead, he argues, "everything turns on a tacit complicity, whereby the author leaves the work, in effect, half-finished so as to 'capture the imagination' of the interpreter."[71]

Unfinished, unfolding, incomplete—like Myanmar's revolution. Ruth has also been working in the presence of something that doesn't really exist, and didn't even in the years of so-called transition: a democratic Myanmar that is both politically—and, for her, spiritually—saved. But in defying the military, just as she evangelized in the face of indifference, she and others act "as if" they live in a world not just where "the revolution must succeed," but in which it already has, and in imagining that world, they work to bring it into being.

Notes

1. Daily briefing in relation to the military coup, Assistance Association for Political Prisoners, October 6, 2022. Available at: https://aappb. org/?lang=en (accessed October 6, 2022).
2. Ingrid Jordt, Tharaphi Than, and Sue Ye Lin, *How Generation Z Galvanized a Revolutionary Movement against Myanmar's 2021 Military Coup* (Singapore: ISEAS–Yusof Ishak Institute, 2021).
3. Iselin Frydenlund, Pum Za Mang, Phyo Wai, and Susan Hayward, "Religious Responses to the Military Coup in Myanmar," *Review of Faith & International Affairs* 19, no. 3 (2021): 77–88.
4. David Graeber, "Foreword," in *Revolution in Rojava: Democratic Autonomy and Women's Liberation in Syrian Kurdistan*, ed. Michael Knapp, Ercan Ayboga, and Anja Flach (London: Pluto Press, 2016), xiv.

5. David Graeber, "Revolution in Reverse," in *Revolutions in Reverse: Essays on Politics, Violence, Art, and Imagination* (London: Minor Compositions, 2007), 52–53.

6. Edmund Leach, *Political Systems of Highland Burma* (Boston, MA: Beacon Press, 1964).

7. E.g. Maran La Raw, "On the Continuing Relevance of E.R. Leach's *Political Systems of Highland Burma* to Kachin Studies," in *Social Dynamics in the Highlands of South East Asia: Reconsidering "Political Systems of Highland Burma" by E.R. Leach*, ed. François Robbine and Mandy Sadan (Leiden: Brill, 2007); Tharaphi Than, "Why Does Area Studies Need Decolonization?" Commentary Board, November 21, 2021, available at: https://criticalasianstudies.org/commentary/2021/11/20/commentary-tharaphi-than-why-does-area-studies-need-decolonization (accessed November 30, 2021).

8. David Graeber, "It Wasn't a Tenure Case—A Personal Testimony, with Reflections," *Public Anthropologist* 1 (2019): 96.

9. David Graeber, "Ready Steady Book," interview by Mark Thwaite, 2007, available at: http://www.readysteadybook.com/Article_page_davidgraeber.html (accessed May 20, 2021).

10. Chris Fuller and Jonathan Parry, "Petulant Inconsistency? The Intellectual Achievement of Edmund Leach," *Anthropology Today* 5, no. 3(1989): 11.

11. James Laidlaw and Stephen Hugh-Jones (eds.), *The Essential Edmund Leach*, vol. 1: *Anthropology and Society* (New Haven, CT: Yale University Press, 2000), 3.

12. Edmund Leach, "Glimpses of the Unmentionable in the History of British Social Anthropology," *Annual Review of Anthropology* 13, no. 1 (1984); David Graeber, "Anthropology and the Rise of the Professional-Managerial Class," *Hau: Journal of Ethnographic Theory* 4, no. 3 (2014).

13. David Graeber, *Lost People: Magic and the Legacy of Slavery in Madagascar* (Bloomington, IN: Indiana University Press 2008); David Graeber, *The Utopia of Rules: On Technology, Stupidity, and the Secret Joys of Bureaucracy* (Brooklyn: Melville House, 2015); Edmund Leach, *Social Anthropology* (London: Fontana, 1982).

14. Leach, *Social Anthropology*, 108. On this point, Graeber also (e.g. *Toward an Anthropological Theory of Value: The False Coin of Our Own Dreams* [New York: Palgrave, 2001, 58]) cites Marx's observation that, unlike a spider weaving its web or a bee building its nest, "the [human] architect raises his structure in imagination before he erects it in reality."

15. Graeber, *Toward an Anthropological Theory of Value*, 88.

16. Leach, *Political Systems of Highland Burma*, 127–128.

17. Frederic Kris Lehman, *The Structure of Chin Society* (Urbana: University of Illinois Press, 1963).

18. Frederic Kris Lehman, "Ethnic Categories in Burma and the Theory of Social Systems," in *Southeast Asian Tribes, Minorities and Nations*, vol. 1,

ed. Peter Kunstadter (Princeton, NJ: Princeton University Press, 1967), 97.

19. Michael Edwards, "Drowning in Context: Translating Salvation in Myanmar," *Comparative Studies of South Asia, Africa and the Middle East* 41, no. 2 (2021).

20. Michael Edwards, "Circulating in Difference: Performances of Publicity on and Beyond a Yangon Train," *Journal of the Royal Anthropological Institute* 28, no. 2 (2022).

21. Joel Robbins, "Afterword: Some Reflections on Rupture," in *Ruptures: Anthropologies of Discontinuity in Times of Turmoil*, ed. Martin Holbraad, Bruce Kapferer, and Julia F. Sauma (London: UCL Press, 2019).

22. Naomi Haynes, "The Expansive Present: A New Model of Christian Time," *Current Anthropology* 6, no. 1 (2019).

23. Graeber, *Revolutions in Reverse*, 52.

24. David Sneath, Martin Holbraad, and Morten Axel Pedersen, "Technologies of the Imagination: An Introduction," *Ethnos* 74, no. 1 (2009): 5.

25. Joel Robbins, "On Imagination and Creation: An Afterword," *Anthropological Forum* 20, no. 3 (2010).

26. Ibid., 306.

27. A notable exception is Amira Mittermaier's *Dreams that Matter: Egyptian Landscapes of the Imagination* (Berkeley: University of California Press, 2011).

28. Robbins, "On Imagination and Creation," 307.

29. Vincent Crapanzano, *Imaginative Horizons: An Essay in Literary-Philosophical Anthropology* (Chicago: University of Chicago Press, 2004), 2.

30. Maurice Bloch, "Why Religion is Nothing Special but is Central," *Philosophical Transactions of the Royal Society B: Biological Sciences* 363, no. 1499 (2008).

31. Lehman, "Ethnic Categories in Burma."

32. Ibid., 105.

33. Leach, *Political Systems of Highland Burma*, xii.

34. Ibid., 16.

35. Ibid., xiv.

36. Ibid., 14.

37. David Nugent, "Closed Systems and Contradiction: The Kachin In and Out of History," *Man* 17 (1982). See also Jonathan Friedman, *System, Structure, and Contradiction in the Evolution of "Asiatic" Social Formations* (Copenhagen: National Museum of Denmark, 1979).

38. Stanley J. Tambiah, *Edmund Leach: An Anthropological Life* (Cambridge: Cambridge University Press, 2007), 429.

39. Edmund Leach, in Edmund Leach and David Nugent, "Imaginary Kachins," *Man* 18, no. 1 (1983).

40. Ibid., 227.

41. François Robinne and Mandy Sadan, "Preface," in *Social Dynamics in the Highlands of South East Asia*, ed. Robinne and Sadan, x–xi.

42. Maran La Raw, "On the Continuing Relevance"; Mandy Sadan, "Translating *Gulmau*: History, the 'Kachin' and Edmund Leach," in *Social Dynamics in the Highlands of South East Asia*, ed. Robinne and Sadan.

43. Sadan, "Translating *Gumlau*," 77–78.

44. Leach, "Glimpses of the Unmentionable," 18.

45. Fuller and Parry, "Petulant Inconsistency," 11.

46. Nayanika Mathur and Liana Chua, *Who Are "We"? Reimagining Alterity and Affinity in Anthropology* (New York: Berghahn, 2018).

47. Graeber, *Toward and Anthropological Theory of Value*, 251–254.

48. David Graeber, "Radical Alterity is Just Another Way of Saying 'Reality': A Reply to Eduardo Viveiros de Castro," *HAU: The Journal of Ethnographic Theory* 5, no. 2 (2015), 6.

49. Raymond Firth, "Foreword," in Edmund Leach, *Political Systems of Highland Burma* (Boston, MA: Beacon Press, 1964), viii.

50. Leach, *Political Systems of Highland Burma*, xiv.

51. David Graeber, "Concerning Mental Pivots and Civilizations of Memory," Preface in *The Chimera Principle: An Anthropology of Memory and Imagination* (Chicago: HAU Books, 2015), xv.

52. Joel Robbins, "On Imagination and Creation."

53. Jon Bialecki, *A Diagram for Fire: Miracles and Variation in an American Charismatic Movement* (Oakland, CA: University of California Press, 2017), 46.

54. Caroline Humphrey, "Schism, Event, and Revolution: The Old Believers of Trans-Baikalia," *Current Anthropology* 55 (2014).

55. Ibid., 216.

56. Robbins, "Afterword: Some Reflections on Rupture," 219.

57. Igor Cherstich, Martin Holbraad, and Nico Tassi, *Anthropologies of Revolution: Forging Time, People, and Worlds* (Oakland, CA: California University Press, 2020), 4.

58. Leach, *Political Systems of Highland Burma*, 7.

59. Tambiah, *Edmund Leach*, 443; on the "denial of coevalness," see Johannes Fabian, *Time and the Other: How Anthropology Makes Its Object* (New York: Columbia University Press, 1983).

60. Leach does mention the coup in the essay, "Buddhism in the Post-Colonial Political Order in Burma and Ceylon," *Daedalus* 102, no. 1 (1973).

61. David Graeber, "Dead Zones of the Imagination: On Violence, Bureaucracy, and Interpretive labor," *Hau: Journal of Ethnographic Theory* 2, no. 2 (2012).

62. See, for example, Fuller and Parry, "Petulant Inconsistency?" 12–13.

63. Edmund Leach, "Rethinking Anthropology," in *Rethinking Anthropology* (Oxford: Berg, 1961).

64. Graeber, "Anthropology and the Rise."

65. Laidlaw and Hugh-Jones, *The Essential Edmund Leach*, 3.

66. Anna Grimshaw, "A Runaway World? Anthropology as Public Debate," *Cambridge Anthropology* 13, no. 3 (1989): 76.

67. Sneath, Holbraad, and Pedersen, "Technologies of the Imagination," 25.

68. Edmund Leach, "Tribal Ethnography: Past, Present, Future," *Cambridge Anthropology* 11, no. 2 (1987).

69. Tanya Lurhmann, *When God Talks Back: Understanding the American Evangelical Relationship with God* (New York: Alfred A. Knopf, 2012).

70. Haynes, "The Expansive Present."

71. Graeber, "Concerning Mental Pivots," xx–xxi.

7

Debt and Political Possibility in Eritrea

Michael Ralph

Peace does not arise from the actions of one party alone.
—Norwegian Nobel Committee[1]

On October 11, 2019, the Norwegian Nobel Committee issued a press release explaining its "decision to award the Nobel Peace Prize for 2019 to Ethiopian Prime Minister Abiy Ahmed Ali for his efforts to achieve peace and international cooperation, and in particular"—the announcement stressed—"for his decisive initiative to resolve the border conflict with neighbouring Eritrea":

> When Abiy Ahmed became Prime Minister in April 2018, he made it clear that he wished to resume peace talks with Eritrea. In close cooperation with Isaias Afwerki, the President of Eritrea, Abiy Ahmed quickly worked out the principles of a peace agreement to end the long "no peace, no war" stalemate between the two countries. These principles are set out in the declarations that Prime Minister Abiy and President Afwerki signed in Asmara and Jeddah last July and September.[2]

The press release is perplexing because it shifts from heaping praise on Prime Minister Abiy Ahmed to noting the strenuous efforts that President Isaias likewise made toward restoring peace. Yet, the narrative insists on crediting Abiy Ahmed with leading the effort:

> An important premise for the breakthrough was Abiy Ahmed's unconditional willingness to accept the arbitration ruling of an international boundary commission in 2002.[3]

War between these two nations derives from the fact that Eritrea fought a nearly 30-year war for formal independence (1961 to 1991) against Ethiopia, a country that—ironically—boasts about being the only one in Africa never to have been colonized. Eritrea made aggressive strides to de-mobilize its military, promote free press, and foster a broad range of employment possibilities for the nation's people for about 7 years following independence until Ethiopia violated its territorial sovereignty in 1998, provoking 20 years of tense military engagement that finally came to an end with the landmark peace deal in 2018 that so impressed the Nobel Committee. But there would have been no need for a peace deal if Ethiopia had never colonized Eritrea, nor spent another 20 years denying its right to territorial sovereignty. Throughout that period, President Isaias made several speeches referring to the conflict as "senseless" and pointing to the specific process the United Nations (UN) had endorsed for delineating the territorial boundaries between the two countries in the presence of impartial international observers. In fact, as President Isaias noted, the boundary had not simply been agreed upon by both nations but archived in a repository available for all to observe. Peace came in 2018 when Dr Abiy finally accepted terms that had been established decades prior. So, why make such a big deal of his "unconditional willingness to accept the arbitration ruling of an international boundary commission" Ethiopia had willfully defied for nearly two decades?

Scholars working on the intersection of finance and imperialism in Africa have shown how protocols for diplomatic engagement and forms of lending characteristic of Italian city-states evolved into protocols for trade and diplomacy that shaped how people of the continent engaged with the Mediterranean world.[4] The scholarly literature has also demonstrated the formative role of experiments in islands off the Atlantic coast in shaping the forms of accounting, labor techniques, and strategies of prediction that would dominate the plantation societies of the Americas from the fifteenth century onward.[5] This scholarship has also explored how Indigenous strategies for adjudicating debt were displaced by colonial conquest during the nineteenth century, while explaining how European colonialism transformed labor markets, as well as quotidian forms of exchange.[6] In this way, the scholarly literature has connected vernacular forms of finance to state structures.[7] The most piercing analyses have critiqued the hierarchies that dominate liberal notions of progress, where African polities are fitted into a developmental horizon that positions affluent nations as custodians who judge which economies are successful and under what conditions.[8] Recent scholarship has grappled with the strategies of profiling used to establish a country's diplomatic standing with implications for the forms of capital it can access—a paradigm with deep roots in notions of race and civilization.[9]

The academic literature on finance, when it bothers to mention the African continent, centers on the forms of prediction, calculation, investment, and exchange introduced by people whose origins lie elsewhere, most notably via European colonization, which dismantled African infrastructure, halted progress, fostered genocide, undermined ingenuity, and contributed to economic and political growth. Other work highlights the role of the United States as an increasingly influential force in shaping economic and political affairs on the continent in the years following World War II, as a Europe depleted by war faced a United States emboldened by the infrastructure achievements of New Deal policies and eager for a greater role as a leader in world affairs. More recent studies of finance in Africa consider the role of China, South Korea, Iran, Saudi Arabia, and the United Arab Emirates in shaping policy and investment initiatives. None of these approaches prepares scholars to grapple with the case of Eritrea—an African country colonized by a neighbouring country within the continent. Our discussions of finance and imperialism in Africa do not center on the role that African countries have played in exploiting other African countries, nor do they center on autonomous solutions that African countries have developed for tackling imperialism.

Typically, when African countries seek to establish a distinct economic and political vision, they are dismissed as well intentioned but naïve (Kwame Nkrumah's Pan-Africanism, Julius Nyerere's African socialism, Patrice Lumumba's defiant stand against Belgian neocolonialism, Burkina Faso under Thomas Sankara), or authoritarian and dictatorial (Zimbabwe's Robert Mugabe). Eritrea offers a unique opportunity to explore a vision for economic and political development that, despite being criticized and undermined, has arguably triumphed as a strategy for grappling with the ravages of finance and imperialism—for, as I will demonstrate, the most impressive and intriguing aspect of the peace deal between Ethiopia and Eritrea is that Ethiopia accepted peace *on Eritrea's terms*. The Nobel Committee's regrettable bias traffics in a pattern of distortion that arguably helped to precipitate and sustain the conflict between these two countries over nearly half a century: the assumption that Ethiopia is the true leader in the region, the more noble party, the more rational, and the more generous interlocutor. In what follows, I discuss some "political possibilities" for democratic governance that Eritrea has explored to establish political legitimacy in the eyes of its populace against an imperial framework that has sought to undermine and invalidate the struggle for formal independence. That strategy centered on developing unprecedented forms of horizontalism and in newfound notions of indebtedness, specifically the significance of sacrifice for forging an enduring sense of political belonging. The sense of debt and obligation does not merely animate and sustain the legitimacy of the Eritrean liberation struggle in the eyes of supporters, it has also had material ramifications as the source of the nation's founding budget and operational framework.

In *Possibilities: Essays on Hierarchy, Rebellion, and Desire*, David Graeber distills an insight from his experience organizing and strategizing with anarchists that resonates with the forms of horizontalism the Eritrean People's Liberation Front (EPLF) has historically insisted upon:

> [A]narchist inspired groups tend to operate on the assumption that no one could, or probably should, ever convert another person completely to one's own point of view, that decision-making structures are ways of managing diversity, and therefore, that one should concentrate instead on maintaining egalitarian processes and on considering immediate questions of action in the present.[10]

Thus, while critics and some observers characterize Eritrea as an authoritarian state governed by an egomaniacal, charismatic leader, the ministers of various state agencies, and the leaders of trade unions, have historically insisted on a division of labor in which roles are determined by constituencies of concerned activists who ultimately determine who will be the anointed authorities of a given domain.

These horizontalist strategies align with the work of Graeber, who goes beyond mere ethnographic observation in suggesting that these principles should even shape how we read and understand different styles of governance—especially forms of authority that differ dramatically from our own experiences and preferences:

> A fundamental principle of political debate, for instance, is that one is obliged to give other participants the benefit of the doubt for honesty and good intentions, whatever else one might think of their arguments. In part, this emerges from the style of debate consensus decision-making encourages: where voting encourages one to reduce one's opponents'

positions to a hostile caricature, or whatever it takes to defeat them, a consensus process is built on a principle of compromise and creativity, where one is constantly changing proposals around until one can come up with something everyone can at least live with. Therefore, the incentive is always to put the best construction on others' arguments.[11]

In should be noted that Graeber's analysis of politics drew heavily from his extensive ethnographic research in East Africa, specifically Madagascar. He held that context in mind as he observed that, "Anarchist or anarchist-inspired movements are growing everywhere; anarchist principles—autonomy, voluntary association, self-organization, mutual aid, direct democracy—have become the basis for organizing within the globalization movement and beyond."[12]

This chapter explores how Eritrea navigated imperialism through several decades of self-defense that entailed forging an enduring sense of political belonging through newfound strategies of horizontalism and an acute sense of indebtedness to the people who gave their lives for independence—the martyrs. The formal parameters of the Eritrean economy as well as the broader economic and political vision take their shape from this sense of obligation. When Eritreans liberated their country in 1991, the United States and the UN persuaded Eritrea to wait two years to hold a formal referendum in exchange for an operating budget. From the vantage point of the international community, Eritrea became a sovereign nation in 1993.

But, as Eritreans had ousted Ethiopian forces and regained formal control of their territory in 1991, they spent 1992 establishing political belonging among the nation's people, especially those who had paid most dearly with their lives and the lives of loved ones. This sentiment surfaces in the Tigrinya term, *hdri*, meaning "promise," or "sacrifice." To understand how Eritreans understand these crucial concepts, it is essential to see how they are deployed in the conversations and events that shape life's most visceral and most intimate moments.

Hdri, *"Promise, Sacrifice"*

It was in her left arm. A sharp pain. Out of nowhere. She was crying and wailing uncontrollably but no one noticed at first because that part was normal. It started when Gebretensae left for the war.[13] She couldn't handle it. She cried and cried until she lost her mind. Her other sons felt awful about it. They loved Gebretensae and believed in him. He was a hero. He always had been. Handsome, young, and charismatic, everyone had always loved Gebretensae. He was a star soccer player. He left Eritrea at a young age to play professionally, which never happened in those days (either in Kenya or Uganda, people disagree about where he went). He was successful as a soccer player, but returned home to visit his family and decided to stay. He refused to accept what was happening in his country. He joined the war against colonial rule. Signing up was easy because his city, Keren, played a pivotal role in the conflict. Dominated by mountains, it was difficult to enter and exit Keren, making it a great place to fight from and a difficult place to capture. The Eritrean Liberation Front (ELF) and Eritrean People's Liberation Front (EPLF) found it increasingly difficult to move troops into Keren, so they depended heavily on volunteers. And Gebretensae was exceptional.

Being from Keren, he knew the terrain. He had just enlisted but, in a matter of months, was appointed commander of Brigade 23. Meanwhile, his mother started losing her grip on reality. She looked for him. Waited for him. Prayed for him. Despite being in and from Keren, he was not allowed to notify family members about where he was stationed, where he would be, and what he was doing. His family respected and admired him. But they also looked for him. Longed for him. Gebretensae knew that, so he would visit. Sometime in 1977, he showed up without notice. He spent the day with his family. They chatted and ate. Told stories. His family enjoyed seeing him and relished the moment. Then, he was gone. Just as quickly as he had come. Gebretensae's mother was better once she had seen him. But, the crying and wailing started back soon after he left. This day, it was worse than usual. And, suddenly, there was pain. She gripped her left arm. "My son is dead," she said. But nobody believed her. She had been losing it for a while. The crying and wailing were normal. The pain made them think she was getting worse. Nobody believed her.

But then, Keren was liberated. And, the other soldiers came home to celebrate. Gebretensae did not come home to celebrate. They never heard what had happened to him. But they knew. They were proud of Gebretensae. He was their hero. Now, he was a martyr. They missed him. They never knew what happened to him. He had enlisted in October of 1975. He died in July of 1977. And in 1992, the government of Eritrea issued his family a martyr certificate (*shilimat suwa'at*).

*   *   *

When the struggle for formal independence officially began in 1961, the leadership of the ELF included exiles from Sudan, Cairo and Addis Ababa, who helped organize fighters from the highland regions into battalions who could defend the country against the forms of violence and intimidation Ethiopia used to pacify the population, revealing that the war for formal independence had a diasporic geography from its inception. By the 1970s, some people involved with the liberation project became concerned that the ELF had not done enough to eradicate long-standing systems of patriarchy, patronage, and religious division in Eritrea. Convinced that an entirely new sense of community would be needed to overcome Eritrea's vast disparity in arms and numbers vis-à-vis Ethiopia, the EPLF was formed. In the years that followed, the EPLF subsumed and displaced the ELF by encouraging religious leaders to appreciate the role of education in social mobility. The EPLF fostered a sense of egalitarianism that translated into active recruitment among women, who joined their cause as fighters, and children, who served them as spies and scouts. In the EPLF understanding of the liberation struggle, all Eritreans were active agents. The people of Eritrea were organized as an interlocking series of associations, within the country and throughout the diaspora, that served as crucial nodes for managing food and arms. These dispersed and interrelated sites of communication also permitted the EPLF leadership to maintain contact with a network of resourceful people whom they drew upon for leadership roles. The EPLF military operation did not use ranks or titles and battalion leaders famously lived as, and among, the soldiers they commanded, as mentioned earlier. The EPLF also pioneered new rituals for grappling with death that differ from the more familiar form of grieving, known (in the language, Tigrigna) as a *hazen*.

A *hazen* is a "theatre, where you go to perform your grief and mourning," in the words of a twenty-something-year-old Eritrean graduate student in anthropology. Guided by the idea that "no one should be alone when they are grieving," a close relative will usually erect a tent near the home that is in mourning and maintain it for twelve days or so. For Eritrean communities in the United States, the *hazen is* usually held inside the home of the grieving family, though if the person who passed away is an important member of the community—and it is believed that the family home cannot accommodate the number of well-wishers who plan to attend—the *hazen* can be held in a community church.

During a *hazen*, people pay tribute to the deceased by crying and wailing. Tributes through wailing are usually gendered—the women closest to the deceased usually enact the loudest, most frequent, and most sorrowful wailing. Men closest to the deceased are usually the most active in trying to console women enacting the most sorrowful wailing. Because men who occupy this role are viewed as trying to temper the crying and wailing, the women closest to the deceased insist on spending most of their time during the *hazen* around other women (in fact, men and women often sit separately at a *hazen*, for this reason). When the deceased is married, supportive women surround the spouse, drawing attention to her as the primary source of action in the "theater" because she will issue the most spectacular enactment of grief.

The *hazen* is understood "as a place where everyone can go and cry and remember" the deceased. Because the emphasis is on paying tribute to a loved one who has died unexpectedly, people adopt a lifestyle that is even more modest than usual. Some avoid taking baths. Others avoid jewelry and other forms of bodily adornment rendered superficial against the tragic loss of life.

The woman closest to the family in mourning usually serves as the host or "manager" of the *hazen*, identifying which community members will bring food—usually one of several stews made with a tomato and garlic base, such as *hamli* (a kale dish, seasoned with local pepper, called *berbere*), *shiro* (made from dried chick peas), *addis* (made from dried lentils), or *teb'he* (made with chicken or beef and seasoned with *berbere*). Dishes are usually served by the host, or host team, from a single pot, carried around the *hazen* rather than the more familiar buffet style of serving associated with festive occasions. Beverages served at a *hazen* include *shahi* (tea made from classic Lipton tea bags, seasoned with cardamom, clove, and sometimes cinnamon), soda, and water. Because funeral arrangements can be quite expensive, whether in Eritrea or in the diaspora, a trusted family member will usually "make a box" during the *hazen* for the grieving family to collect money from guests. Monetary gifts are carefully recorded in a notebook that is given to the family, along with the funds, once the *hazen* is complete.

Death is familiar to the small country that has lost thousands of people during the past half century or so of warfare. In fact, the greatest national holiday is arguably Martyrs' Day. "Martyred" is even used as a title, before the first name, as with "Dr." or "Mr." But you do not honor a martyr with a *hazen*. There is an entirely different ritual dedicated to "the remembrance of martyrs" (*zikri sem'a'tat*).

The "remembrance of martyrs" is usually reserved for more formal Eritrean gatherings, like a community or association meeting. The association is the most basic and most familiar aspect of social life in Eritrea. Most Eritreans are involved in several, interlocking, voluntary associations. In fact, the organization of associations that promote leaders from within based on insight and ingenuity, and without regard to religion, gender, or age, is widely regarded—by veterans as well as by scholars—as the principle that enabled Eritreans to win the 30-year war for formal independence against Ethiopia despite a dramatic numerical disadvantage.

At the start of an association meeting, the appointed leader will say something that translates to, "Ok, everybody, it is time to perform 'the remembrance of martyrs' (*hi'jee, zikri sem'a'tat kin jih'mir eena*)." Unlike other announcements, which inevitably take place over the din of idle chatter, the room falls entirely silent when it is time to perform "the remembrance of martyrs." If someone is a wearing a hat, that hat is removed. After the announcement, the person issuing it will say: "Attention" (*t'ten'Qet*), as people stand at attention, feet together; then, "Take your position" (*seT'bel*), as members of the community stand side by side. Then, the community observes a moment of silence until the person who issued the call says, "You may rest at peace" (*b'selam Erefu*). At that point, everyone looks up, raises their left fists and says, "Glory to the masses" (*Awet n'Hafash*). Then, business may be conducted, as usual. Meetings are opened and closed with the "remembrance of martyrs."

When asked why "remembrance of martyrs" is used to honor fallen soldiers rather than a *hazen*, a 20-something-year-old woman who is a member of the Philadelphia branch of YPFDJ (the primary youth division of the governing party, known in English as the People's Front for Democracy and Justice, or PFDJ), noted that June 20, Martyrs' Day, in fact offers the entire nation the opportunity to be sad, to grieve for martyrs. But, during the "remembrance of martyrs," she noted, "we think of them as a collective body": "The reason we do it is to remember them—it is a part of the struggle ... acknowledging who we are fighting for ... not letting them die." She continued:

Usually, when people die, they are only remembered on special occasions. [This] ritual ['remembrance of martyrs'] is used to keep the martyrs at the forefront: [it] creates stasis for the group, giving [martyrs] a piece of the present since they can't be with us.

Martyrs, by definition, "can't be with us" in the present—in the era of independence their sacrifice made possible. But the *particular kinds* of sacrifices attributed to martyrs are essential to the political projects they inspire. The Eritrean martyr is not only someone who gave his life for independence, but also someone dedicated to the quest for political legitimacy in a world where privileged nations exert disproportionate control over the power of sanction.

Facing a dramatic numerical disadvantage, Eritreans conscripted people of all ages, genders, and walks of life for their decolonization effort. The liberation strategy ultimately involved a dedicated effort to try to eradicate ageism, chauvinism, and religious prejudice in order to forge a collective vision of independence. Tactically, the Eritrean approach involved an elaborate system of trench warfare, that included garages, schools, armories, and clinical facilities.

The critical role of medical expertise in the liberation struggle underscores the scientific authority that makes the martyr certificate possible. The martyr certificate is premised on clinical practices Eritrean doctors and soldiers use to conduct forensic analysis and to thus develop scientific explanations for cause of death. The martyr certificate is made possible by vernacular medical protocols Eritreans developed during the liberation struggle for identifying and documenting cause of death.

Figure 7.1   Martyr certificate

First-hand accounts of the war for independence that detail the production of martyrs from dead soldiers center on the bravery and ingenuity
comrades exhibited under extraordinarily difficult circumstances. Still,
even these narratives, which discuss in great detail the virtues and capabil-
ities of soldiers rather than the specific circumstances surrounding their
deaths, nevertheless involve a discussion about how the bodies of injured
and ultimately deceased soldiers were cared for and honored through
interment in the complex geography of the mountainous region and the
labyrinthine context that defined the principal theater of combat. In other
words, the pervasive presence of unmarked graves scattered throughout
mountainous trenches where martyrs were identified and interred trans-
forms the vast landscape of Eritrea into a sacred burial site in a nation
where it is already common to say: "the land is blessed" (*Halal meryet*).
Martyr certificates attest to fallen soldiers responsible for helping to
bestow upon their nation the ultimate blessing through forensic docu-
ments that confirm their priceless sacrifice at a time when others fled or
were conscripted into the colonial project.

From that perspective, martyr certificates are not merely forensic objects
but honorifics. Eritreans often frame and hang them in their homes in lieu
of photos of the deceased loved ones who are deemed national heroes and
honored with the most sacred of all holidays, "Martyrs' Day." In this way,
the "martyr certificate" condenses the war for formal independence into
an artifact, or emblem, dedicated to the production of political legitimacy.
But, more importantly, it is a proxy for the kind of sacrifice that creates a
sense of shared indebtedness to martyrs for all Eritrean people. That sense
of indebtedness also serves as the explicit justification for the forms of sacrifice used to generate Eritrea's first national budget.

Hdri, *"debt"*

"*Hdri*" means "promise" or "sacrifice." But, it also means "debt."

> If democracy is simply a matter of communities managing their own
> affairs through an open and relatively egalitarian process of public dis-
> cussion, there is no reason why egalitarian forms of decision-making
> in *rural communities* in Africa or Brazil should not be at least as worthy
> of the name as the constitutional systems that govern most nation-
> states today—and, in many cases, probably a good deal more worthy....
> The "democratic ideal" tends to emerge when, under certain historical

circumstances, intellectuals and politicians, usually in some sense navigating their way between states and popular movements and popular practices, interrogate their own traditions—invariably, in dialogue with other ones—citing cases of past or present democratic practice to argue that their tradition has a fundamental kernel of democracy. I call these moments of "democratic refoundation." From the perspective of the intellectual traditions, they are also moments of recuperation, in which ideals and institutions that are often the product of incredibly complicated forms of interaction between people of very different histories and traditions come to be represented as emerging from the logic of that intellectual tradition itself.[14]

[Eritrea] started off its independent existence with one great asset—no debt was owed to any foreign government, bank, or multilateral institution.[15]

Audience member: "I think in my little handout, here, it says that Eritrea gained its independence in 1993."
President Isaias Afwerki: "Formal."
Audience member: "—*formal* independence, from Ethiopia—"
President Isaias Afwerki: "Not *from* Ethiopia."
[awkward silence]
President Isaias Afwerki: "*Not from* Ethiopia."
Audience member: "Alright."
President Isaias Afwerki: "Ok."[16]

The EPLF has always framed the liberation project as an effort to restore autonomy and facilitate decentralized, democratic governance. In fact, as noted above, the liberation project relied on building appreciation for the EPLF among the populace. Soldiers relied on people throughout the country for food and shelter, to hide them from colonial troops, and to help them transmit essential communications.

Most crucially, from the dawn of formal independence, the Eritrean government has implemented protocols designed to assure the nation—and observers including international governing agencies—that it governs through the will of the people. This explains why Eritrean president, Isaias Afwerki, stressed the priority placed on governing by consensus during a 1999 lecture at Princeton University—one of his few public appearances. The visit came a year into repeated violations of border demarcations the

UN had established for what counts as Eritrea and Ethiopia, respectively. The fighting would ultimately become so intense that, after Eritrea made historic peace agreements with Ethiopia, Somalia, and Djibouti in 2018, some veterans and military officials would refer to the period between 1998 and 2018 as a war unto itself. But already in 1999, as the question an unidentified Princeton University audience member posed to President Isaias reveals, observers wanted to know what had "altered the stance of the Ethiopian government towards Eritrea" since the moment that independence was declared in 1991.

In his response, President Isaias emphasizes that the Eritrean liberation project was not a secessionist movement, as it had been characterized by Ethiopian colonial officials, "Eritrea did not get its independence from Ethiopia, at all." In fact, he insists that the war for formal independence was driven by a dogged fight against unjust forces: "We have our just cause. We fought for a long time—for over three decades. [Shrug] Or, for half a century."[17]

The periodization is important. While President Isaias realizes that the Eritrean liberation struggle was characterized by thirty years of continuous warfare, he suggests that—from a different vantage point—Eritreans have been fighting to repel Ethiopia since the two countries became federated in 1952 through a deal brokered by the UN that gave Ethiopia disproportionate power over Eritrea. Hence the reference to "half a century":

> And when '91 came, we said: "We are postponing the unilateral declaration of independence to go through a legitimate political process, to assure the international community—and be assured—that we have exercised this fight through a referendum."

As mentioned earlier, the United States, had in fact, played a critical role in persuading Eritrea to "delay a referendum on sovereignty for two years."[18] Thus, contrary to the "fictional dichotomy" the United States government would later adopt of "'good' Ethiopia," its friend and ally in the region, helping to suppress a dastardly Eritrea—President Isaias notes that Eritrea was encouraged by the United States to pursue a patient and comprehensive agenda for democratic governance:[19]

> Then, people were saying, "Well, a referendum could be expedited if the Ethiopian government agrees to the referendum process." We said, "No. Not at all. We are not asking for the blessing of the Ethiopian gov-

ernment—or anybody else, for that matter. We would like to exercise this right [to self-determination] through a referendum. And, we would like the international community to come help us organize and witness the desire, or the wish, of our population." No one was invited to offer Eritrea independence on a silver platter.

Not at all. We rejected that ...[20]

The 1993 referendum that Eritrea held was in fact the legacy of a request it had made to Ethiopian occupying forces as early as 1980 to put the political wishes of the nation's people to a test through a referendum that demanded Eritreans be permitted to vote for whether they preferred to be (1) autonomous yet linked to Ethiopia, (2) federated, or (3) independent. That desire was dismissed. When Eritrea finally did hold a referendum, two years after declaring military victory, the 99.83 percent who voted in favor of independence included 98.5 percent of eligible voters in a process viewed by the nation's people, as well as by the "international community" as a "legitimate political process."

Eritrea waited for two years after 1991. When the liberation struggle officially drew to a successful close in May 1991, Isais Afwerki, as EPLF leader, asked the entire military to keep working without pay until the referendum so that the emergent nation could consolidate its economic resources.

In November 1991, the EPLF announced the parameters of their program for national service: all citizens between the ages of 18 and 40 were expected to register for it. In addition, people not working or attending university could be summoned for military service for a period extending from 12 to 18 months. Further, university students were mobilized to spread literacy in rural areas. Meanwhile, soldiers were tasked with a range of public works projects, including road construction, terracing hillsides, and building earthen dams and catchment basins—projects reminiscent of the United States Civilian Conservation Corps in the 1930s.[21]

At a meeting of the UN Economic and Social Council in July 1993, President Isaias Afwerki explained why it was so important to calibrate the "interests" of "donors and recipients": "What is required, and what has been conspicuously lacking, is international assistance commensurate with the needs of the country ...".[22] President Afwerki was most concerned with the "impact of assistance on recipient countries"—"whether it inspires or dampens their creativity and self-respect."[23] "What mechanisms and instruments," he asked, "can be developed to inhibit mentalities and attitudes of permanent dependence?" Afwerki then shared his government's thoughtful assessment of the matter:

> Our government believes that all assistance granted or disbursed must include in-built mechanisms of sustainability with a view of [generating], at least partially, the funds for other development projects.[24]

The year following the referendum, some donor nations pledged $250 million toward development in Eritrea. The fund was to be administered by the World Bank on "highly concessionary and favorable terms."[25] But Eritrean government officials quickly parted ways with World Bank experts who sought a strong role in shaping the financial trajectory of the country. Eritrea is arguably the lone example of an African nation that has not participated in structural adjustment programs and bypasses the policy recommendations of international lending agencies and international governing agencies concerning the nation's economic and political trajectory.

And yet, recall that Gebretensae's family received a martyr certificate in 1992. While the EPLF was waiting to conduct its referendum, it began printing commemorations for the people who had given their lives in the war for formal independence. The national government organized economic priorities by compelling veterans to work for free until the 1993 referendum and by positioning the sacrifices of the martyrs and the soldiers as essential to the founding financial framework of the nation. Independence in Eritrea was visceral. Material. The process involved furnishing grieving families with forensic evidence of the role their loved ones had played in achieving formal independence. That role paid dividends after formal recognition of this tremendous sacrifice Eritreans had endured, as President Isaias explains:

> In 1993, in a referendum [that was fair and free] the choice of the population was expressed. And, in that referendum, *we* got our independence. No one *gave us* our independence.[26]

Then, clarifying that independence cannot be delivered by enemies, allies, nor by purportedly disinterested observers, President Isaias reiterates: "We did not get our independence from anyone. Not Ethiopia. Not Somalia. Not Sudan. Not even the international community."

But what *was* the role of the "international community"—the only entity President Isaias names that is not a nation? The international community was there to *witness* an exercise of free choice of the Eritrean people, which culminated in the independence of this small country.

President Isaias then shifts back to the immediate context of the question, in the attempt to clarify what is at the root of recent Ethiopian efforts to transgress borders. He notes that the borders fixed by the UN at the dawn of Eritrea's formal independence were the same borders that maps depicted in primary school textbooks, as well as the same borders depicted in maps that the Emperor Haile Selassie had produced in the United States to depict the vast territory he controlled. "What has changed?" President Isaias asks.

President Isaias offers a generous explanation: that the Ethiopian government did not, in fact, have a clear agenda when transgressing Eritrea's border in 1998. He hypothesizes they might have erred in creating maps depicting new borders; and, since those maps do not resemble any depiction of the demarcations between Ethiopia and Eritrea produced during the twentieth century, they became trapped in a "vicious circle," where one lie was used to cover up the first lie, a third lie is generated to cover up the first two, and so on. Meanwhile, President Isaias maintains:

> We will patiently pursue our policy of dialogue. We will work with the international community to find a peaceful solution to the problem. We are against the war. We will try to avoid war. We do have a legitimate right to self-defense. But, again, we find this war a senseless war.[27]

This desperate plea to avoid war despite fighting a war is what Graeber understands as the "contradictions" of any democratic process:

> The fact that this ideal is always founded on (at least partly) invented traditions does not mean it is inauthentic or illegitimate or, at least, more inauthentic or illegitimate than any other. The contradiction, however, is that this ideal was always based on the impossible dream of marrying democratic procedures or practices with the coercive mechanisms of the state.[28]

Despite implementing strategies of horizontalism, Eritreans never identified their liberation struggle as anarchist. But then, as David Graeber notes in *Possibilities*:

Many of the key principles of the movement (self-organization, voluntary association, mutual aid, the refusal of state power) derive from the anarchist tradition. Still, many who embrace these ideas are reluctant, or flat-out refuse, to call themselves "anarchists." Similarly with democracy. My own approach has normally been to openly embrace both terms, to argue, in fact, that anarchism and democracy are—or should be—largely identical. However, as I say, there is no consensus on this issue, nor even a clear majority view.[29]

This insight raises the question of whether prevailing political designations—whether "democratic," "anarchist," or even "authoritarian"—are adequate to the task of understanding the broad range of governance strategies that exist throughout the world, especially recent efforts to interrogate the state form.

In light of how often President Isaias invokes the "international community," and how much he stresses political legitimacy, it is worth noting that Eritrea is the only country to bear the UN's iconography on its national flag. It is also crucial to note when and how the "senseless war" at the border drew to a close. This context is essential to understanding why, shortly after being elected in April 2018, Ethiopia's newest prime minister, Dr. Abiy Ahmed, announced that his country was ready to accept the peace agreement that had been pending for twenty years. On Eritrea's most important national holiday, Martyrs' Day, President Isaias Afwerki declared that we would "send a delegation to Addis Ababa to gauge current developments directly in depth as well as to chart out a plan for continuous future action," lamenting that the "Eritrean people, but also the Ethiopian people, have lost an opportunity of two generations."[30] Prime Minister Abiy responded by thanking President Isaias in Tigrinya, and expressing his heartfelt appreciation that his overture was accepted on Martyrs' Day.

During the colonial era, Ethiopia had banned Eritrean languages, including Tigrinya, forcing colonial subjects to speak Amharic. Even more significantly, the Ethiopian government had never acknowledged the political significance of Martyrs' Day, instead depicting Eritrea as an unruly province bent on secession. Prime Minister Dr. Abiy's overture acknowledged Eritrean autonomy, politically and linguistically. In the process, Prime Minister Abiy also affirmed the political legitimacy of the Eritrean struggle for independence in the only terms that Eritreans would accept—by acknowledging the sacrifice of the martyrs in whose death lay the gift of formal independence.

Notes

1. "The Nobel Peace Prize for 2019," press release, October 11, 2019, available at: https://www.nobelprize.org/prizes/peace/2019/press-release/ (accessed October 12, 2022).
2. Ibid.
3. Ibid.
4. Michael Ralph, *Forensics of Capital* (Chicago: University of Chicago Press, 2015).
5. Toby Green, *Fistful of Shells: West Africa from the Rise of the Slave Trade to the Age of Revolution* (Chicago: University of Chicago Press, 2019); Dale Tomich, *Through the Prism of Slavery: Labor, Capital and World Economy* (Boulder, CO: Rowman and Littlefield, 2004).
6. William Pietz, "The Problem of the Fetish: I," *Res: A Journal of Anthropology and Aesthetics* 9 (Spring 1985): 5–17; Frederick Cooper, *Decolonization and African Society: The Labor Question in French and British Africa* (Cambridge: Cambridge University Press, 2010); Keith Hart, *The Political Economy of West African Agriculture* (Cambridge: Cambridge University Press, 1982).
7. Patrick Bond, *Uneven Zimbabwe: A Study of Finance, Development, and Underdevelopment* (Trenton, NJ: Africa World Press, 1998).
8. Samir Amin, *Neocolonialism in West Africa* (New York: Penguin, 1971); Walter Rodney, *How Europe Underdeveloped Africa* (New York: Verso, 2018 [1972]).
9. Ralph, *Forensics of Capital*; Cedric Robinson, *Black Marxism: The Making of the Black Radical Tradition* (Chapel Hill, NC: University of North Carolina Press, 1983).
10. David Graeber, *Possibilities: Essays on Hierarchy, Rebellion, and Desire* (Oakland, CA and Edinburgh: AK Press, 2007), 301.
11. Ibid., 301–302.
12. Ibid., 302.
13. Gebretensae Debrezion Nuguse enlisted in the Eritrean People's Liberation Front in October of 1975 and was soon appointed commander of Brigade 23. Though such ranks involved a greater role in leadership and strategy, officers lived among and as ordinary soldiers, without any greater material benefits, nor even stripes or bars to indicate higher status.
14. Graeber, *Possibilities*, 331–332.
15. Roy Pateman, *Eritrea: Even the Stones are Burning* (Asmara: The Red Sea Press, 1990), 240.
16. President Isaias, Invited Lecture, Princeton University, 1999.
17. Ibid.
18. Pateman, *Eritrea: Even the Stones are Burning*, 238.
19. Consider that Obama's former National Security Adviser, Susan Rice, delivered the eulogy at the funeral of Ethiopia's late prime minister,

Melese Zenawi. Rice's heartfelt tribute to the man she called "a true friend" affirmed US support for Ethiopia, despite documented transgressions of Eritrean territorial integrity. Bronwyn Burton, *Eritrea: Coming in from the Cold*, Issue Brief (Washington, DC: Atlantic Council, Africa Center, December 2016), p. 4.

20. President Isaias, Princeton lecture.

21. Ruth Iyob, *The Eritrean Struggle for Independence: Domination, Resistance, Nationalism 1941–1993* (Cambridge: Cambridge University Press, 1995), 136; Dan Connell, *Conversations with Eritrean Political Prisoners* (Asmara: The Red Sea Press, 2005), 249.

22. Iyob, *The Eritrean Struggle for Independence*, 144.

23. President Isaias, Princeton lecture.

24. Ibid.

25. Pateman, *Eritrea: Even the Stones are Burning*.

26. President Isaias, Princeton lecture.

27. Ibid.

28. Graeber, *Possibilities*, 334.

29. Ibid., 330.

30. President Isaias, Princeton lecture.

8

Common(s) Currency: Collectivized Hoards and the Regulation of Money

Gustav Peebles

The sociology of everyday communism is a potentially enormous field, but one which, owing to our peculiar ideological blinkers, we have been unable to write because we have been largely unable to see the object.

—David Graeber[1]

My first inkling that central banks—and the national currencies they manage—might harbor talismanic properties occurred all the way back in 1992, when the Swedish krona suffered a massive devaluation at the hands of "the market." As the krona's trading value was relentlessly questioned by the market for months, the Swedish Central Bank (the "Riksbank") came to its valiant but pyrrhic defense, hopelessly trying to maintain its "peg" by continually ratcheting up the interest rate—at one point, all the way to a shocking and untenable 500 percent. During this raucous episode, desperate holders of kronas came rushing to the central bank coffers, trading their now less trustworthy kronas for the more reliable foreign reserve holdings that sat immobilized in the Riksbank's vault.

Despite its status as a central bank, the world was witnessing a classic "bank run," with people who held Riksbank liabilities (i.e. the krona) suddenly hoping to cash them in for the items that (partly) guaranteed their value. The country of Sweden lost immense amounts of economic value during those months, as the national treasury was drained of its foreign currency reserve and simultaneously engorged with national currency. In her defense of governmental decisions at the time, then Finance Minister Anne Wibble disingenuously explained away these losses, stating "it is not as if society has lost that money. We have it in Swedish kronas, whereas before we had it in foreign currency."[2]

Since 1992, the world has seen an entire array of runs on central banks, from the United Kingdom to Mexico to Argentina to Thailand. But for unknown—perhaps talismanic—reasons, such bank runs are referred to as "currency crises," rather than acknowledging that they precisely mimic a traditional run against a private bank. It's as though we cannot tolerate this affront to national pride, which sullies a nation's reputation by revealing its currency to be a mere paper promise, issued and guaranteed by a central bank that might not be as august and upstanding as everyone had previously believed.

In each currency crisis I have witnessed since, much of the local media of the afflicted country sets off to look for a scapegoat. Sometimes it devolves into the ugliest of conspiracy theories (just ask George Soros), but it never fails to train its ire at ... _foreigners_: it must have been foreigners who brazenly questioned the trustworthiness of our central bank; it must have been non-locals who had no true investment in the nation's economic health; it must have been outsiders who raided our vault.

People inside the markets, who witnessed the actual trading, quickly retort that _none_ of this is true—locals abandon the national medium of exchange as quickly as everyone else. Just as in private bank runs, no one wants to be left "holding the bag"; but somehow this provincial trope and its underlying sentiment always emerges during currency crises. Notably, private bank runs do not seem to produce a similar rhetoric, which instead tend to focus on the malfeasance or negligence of the private bank's internal hierarchy and management, and can even result in criminal prosecution of same.

How could currency, this seemingly neutral device for quotidian trading and planning for the future, garner such citizen vitriol and breathless media coverage, and why would blame consistently be leveled at supposed outsiders? I will propose here that we witness such jingoistic defenses of currency because attacks on it are perceived as attacks on something inside a national Commons; as a national Commons, they may have metaphysical powers that reach beyond their mere economistic powers (as explored later). If this is true, it becomes more obvious why people rise up against these attacks, much as populations the world over have responded, over several centuries, to the privatization of their communal property, owned and governed in a local Commons.

Admittedly, arguing that central banks—those icons of capitalist machinery and hierarchy— might actually be inside a national Commons might raise a few hackles. But I take inspiration from David Graeber's notion of "everyday communism." Using the example of a plumber who needs a wrench from his colleague, who doesn't even dream of charging a fee for its brief use, Graeber asserts that "this [everyday communism] is what makes society possible. There is always an assumption that anyone who is not actually an enemy can be expected to act on the principle of 'from each according to their abilities'."[3] Moreover, he proposes that often such standardized and ubiquitous—though unacknowledged— structures of everyday communism might well undergird many modes of seemingly individualistic exchange.

Marx helps us see that these collectivized central bank reserves are no different than standard hoards; indeed, because they are shared with a broad public, he argues that they produce even stronger emotional attachments than individual hoards. Writing of the Bank of England's gold reserve, he states, "[T]he sanctity and inviolability of the reserve is thereby carried much farther than among the hoarders of old."[4] All of this suggests that central banks and the currency infrastructure they oversee are somehow cherished by a given national population, and seen as something to which they are intimately attached, just as locals the world over have been intimately attached to—and have vociferously defended—other local Commons.[5]

Currency as Commons

[B]y naming the commons, we can learn how to reclaim it.

—Bollier[6]

In currency crises we are witnessing a raid on what Ostrom christened a "Common Pooled Resource" (CPR).[7] In these moments, private holders of currency (a type of banknote) proclaim that they no longer want to hold these representative units of the communal reserves; they rush to trade it, to seize a portion of the pooled resource and privatize it, running away with this newly privatized value and leaving the Commons diminished. In previously holding the banknote, the holder had agreed to trust this Commons and its management by a central bank; by trading it in for the immobilized value that sat in a communal hoard-cum-reserve, the holder—whether for nefarious or sound reasons—has abandoned that same Commons.[8]

As stewards of national currency, central banks must constantly navigate this tension-laden dialectic common to all Commons, wherein the central object of value sitting accumulated in its reserve is either waxing or waning in size and power. Due to the way banking "best practices" have circled the globe over 200 years, telling the story of how these currency reserves have been built and managed will necessarily rely on some broad-brush sketches. Local variations are important, but they do not undermine the general thrust of this historical development; indeed, these variations affirm one of Ostrom's central axioms: Commons must adapt and respond to local conditions, and there can be no "one size fits all" solution.

Stewarding the growth and stability of these reserves requires intricate cooperation and norm-following by a wide array of both public and private interests. As Ostrom insisted, "Many successful CPR institutions are rich mixtures of 'private-like' and 'public-like' institutions defying classifications in a sterile dichotomy."[9] Following a sort of gravitational model, central banks stand as the sun in a national solar system of private banks and depositors, attracting or repulsing new members—new commoners—every day.

Like many Commons, the reserves of central banks take on a sort of magical luster, capable of fecundity.[10] Circulating currency, as a liquid asset for members of the banking Commons (whether corporate bank or individual cash holder), is simultaneously a liability from the perspective of the CPR; as such, currency symbolizes a dyadic credit/debt relationship between the holder of the banknote and the communal owner of the reserve. And yet, as will become clear below, the CPR is itself nurtured by the pooled assets of these same currency holders. Cash (currency), in other words, emanates from this CPR, allowing all people who trust the CPR's promises to go about their daily business of trading and planning for the future.[11]

Typically, hoards are often accused of being "dead" or "sterile," but in the case of currency reserves, they are fertile in the extreme, giving birth to the entire currency system.[12] Just as with a typical grazing Commons, central banks strive to maintain a stable currency through which commoners are allowed to build their own personal value, while the central bank reserves represent the (ideally) untouchable "principal" that fructifies the broader economy.[13]

As Thomas Weguelin, a nineteenth-century Governor of the Bank of England, testified before the British parliament long ago, "The reserve of bullion in the Bank of England is, in truth, the central reserve or hoard of treasure upon which the whole trade of the country is made to turn."[14]

We are accustomed to stereotyping the Commons as small, as always under attack, and as zones of warmth, empathy, and community. Contrariwise, central banks and the currency systems that they safeguard are hard to romanticize. But what if the talismanic powers of central bank hoards emerge from their unacknowledged representation of a giant community, of an idiosyncratic blend of the public and the private, of an ability to draw together an otherwise scattered and solipsistic citizenry into one community of conjoined interest? If so, we would do well to name them as a Commons, and then carefully consider not only if they are worth saving, but also if they can be constructed and managed in a more fair fashion. As Maurer asks, "who writes and controls these accounts? How are they ordering and re-ordering the world?"[15]

Building the Hoard

> All commons have a history
>
> —Standing[16]

Grasping the history of the banking Commons requires that we imagine daily life without access to banking services. "The Father of Savings Banks," the Scottish pastor, Henry Duncan, observed that his impoverished congregants in Scotland were, in today's terms, "financially excluded." In his day (the early 1800s), a deposit account was a privilege for the relatively wealthy, and the lion's share of the British citizenry had no formal bank account.[17] Duncan set about to democratize banking, for he believed that it could provide countless financial and moral benefits to his charges.

Importantly, Duncan's crusade hinged on the many perils of holding a private hoard at home. He wrote:

> Those who know anything of the situation and habits of the lower orders will readily be aware of the temptations and discouragements to which such a plan [to store wealth for a rainy day] is necessarily subjected.... The temptation to break in upon the little stock on every emergency might be too strong to resist. At all events, the progressive addition of interest would be lost during the period of accumulation.... A similar effect must have resulted from the frequent instances which occur of the failure or knavery of those adventurers to whose hands the unwary are induced.[18]

According to this logic, a private hoard requires expertise and diligence, neither of which Duncan expected of his flock. Further, private hoards were hard to protect not only from lurking thieves and other assorted "knaves," but even from family members who would invariably catch wind of its existence and plead with the owner to share it. Duncan also avers (along with countless other advocates of financial inclusion through the ages) that a given amount of money, while hidden in a mattress, accrues no interest. But once it has attached itself to the larger bank hoard, it can steadily increase in value, seemingly magically.

Pre-fiat deposit banking operated on the principle that as much underutilized money as possible should be shared.[19] By building a collectivized hoard, banks could "magically" transform sterile money into fecund money. Via the interest rate, one member of a deposit institution could acquire usufruct rights over a portion of a communal hoard whenever it was sitting idly (tellingly, usufruct rights are the standard property mechanism for other Commons).[20] Keynes referred to the interest rate as the "liquidity preference" for precisely this reason; he believed the interest rate governed the individual choice between private hoarding versus joining a communal deposit institution (or investing), which incentivized the holder of money to share with anonymous others.[21] Keynes' insight clarifies why money in a mattress is viewed as a selfish hoard, whereas money placed in a deposit bank functions as a communal sharing tactic.[22] Equally, during Duncan's era, the interest rate was the premier incentive for attracting new depositors to these new institutions (along with moralizing rhetoric), gradually convincing everyday citizens to move their money into these larger pools of savings.[23]

Gradually, these deposit bank reserves were socialized at yet another higher level still—into the national central banks. In the era prior to the nationalization of currency, private banks could hold a communal reserve stored in a vault, while allowing their depositors and borrowers to walk the streets with paper liabilities representing this same reserve. For reasons too extensive to be detailed here, this led to the endemic bank runs of the nineteenth century. In an attempt to solve this damaging pattern, national and international debates ensued about how to control and regulate national currency supplies, focusing largely on how to convert these countless unreliable private bank currencies into one, reliable, public currency.[24]

John Fullarton, an economist upon whom Marx heavily relied in his own writings, analyzed and recounted this era as follows:

> In this country [England], where the banking system has been carried
> to an extent and perfection unknown in any other part of Europe,
> and may be said to have entirely superseded the use of coin except for
> retail dealings and the purposes of foreign commerce, the incentives
> to private hoarding exist no longer, and the hoards have all been trans-
> ferred to the banks, or rather, I should say, to the Bank of England.[25]

In other words, as a result of a series of legislative reforms and evolution
of banking practices, the Bank of England gradually became *the* national
hoard, agglomerating unto itself all the private hoards that had previously
been hiding in mattresses across the land. This agglomerated, national,
hoard also was then believed to regulate the currency supply, as the Bank
of England (like other central banks after it) gradually attained monopoly
control over currency issuance. Once the promise to convert to specie was
suspended or abandoned in country after country, these national reserves
were clearly no longer explicitly claimable by individual members, but
instead represented a true common resource, owned by all, though only
managed by a few.

Seen from this angle, we can see that the spread of deposit banking was,
surprisingly, *the inverse of enclosure.* During this period, what had been
deemed a fiercely privatized good—precious personal savings—was being
pushed into a new Commons. In the process, both the individual and the
community saw *material* gains, while they also gave up certain rights.[26]
Perhaps, in fact, this process represents an early variant of what Taylor has
termed "predatory inclusion."[27] Be that as it may, the many bank runs of
the nineteenth century (and since) all bluntly confirmed that depositors
were relinquishing fee simple control over their private savings, allowing
them to instead enter into a Commons with new rights held by the group.
During a bank run, the private depositor became jarringly aware that the
money they believed was firmly their own also had countless other claim-
ants upon it. Had they kept it in the mattress, they would have no cause
for concern as a financial panic gripped their neighborhood bank. Having
instead joined the emergent banking Commons for its many benefits, they
also learned of its attendant costs.[28]

Affirming my argument further, it is also worth highlighting that bank
runs represent the standard "tragedy of the Commons," but played out
at an accelerated speed. As depositors awaken to the possibility that the
communal hoard may not be as extensive as they had believed, they all rush
to reacquire what they had stored for safekeeping at the bank. If they still

trusted the banking Commons, the communal hoard would live another day, but once the trust has evaporated, each depositor fears that they will be the only one who will lose their private portion of the communal hoard. As a result of this "herd mentality," private hoards blossom once again as the communal hoard is raided and depleted, much as an unregulated Commons can devolve into myriad private parcels if the bonds of social trust break down.[29] *A contrario*, this also shows that regular depositors, by simply agreeing to keep their money at local banks, are helping to sustain and nurture the system through their mundane behavior, what Elyachar has coined "phatic labor."[30] Considering all this, perhaps it is time to recognize that national currency systems may be a fecund Commons, regulated (whether for good or ill is another question) by non-profit stewards, rather than for-profit CEOs.[31]

Owning the Hoard

The Federal Reserve System is not "owned" by anyone.
—United States Federal Reserve website FAQs[32]

Citizens of many nations are so accustomed to their own deposit banks being private that it can be hard to countenance the idea that the very root of the system might be communally owned. In their administrative structure, central banks are intended to be bankers to the private banks, rather than having direct customer-based lines to individual citizens. No daily contact—or rather, no transparent daily contact—with citizens might push central banks ever further into a stratospheric remove from daily life. Consequently, many people are unaware of their own role in building and sustaining the national currency system.

Indeed, how many people even bother to ascertain who, in the legal sense, owns the central banks that backstop the currency they hold? The academic literature dedicated to the topic is quite scant outside of a subset of monetary economists and legal writers.[33] Typically, known hoards have identifiable owners, but it would seem that few people ponder who owns the gargantuan reserves-cum-hoards held by central banks.[34] As recounted above, public rhetoric during currency crises—the breakdown of the central bank system—provide us with a hint that "the people" of a given nation dimly sense that these reserves are rightly theirs—part of a national patrimony.

But normally, as with all good infrastructure, central banks should not experience such crises, and should instead chug along in the background, doing their boring and mundane labor while the rest of us skirt along on their fluid operation—much as we fail to notice the intense daily maintenance that goes into operating a highway bridge until it collapses.[35] Much to their chagrin, central bankers' daily work has become more common knowledge precisely because of the seemingly endless crises, starting with the European crises of 1992, followed by the Asian crisis of the late 1990s up to the 2008 financial crisis, the euro crisis, and now COVID-19. Novel techniques to push and pull the economy have emerged, and central bank chiefs have become household names. Still, arcane language and complex operations keep many of us from prying too deeply into central bank administration.[36] Like the aforementioned highway bridge, many of us find ourselves simply assuming trust in our central bank, for it may be too cumbersome and futile to dig any deeper.

As with any Ostromian Commons, we have contracted the governance of these robust and complicated systems to local experts, all hailing from multiple locations within the nested system.[37] Central bankers, treasury officials, and private sector actors carry on fine-tuned discussions every day about how best to sustain and nurture the system. Both quotidian and radical challenges to the monetary system are addressed in consultation, listening to groups "on the ground" who are witnessing the ebb and flow of money at various points along the chain.[38] Different countries have different traditions of how competitive versus cooperative these consultations can be, but few countries refuse to have the conversation at all. Aside from being "nested at scale," this also fits with Ostrom's notion of "polycentric governance," which she describes as "many centers of decision making that are formally independent ... [which can] enter into various contractual and cooperative undertakings or have recourse to central mechanisms to resolve conflicts," even when they are in seemingly competitive relationships.[39]

Just as Ostrom's model would suggest, naming such a system as either "state or market" becomes somewhat nonsensical.[40] Rather, a mutually reinforcing set of private and public operators—running from individual to central bank—all thrive from and nurture this vast infrastructure. Ostrom herself hinted at all of this, when she bluntly insisted that "No market can exist for long without underlying public institutions to support it. In field settings, public and private institutions frequently are intermeshed and depend on one another, rather than existing in isolated worlds."[41]

Fascinatingly, even when statute clarifies exactly who owns a central ·
bank (e.g. Italy, or the regional Federal Reserve banks of the American
system), it is not classic "fee simple" ownership. Rather, ownership shares
are typically *not* transferable but are instead considered a prerequisite to
membership, just as with more standard cooperatives. More telling still,
many central bank reserves are specifically not "marked to market" and
sometimes do not even *have a market* in which to sell,[42] which also mimics
the classic way in which items inside a Commons cannot be sold and often
cannot even be priced.[43]

Investigating the role of bankruptcy also confirms the odd status of
central banks and their currency systems that we are trying to pin down
here. In the world of private goods and markets, bankruptcy proceedings
reliably clarify ownership over assets. Central banks, contrariwise, cannot
go bankrupt.[44] Rather, hyperinflation and international currency crises
govern "the bottom line" of central banks.[45] In those instances, central
banks' status as inside a Commons becomes manifest, for the only people
who lose are the holders of the central bank's currency (i.e. its circulating liability), which is the asset of the people who rely on the central bank
system. Indeed, one well known central banker has referred to inflation as
"share dilution," comparing cash to equity.[46]

In his book, *Plunder of the Commons*, Guy Standing divides governance
and use of the Commons into three groups—Stewards, Gatekeepers, and
Commoners.[47] Stewards are the "titular owners ... expected to uphold
[the Commons'] integrity on behalf of the commoners." Gatekeepers are
"vital for the commons, as monitors tracking what happens and as inter-
mediaries negotiating between commoners, property owners, and those
seeking to commodify the commons."[48] Finally, commoners are "all those
who have access to the commons, who rely on them for their livelihood
or way of living, and who participate in the governance, preservation and
reproduction of a commons."[49] This nicely describes the management of
national currency systems as well—the central banks are the stewards,
the private banks are the gatekeepers, and the currency holders are the
commoners. It seems especially important to note that central banks'
chairpeople never receive remuneration even remotely similar to that of
the private banks' chairpeople. Though they preside over the operation of
everyone else's ability to profit—and even profit at potentially grotesque
levels—they themselves are not expected to profit from their stewardship.

We can, of course, vociferously disagree that there is not nearly
enough input from the commoners themselves, and that national cur-

rencies are governed by an all too rarefied and wealthy assemblage of players; many alternative currency formations have been built upon precisely this critique.[50] Further, the commercial bankers-cum-gatekeepers may be abusing their access and thus too easily over-appropriating from the Commons.[51] Finally, the system necessitates endless growth, which is also worthy of critique in this era of looming climate catastrophe. But those are all critiques of the *governance* of the banking Commons, rather than negating the idea itself that the central bank currency system *is* a Commons. Users of currency—commoners—ignore the day-to-day governance of the currency until a raid on the public hoard occurs; this is perceived as an attempt to privatize that which is public—a repeat of enclosure tactics that are so well documented in the literature. Not surprisingly, we find that when this occurs, the commoners make their input heard quite well.

Magic of the Hoard

> Inalienable possessions are the representation of how social identities are reconstituted through time.
>
> —Weiner[52]

Commons generate so much friction not only because they are engines of economic growth for a given community, but also because they embody and symbolize the groups that collectively own them. Commoners are invested both financially *and* culturally in sustaining their Commons. In this sense, Commons are a communally owned valuable that must be held *outside* of the sphere of profane market exchange and guarded from it. Here it is worth reiterating how central bank currency systems are manifestly not for sale, and people would generally react in horror if they discovered that they were. Even a central bank with as sullied a recent history as Argentina's cannot be imagined as something that could land on the auction block, even though its assembled assets would be attractive to many a buyer. And yet, all of the objects that circulate as a result of this "grounding" central bank currency system *are* for sale, including the private banks that act as local experts within the system.

Within anthropological theory, valued objects that cannot circulate inside a market can be referred to as "inalienable possessions," following the arguments made by Annette Weiner in her landmark text of the same name.[53] Weiner carefully catalogued a range of such objects, across the world in both time and space, claiming that the category existed as a "human universal."[54] Importantly, these objects have often previously circulated, but then become de-commodified as they become inalienable. At that moment, she explains, they acquire sacrality, while they are simultaneously credited with activating societal power, growth, and regeneration.

This returns us to the magic of the Commons—how it can acquire generative powers "beyond its exchange value," as Weiner would say. As discussed above, central bank reserves follow the standard logic of fertility that governs more typical Commons. But central banks have additional magical powers that derive from their sovereign status, standing simultaneously both inside and outside the market. Aside from their surprising inability to go bankrupt, central banks share another important "sovereign exception."[55] To wit, they are well known as the "lender of last resort"; indeed, this is considered the pillar of their capacity to grant stability to the banking system, as described by Bagehot long ago in his benchmark study of the money market, *Lombard Street*.[56] Even though many central banks have fewer assets than some of the largest international private banks, there is effectively no limit (other than hyperinflation) on their ability to lend to private banks in need.[57] With merely the click of a keyboard, central banks can "explode their balance sheet" in ways that private banks cannot. In so doing, they take on the "toxic" assets of failing institutions as collateral, injecting "base money," that is, central bank-issued liabilities into the failing institution's coffers. Doing so allows central banks not only to backstop failing institutions but also to push the toxic assets into the Commons, where they can be sacralized and then returned to the market at a later date (if the central banks so choose).

But these standard practices also magically transform the diminishing assets of a flailing private bank into hard currency.[58] The currency that central banks conjure from commoning these private goods keeps its value because it is a liability owned by a sovereign public. So long as the market trusts this sovereign public, its currency tends to be trusted too.

Perhaps because of enduring suspicions of banking, we have forgotten these standardized and repetitive tales of central banks commoning privately held goods through the economy that they oversee. Instead, we often treat enclosure as a one-way street, always heading toward privatization, while failing to pay as much attention to the building of Commons. In actuality, it may be better to think of enclosure and commoning as an ongoing dialectic, with new Commons being built even while others are being destroyed. This fits better, after all, with the understanding that all

Commons must be "living organisms," capable of nimbly responding to ever-changing socioeconomic circumstances.

All of this was covered once before by Marx, who carefully noted the migration of private hoards into public ones in *Capital*. Indeed, the agglomeration of private hoards into "socialized" ones stood as one of the empirical pieces of evidence he relied on to argue that capitalism necessarily led to socialism. As he explained, the evolving credit system he was witnessing in Fullarton's nineteenth-century United Kingdom represented the moment when countless "private capitals" become "social capital," thereby causing the "abolition of capital as private property within the confines of the capitalist mode of production itself."[59]

As vital Commons in our midst, perhaps central bank systems have acquired a sort of "sacredness" that grants them all of their fecund powers; these fecund powers, in turn, are what allow them to regulate the profane economy that they oversee. After all, no other entity in the economy can issue an almost limitless supply of IOUs that are not even redeemable with the original issuer (except as payment of taxes), to say nothing of a central bank that abandons its gold peg, leaving all cash holders with a broken contract and itself with the accumulated gold.[60] In a perfect display of Schmitt's argument, such behavior is, in fact, considered fraudulent when practiced by others.

Such practices also harmonize perfectly with Graeber's argument that everyday communism is marked by a refusal to delineate and maintain a "bottom line": "When keeping accounts seems insane in this way, we are in the presence of communism."[61] And so we learn that, while all other parties in the economy are famously governed by the iron law of scarcity, central banks are governed by the plastic law of abundance.

Graeber often mischievously enjoyed pointing out bizarre idiosyncrasies of social life that lay hidden in plain sight. I can readily picture him gleefully reframing this potentially boring story of central bank history and practice as no different than a king who can, almost magically, issue limitless debts to his subjects. Defending the value of the currency seems *ipso facto* noble to many of us, but Graeber would surely emphasize how this same defense on our behalf simultaneously makes us utterly dependent on the credit that we've agreed to grant this sovereign, who now lords it over us. "Exploding the balance sheet"—as central banks do during times of crisis—is typically depicted as a sacrifice, taking on risky debts that others in our society could no longer hold. But it is also a blistering display of sheer might, reserved only for those quasi-magical beings who can successfully claim the mantle of sovereignty.

Always hoping to dismantle hierarchies, Graeber would often also seize upon hypocrisies such as those represented by the sovereign exceptions of central banks. But instead of banishing the hypocrisy, he would ask that its privilege be distributed to others—why can't *everyone* hold the sovereign exception to issue limitless credit, he would wonder. Graeber's tactics thus push me to close with an important political question: if, during the blossoming of the capitalist era, banks and central banks have long had this clear and consistent preference to force—or at least, cajole—us to share and to "common" *our* private capital, why do they not espouse this same technique for countless other goods in the economic system?[62] David Graeber would want to know.

Notes

1.   David Graeber, "Communism," in *The Human Economy*, ed. Keith Hart et al. (Cambridge: Polity Press 2010), 207–208.

2.   Carl Hamilton and Dag Rolander, *Att Leda Sverige in i Krisen* (Stockholm: Norstedts, 1993); Gustav Peebles, "The Crown Capitulates: Conflations of National Currency and Global Capital in the Swedish Currency Crisis," in *Market Matters: Exploring Cultural Processes in the Global Marketplace*, ed. Christina Garsten and Monica Lindh de Montoya (Basingstoke: Palgrave, 2004), 180–206.

3.   Graeber, "Communism," 206.

4.   Karl Marx, *Capital, A Critique of Political Economy*, vol. 3, translated by David Fernbach (New York: Penguin Books, 1981), 696.

5.   Seung-kyung Kim and John Finch, "Living with Rhetoric, Living against Rhetoric: Korean Families and the IMF Economic Crisis," *Korean Studies* 26, no. 1 (2002), 125ff. During South Korea's currency crisis of 1997, citizens even sacrificed cherished family gold in a vast national effort to save the currency's value.

6.   David Bollier, *Think Like a Commoner* (Gabriola Island, BC: New Society Publishers, 2014), 3.

7.   Elinor Ostrom, *Governing the Commons* (Cambridge: Cambridge University Press, 1989).

8.   Nineteenth-century economists, including Marx, used "hoard" and "reserve" interchangeably in their writings. I am revivifying the archaic usage because it better hints at the metaphysical power of reserves.

9.   Ostrom, *Governing the Commons*, 14; Paul Tucker, *Unelected Power: The Quest for Legitimacy in Central Banking and the Regulatory State* (Princeton, NJ: Princeton University Press, 2018), 59. In this recent book, Tucker

(a retired central banker himself) frames national currency systems as sitting in a unique place within governments, oddly straddling the Commons and public goods.

10. Though this chapter opens with the example of foreign currency reserves, it will become clear throughout that I am arguing that the entire central banking system should be considered a Commons, not only its foreign exchange holdings. The reaction of national publics to the depletion of forex reserves offers a palpable reason for studying the entire system within which they are held. As for the difference between forex reserves and banking reserves, for the purposes of this chapter, it is a distinction without a difference. Both can be depleted in "runs," and both are built up, gradually over time, through the actions of commoners and the sound management by the Commons' "stewards" (see below).

11. Geoffrey Ingham, *The Nature of Money* (Cambridge: Polity, 2004); Bill Maurer, "Money as Token and Money as Record in Distributed Accounts," in *Distributed Agency*, ed. Paul Kockelman and N.J. Enfield (Oxford: Oxford University Press, 2017).

12. In rare instances, a currency can be successful without a centralized hoard that backs it (e.g. Bitcoin), but this is the exception rather than the rule. Even in such cases, something more metaphysical must undergird the circulating currency's value, such as "trust in the community." If there is no immobilized and stable value that the circulating currency represents, the latter will have no value itself.

13. Having the power to fructify has often been associated with magic, so we should not be surprised that central banks have an aura of sacrality to them, and we should no longer wonder why they are all built to resemble churches and other temples. A simple google image search will reveal that both the interiors and exteriors of private and central banks have often been modeled on temple architecture.

14. Marx, *Capital*, vol. 3, 633.

15. Bill Maurer, "Cashless, Ancient and Modern," in *The Archaeology of Money*, ed. Colin Haselgrove and Stefan Krmnicek (Leicester: Leicester Archaeology Monographs, School of Archaeology & Ancient History, University of Leicester, 2016), 209–225.

16. Guy Standing, *Plunder of the Commons* (London: Penguin Random House, 2019), 40.

17. Oliver H. Horne, *A History of Savings Banks* (New York: Oxford University Press, 1947).

18. Ibid., 42–43; see also Henry Duncan, *An Essay on the Nature and Advantages of Parish Banks, for the Savings of the Industrious*, 2nd edn (Edinburgh: Oliphant, Waugh and Innes, 1816).

19. At least during Duncan's era. The era of fiat money has complicated this; nevertheless, today all customers' deposits are still assembled in a giant pool and this impacts the amount of money that the bank can loan out, even if it is far from the only controlling variable. According to both the

Bank of England and proponents of Modern Monetary Theory, the logic is different today. But since I am here tracking a historical moment, we don't need to worry about how fiat currency may have changed the system today. See Michael McLeay, Amar Radia, and Ryland Thomas, "Money Creation in the Modern Economy," *Bank of England Quarterly Bulletin* 54, no. 1 (2014): 14–27; and Stephanie Kelton, *The Deficit Myth* (New York: Public Affairs, 2020).

20. Even considering vociferous critiques of the "loanable funds theory" by Modern Monetary Theory, it remains the case that individual borrowers are paying a rate to a bank to temporarily use a portion of its assets, regardless of the assets' origin.

21. John Maynard Keynes, *The General Theory of Employment, Interest, and Money* (Amherst, MA: Prometheus Books, 1997 [1936]); Jonathan Levy, "Primal Capital," *Critical Historical Studies* 6, no. 2 (2019), 161–193.

22. See Gustav Peebles, "Hoarding and Saving," *Oxford Research Encyclopedia of Anthropology* (online publication: 2020) for a review of anthropological work on hoarding and saving.

23. Lest this sound like a provincial story from Britain, Duncan's effort to democratize banking access for the masses stood as an inspiration to reformers across much of the nineteenth-century world (see Horne, *A History of Savings Banks*, 52).

24. Eric Helleiner, *The Making of National Money: Territorial Currencies in Historical Perspective* (Ithaca, NY: Cornell University Press, 2003).

25. John Fullarton, *On the Regulation of Currencies: Being an Examination of the Principles on Which it is Proposed to Restrict, Within Certain Fixed Limits the Future Issues on Credit of the Bank of England, and of the Other Banking Establishments Throughout the Country* (London: John Murray, 1844), 72.

26. But we reserve judgment on whether they have benefitted spiritually. Many of the critiques of capitalism rest on this distinction: not questioning the material bounty that it can produce, but instead contesting the damage it can do to both individual and community spirit.

27. Keeanga-Yamahtta Taylor, *Race for Profit: How Banks and the Real Estate Industry Undermined Black Homeownership* (Chapel Hill, NC: UNC Press, 2019).

28. This story is, incidentally, repeating itself once again today, with the advent and spread of microfinance, which is today's forward spear of the same effort toward financial inclusion that Duncan advocated long ago.

29. Fullarton covers this, calling it a "sponge mechanism," in *On the Regulation of Currencies*.

30. Julia Elyachar, "Phatic Labor, Infrastructure, and the Question of Empowerment in Cairo," *American Ethnologist* 37, no. 3 (2010), 452–464.

31. This is not to suggest, of course, that these stewards do not monetize their connection to the public hoard in other ways, as the recent controversy over US Federal Reserve Chairwoman Janet Yellen's speaking fees

attests (see Kalyeena Makortoff, "Janet Yellen Has Made at Least $7m from Speaking Fees, Records Show," *The Guardian*, January 1, 2021).

32. Board of Governors of the Federal Reserve System, "Most Frequently Asked Questions," updated September 11, 2020, available at: https://www.federalreserve.gov/faqs.htm (accessed March 8, 2023).

33. Morgan Ricks, *The Money Problem: Rethinking Financial Regulation* (Chicago: University of Chicago Press, 2016); Tucker, *Unelected Power*; Piergiuseppe Spolaore, "Ownership and Governance of Central Banks: Insights from the Italian Experience," *European Company and Financial Law Review* 17, no. 6 (December 2020), 619–656.

34. Here we ignore the predictable range of fringe conspiracy theorists who traverse dark corners of the blogosphere.

35. Elyachar, "Phatic Labor, Infrastructure, and the Question of Empowerment in Cairo," 455

36. Douglas Holmes, *Economy of Words* (Chicago: University of Chicago Press, 2013).

37. This is an important term of art. One of the reasons that libertarian "free bankers" are so excited to eliminate the central bank system is that they believe that regular depositors would suddenly awaken, and then maintain more vigilant surveillance over their own depository institutions; free bankers believe that the current system causes us to too easily let our banks engage in nefarious and irresponsible behavior, and that the centralized system creates the conditions for rife "moral hazard," by causing regular depositors to not care how responsible or irresponsible their own bank may be. Either way, their stance illuminates the fact that, in becoming banked, we are implicitly agreeing to a wider contract with the central bank system that governs our local bank.

38. Robert Bruner and Sean D. Carr (eds.), *The Panic of 1907: Lessons Learned from the Market's Perfect Storm* (Hoboken: John Wiley & Sons, 2007); William D. Cohan, "Three Days that Shook the World," *Fortune Magazine*, December 16, 2008; Hamilton and Rolander, *Att Leda Sverige in i Krisen*; Ingham, *The Nature of Money*; Marcia Stigum and Anthony Crescenzi, *Stigum's Money Market*, 4th edn (New York: McGraw-Hill, 2007).

39. Elinor Ostrom, "Beyond Markets and States: Polycentric Governance of Complex Economic Systems," *American Economic Review* 100, no. 3 (June 2010), 643.

40. The United States Federal Reserve System makes this eminently clear, by having sui generis status both inside and outside the government, and, as the Fed itself clarifies, "is not 'owned' by anyone." I find it also quite suggestive that the United States Federal Reserve system was founded as a dispersed unity of "regional" reserve banks specifically sensitive to America's farm economy, and built at the height of American popularity for the global cooperative movement, when the United States was witnessing an explosion of cooperativist "granges." Richard Grossman, *Unsettled Account: The Evolution of Banking in the Industrialized World since 1800*

(Princeton, NJ: Princeton University Press, 2010); Marc Schneiberg, Marissa King, and Thomas Smith, "Social Movements and Organizational Form: Cooperative Alternatives to Corporations in the American Insurance, Dairy, and Grain Industries," *American Sociological Review* 73, no. 4 (August 2008), 635–667.

41. Ostrom, *Governing the Commons*, 15; James Ferguson, *Give a Man a Fish: Reflections on the New Politics of Distribution* (Durham, NC: Duke University Press, 2015), 178.

42. Willem H. Buiter, "Can Central Banks Go Broke?" *CEPR Policy Insight* no. 24 (London: Centre for Economic Policy Research, 2008); David Archer and Paul Moser-Boehm, "Central Bank Finances," *BIS Papers* no. 71 (Bank for International Settlements, April 2013).

43. Archer and Moser-Boehm, "Central Bank Finances"; Standing, *Plunder of the Commons*, 46.

44. Buiter, "Can Central Banks Go Broke?"

45. Noting this constraint has become a central pillar of the newly emergent "Modern Monetary Theory."

46. Ferguson, *Give a Man a Fish*, 178. Here Ferguson points out that corporations, while typically understood as private actors, are actually collectively owned; David Andolfatto, "Money and Inflation," MacroMania (blog), July 21, 2010, available at: http://andolfatto.blogspot.com/2010/07/money-and-inflation.html (accessed March 8, 2023); David Andolfatto (@dandolfa), "'A Big Enough Helicopter Drop Could Even Find the Fed Running on Negative Equity Capital—Something No Ordinary Bank Could Long Get Away With.' But the Fed Is Not an Ordinary Bank—All Its Liabilities Can be Thought of as 'Equity'," Twitter, October 27, 2020, 11:47 p.m.

47. Standing, *Plunder of the Commons*, 50–51.

48. Ibid.

49. Ibid., 29.

50. Bill Maurer, *Mutual Life, Limited: Islamic Banking, Alternative Currencies, Lateral Reason* (Princeton, NJ: Princeton University Press, 2005); Gustav Peebles, *The Euro and Its Rivals* (Bloomington, IN: Indiana University Press, 2011).

51. Current innovations in digital money are, in fact, threatening the copious profits that private banks have been gleaning from their position within the central banking system.

52. Annette B. Weiner, *Inalienable Possessions: The Paradox of Keeping-While-Giving* (Berkeley: University of California Press, 1992), 11.

53. Ibid.

54. Ibid., 154.

55. Carl Schmitt, *Political Theology: Four Chapters on the Concept of Sovereignty*, translated by George Schwab (Chicago: University of Chicago Press, 2005).

56. Walter Bagehot, *Lombard Street: A Description of the Money Market* (New York City: Charles Scribner's Sons, 1910).

57. Buiter, "Can Central Banks Go Broke?"

58. Perry Mehrling, *The New Lombard Street: How the Fed Became the Dealer of Last Resort* (Princeton, NJ: Princeton University Press, 2011); Kjell Nyborg, *Collateral Frameworks: The Open Secret of Central Banks* (Cambridge: Cambridge University Press, 2016); Ricks, *The Money Problem: Rethinking Financial Regulation*; Stigum and Crescenzi, *Stigum's Money Market*.

59. Marx, *Capital*, vol. 3, 567.

60. Chris Gregory, *Savage Money* (Amsterdam: Harwood Academic Publishers, 1997); Gustav Peebles, "Rehabilitating the Hoard: The Social Dynamics of Unbanking in Africa and Beyond," *Africa* 84, no. 4 (2014).

61. Graeber, "Communism," 208.

62. Again, the Modern Monetary Theory branch will counter that the money should never have been seen as a private hoard to begin with. But the logic still holds, asking why a system of collective management couldn't be attached to all manner of other goods, regardless of origin.

9

Notes on Confronting the System

David Pedersen

Some Marxist groups had set up stages and megaphones and were making speeches and were planning a march. So, we said we don't need to do this. We pulled a small group together and decided to have a "real assembly."

—David Graeber[1]

In early 2001, David Graeber sent me several chapters of his unpublished manuscript, *Toward an Anthropological Theory of Value*. We had begun to correspond in advance of participating together on a panel that I was organizing for that year's annual meeting of the American Anthropological Association. Titled "Signifying Value: Towards a Realist Semeiotic Anthropology," the panel included several people connected to the University of Michigan Doctoral Program in Anthropology and History (DPAH) where I was a graduate student.[2] These participants included Paul Eiss, a fellow graduate student, Sharad Chari, a postdoctoral member of the Michigan Society of Fellows, Julie Skurski, a professor in the Anthropology Department, and Fernando Coronil, erstwhile Michigan Society Fellow and a professor with appointments in both history and anthropology at Michigan. The panel discussant was Terence Turner, who then was a faculty member of the Department of Anthropology at Cornell University.[3] Earlier, Turner had been a teacher of Graeber, Coronil, and Skurski at the University of Chicago (and before that, a professor of Skurski and Coronil at Cornell, where Turner had begun his career before moving to Chicago in 1968).[4]

This short chapter recalls some of David's contributions to the panel and explores how his approach to value in his chapters at the time yielded a way of "confronting the system," both in the sense of studying a central anthropological object (a cultural system) and of enacting a political project (overcoming capitalism, especially its form of rule.) He found great continuity between these two endeavors, dissolving in practice any necessity of choosing between them. As an anthropologist, he was committed to learning and writing about cultural systems that were radically different and exterior to what he recognized as capitalist ones. As an activist, he directly sought to build similarly alternative systems like the "real assembly" in Zoccotti Park that defined the Occupy Wall Street Movement. The seamless exuberance he brought to both kinds of projects is related to the way that he understood the discipline of anthropology and the concept of value within it, some of which I experienced when we first interacted in 2001.

Dialed-in Disciplinary Settings: Locus, Focus, Scope

As I read the three chapters that David had sent, I immediately noticed the density of references to published ethnographies written by anthropologists. His chapters carried a quality of erudition and disciplinary foundationalism, showing that quite a significant group of university-based anthropologists used the concept of value to denote a central theory-object within their studies. One could perceive a field-affirming conversation.

The chapters were structured to show that all these value-concept users were seeking to advance a framework that would be applicable beyond their particular case. His chapters also pointed out the limits of these various conceptualizations of value and concluded with a specific framework that Graeber endorsed as superior to all others, because it could account for the greatest diversity of processes and events. David's style of writing is distinctive, but this logic of survey, critique, and advancement/resolution is quite typical of disciplinary-specific academic debate. The guiding assumptions are that the end-goal of inquiry is to develop the fullest covering model and that to engage in this project contributes to the relative health of the discipline. Vitality is achieved when many discipline-members agree on a central theoretical framework that they bring into relation with their otherwise highly diverse empirical research.

Figuratively, an edifice-like composite of knowledge may be gradually constructed upon such a shared foundation. At sufficient size and grandeur, other researchers, and even other disciplines, may seek to emulate this creation by similarly adopting its basic design via theory and method. Exactly this had happened with anthropology's conceptual focus on "culture" and various frameworks for its study, notably "structuralism," as well as reactions to that framework, which had come to guide inquiry across multiple disciplines and fields in the humanities and social sciences throughout the second half of the twentieth century.[5] After reading David's three chapters I got the strong sense that there was, in fact, a big disciplinary focus on "value" and a holy-grail-like quest for the most encompassing model.

Another quality reflected in the three chapters only became clear after David and I spoke by telephone. I remember that he had called while traveling on the Amtrak train service between New York City and New Haven, Connecticut. He kicked off the conversation by reflecting on the novelty of using a hand-held portable telephone. I also remember his enthusiastic description of a new social movement in France focused on rediscovering not only the scholarship, but especially the political engagement of Marcel Mauss. David happily endorsed this project, emphasizing that Mauss was uniquely admirable for his passionate coupling of academic anthropological scholarship and political activism.[6]

As we discussed the upcoming American Anthropological Association (AAA) panel, including the participants and their varied research, David immediately raised what he felt was a pressing issue. The discussant for the panel was going to be Terence Turner, whose approach to value lay at the center of David's three chapters and that David had endorsed as offering the definitive covering model. David told me that because of Terry's participation, we should be sure to include ample research on non-capitalist contexts and "small-scale" societies. He told me that Terry would be looking for that and likely would criticize the panel if it did not adequately cover such ground. We agreed that David's contribution would explicitly address this kind of research context, based on his fieldwork in Madagascar, and that all the other participants would be asked in advance to develop some reflections on the issue of spatiotemporal scope and the focus on capitalist versus non-capitalist contexts as these issues related to their papers.

I recall these memories of this time because they point to instances where a kind of anthropological common sense appeared in relief. With the passage of two decades, I now recognize this as a series of dialed-in settings, definable according to what I will name as the locus, focus, and scope of inquiry and analysis. Reversing the trajectory of my interactions with David that I have reconstructed helps illuminate these settings and hints at the naturalizing and eternalizing forces that make the settings seem more like objective dimensions of reality, rather than chosen and affirmed orientations. David's reiteration of Turner's distinction between capitalist and non-capitalist is a well-wrought distinction in the discipline of anthropology. The issue reflected in David's concern was that Terry held strongly to this sort of distinction and that anthropological research, properly conducted, should include inquiry into non-capitalist contexts, specifically. The locus from which research should occur—literally "the where" that makes research count as anthropology—must be overtly definable in relation to an existing boundary between two separate and distinct realms: one with capitalist relations and one without. Anthropology and anthropologists should know and respect this border.

Besides locus, David's reiteration of Terry's concerns also reflected assumptions about the spatiotemporal scope of inquiry and analysis. In basic terms, the spatial scope should be "small." Typically, this means a unitary population and regularized settlement that both residents and an anthropologist could immediately perceive and comprehensively distinguish from other separate and discrete places. The temporal scope of the dialed-in locus-setting remained less spoken. All the research was assumed to have been gathered by the researcher during their situated fieldwork over a specific time-period. It was of that historical moment. This was "the when" that went with "the where." Like a photograph, this present was assumed as self-evident and its clear boundary from the past and the future did not require specification.

Another dialed-in setting, implicit in all the papers, was that research would focus on phenomena related to the formation and existence of *value*. Debates about what this proper focus should entail would be at the center of our AAA panel, while the other two settings, the locus and scale of analysis, would be pre-set. Finally, David's excitement over Mauss echoed the capitalist/non-capitalist distinction specified by Turner, as well as another important distinction, that between academic discipline-based scholarship and political activism. David's enthusiasm grew from recognition that Mauss had focused on both with equal energy and enthusiasm, even if the domains were assumed to be quite different and distinct.

Overall, my interactions with David and his contribution to the panel that day showed the importance of getting these settings right, much like variables, so that our anticipated interactions among panel members and audience, like another variable, could ensue within a range of possibility. Amidst everything, proper anthropology had to include consideration of objectively small-scale non-capitalist contexts in the ethnographic present. Such inquiry should be carried out with a focus on value with the goal of developing the most encompassing explanatory model. Admirable anthropologists engaged as well in political activism, which was pursued from a different locus than their research and assumed to be a separate domain of activity. Distilled according to the distinctions of locus, focus, and scope, these dialed-in settings were the disciplinary common sense that David sought to establish and see reflected in our panel.

Dialed-in Focus Setting: Value

What is the particular focus on value that David was endorsing via the yet-to-be published book chapters that he shared and that he was seeking to dial-in, together with the locus and focus settings via our phone conversation?

His book chapters argued that there are essentially three different ways that scholars have focused on value. Each of these different foci entails a different object and therefore a different theory. Some name value as that which determines exchangeability. Others treat value as standards of goodness. A third perspective understands value as "meaningful difference": the relative position of something within a closed set of possible contrastive positions. David's review showed the innovative ways that scholars sought to develop value as a category capable of accounting for more than one of what otherwise had been assumed to be three fully distinct phenomena.

Graeber points to the scholarship of Nancy Munn, Jane Fajans, and especially Terry Turner as the only examples of treating all three of the different understandings of value as mutually constituting moments within a single process, rather than as separate objects and concerns. David devotes much of the third chapter to summarizing various features of Terry's inclusive approach to value, sometimes in Terry's words, but most often in his own sprightly prose.[7] With the distance of two decades, I believe that if this puzzle-like chapter, with its many pieces, were easier to assemble, more scholars would adopt or at least address in detail Graeber's rendering of Terry's framework.[8]

One important piece in the puzzle is David's description of Terry's interpretation of Marx regarding value as a structural arrangement that expresses relative social importance or significance. This is different than an objective quality located in material objects or people's minds. David expressed how Terry had interpreted Marx as clarifying the way that capitalism could be understood as a historically specific way of defining and differentially distributing the total social activity necessary for the development and reproduction of a whole social group. David conveys Terry's perspective through the example of a pie chart that could show the distribution of social activity as it is directed toward all that is produced in the USA. "[I]f Americans spend 7 percent of their creative energies in a given year producing automobiles, this is the ultimate measure of how important it is to have cars."[9] According to Terry's formulation, as explained by David, this distributional process also could be explored in non-capitalist contexts, including the way that subgroups effectively accumulated relative surpluses of such activity via circulating symbolic forms.

The importance of this piece of the puzzle is that it emphasizes the distribution of human activity within a total system. Recalling the dialed-in settings that David had urged our panel to adopt, in part at the behest of Terry, to "confront the system" means to ethnographically determine exactly this distributional structure. It is a fully formed, finished, and discrete system that confronts the anthropologist, since distribution implies an a priori framework and closed set of possible positions.[10] In a conversation at the AAA conference, Terry explained this perspective through the example of a podium awards ceremony at the end of a sports event. He pointed out that the place of the medal-receivers was relative to the closed totality of the whole event. Competitors, such as in a completed Olympic skating event, were defined as overall winner, second place, and third place.[11]

Confronting the System

David's paper at the panel and the subsequent chapters of his book that he did not share at the time all highlight his ability to seek out such structures of distribution through careful ethnographic research, though David also liked to emphasize human creativity and innovation within the system. He understood "capitalism" as one dominant systemic formation and he was acutely aware of its manner of drastically limiting the possibilities of human life, especially via its institutional form of rule. As an anthropologist, he sought to find, describe, and explain the variability of such congealing, focusing especially on fully exterior "non-western" non-capitalist systems. As a politically engaged scholar, such a focus on counter-examples contributed to de-universalizing, de-naturalizing, and de-eternalizing capitalism, including its specific state form.[12] David emulated exactly this through his enforcement of the dialed-in settings at the AAA conference panel that day.

David confronted dominant systems not only by finding and studying alternatives, but also by building them. At the time of our conversations and the AAA panel, he was inspired by the MAUSS project in France. A decade later he was working closely with other founding members of the Occupy Wall Street Movement. As the opening epigraph captures, David had specifically called for building a fully formed counter-example—"a real assembly"—right in Zuccotti Park, which he explicitly distinguished from what he characterized as a different protest modality predicated on marching and chanting with a megaphone.[13]

David's anthropological practice merged seamlessly with his politics. Both entailed privileging fully formed non-capitalist alternatives, which could stand as destabilizing counter-examples to a similarly bounded capitalist domain. As a kind of external critique, it entailed holding up one social whole as a fully exterior standard—value as what was most important to produce for the whole—against which to judge another separate and distinct social whole and the relative presence or absence of that same free-floating reckoning of value.

Spin the Dial

The mildly audacious phrase "realist semeiotic" in our panel title gestured to Charles Peirce, but also was meant to indicate that we were treating "value" as an encompassing (general) process of mediation and not as a singular object to be positively identified. In retrospect, we could have used the triadic relation of form/content/meaning. In this, we would have more explicitly signaled our affinity with interdisciplinary scholarship directly concerned with capitalism and that has made capitalist "value-forms" the target of study and critique. In this framework, the orienting question has been how and why open-ended human life tends to take the capitalist form of value-producing labor?[14] The answers are complex, but they point to a continuously open, dynamic, interactive, contradictory and, above all, mediated process that envelops the planet. To get to this perspective has required "spinning the dial": multiply modulating the locus, focus, and scope of inquiry and analysis rather than adhering to the common sense of only one academic discipline. The return on this dial-spinning, so to speak, has been much better recognition that what at first may have appeared as separate and different from immediately legible capitalism, actually was part of it, now understood as a relationally encompassing, open-ended, and contradictory process. This more inclusive perspective yields the possibility of more immanent kinds of critique, showing that the inclusive process is failing on its own terms and destroying its necessary conditions. This is different than the external critique generated by the kind of anthropological knowledge and political activism that David led. But it shares the same goal to which he devoted his remarkable life and for which we remember him: to bring into being a world that does not yet exist.[15]

Notes

1. David Graeber, "You're Creating a Vision of the Sort of Society You Want to Have in Miniature," interview by Ezra Klein, *Washington Post*, October 3, 2011, B 1.

2. "Semeiotic" is how Charles S. Peirce named his theory of sign relations. Interpreters of Peirce have adopted this spelling to distinguish his triadic framework from Ferdinand de Saussure's dyadic "semiology" and "semiotic." See the many articles that use Peirce's term in the journal *Transactions of the Charles S. Peirce Society*. I also used "realist" in the spirit of Peirce's development of the concept. See Kelley Parker, "Peirce's Semeiotic and Ontology," *Transactions of Charles Peirce Society* 30, no. 1 (Winter 1994), 51–75.

3. Since the 2001 panel, Fernando, Terry, and David have all passed. Julie Skurski is a professor on the graduate faculty at the City University of New York (CUNY). Sharad Chari is a professor in the Department of Geography at UC Berkeley. Paul Eiss is a professor of anthropology and history at Carnegie-Mellon University. I also must recognize the late Nancy Munn, though she was not directly part of our panel, and I did not have the fortune to know her as I did Fernando, Terry, and David. Fernando and Julie did tell me of their regular movie theater trips with Nancy, followed by intense discussions and debate during their time together at the University of Chicago. Terry had told me of how he and Nancy had collaborated on the project of transposing Marx's value form analysis into a modality suitable for ethnographic research in non-capitalist contexts.

4. At this time Victor Turner had been recruited to the University Chicago from Cornell. He helped to bring Terence Turner to Chicago as well, along with three Cornell graduate students, including Coronil and Skurski. See Mariana Coronil, Laurent Dubois, Julie Skurski, and Gary Wilder, "Introduction: Transcultural Paths and Utopian Imaginings," in *The Coronil Reader*, ed. Fernando Coronil et al. (Durham, NC: Duke University Press, 2019), 1–44.

5. Among many reviews of this theoretical trajectory in the discipline of anthropology, see Sherry Ortner's, "Theory in Anthropology Since the 1960s," *Comparative Studies in Society and History* 26, no. 1 (1984), 126–166.

6. This was the "Mouvement Anti-Utilitariste dans les Sciences Sociales," or MAUSS. See David Graeber, "Give it Away," available at: http://www.freewords.org/graeber.html (accessed November 15, 2022).

7. Years after its publication, a colleague of Terry's once remarked offhandedly to me, "The book is an act of ventriloquism."

8. The editors and contributors to a two-volume edition of the online journal HAU devoted to "value" cited Graeber's book, though no author addressed its argument nor the centrality of Turner.

9. David Graeber, *Toward an Anthropological Theory of Value: The False Coin of our Own Dreams* (New York: Palgrave Macmillan, 2001), 55.

10. Gesturing to the uneven "distribution" of phenomena has become a popular way to refer to dominative relations within a closed system. For example, Judith Butler has explained that "'[p]recarity' designates that politically induced condition in which certain populations suffer from failing social and economic networks of support more than others, and become differentially exposed to injury, violence, and death.... [P]recarity is thus the differential *distribution* of precariousness" (emphasis added). Judith Butler, *Notes Toward a Performative Theory of Assembly* (Cambridge, MA: Harvard University Press, 2015), 33.

11. Terry offered this example in the context of a memorable and extended discussion with me, Fernando Coronil, and Paul Eiss at the AAA meetings. Paul directly addressed Turner's medal awards ceremony example directly in a later article "Beyond the Object." Paul K. Eiss, "'Beyond the Object': Of Rabbits, Rutabagas, and History," *Anthropological Theory* 8, no. 1 (2008): 79–97.

12. For a powerful critique of exactly this kind of project as reflected in the work of Marcel Mauss, see Edward LiPuma and Moishe Postone, "Gifts, Commodities, and the Encompassment of Others," *Critical Historical Studies* 7, no. 1 (Spring 2020): 167–200.

13. Graeber, ""You're Creating a Vision ...," interview by Ezra Klein.

14. See the English-language debates in Diane Elson, *Value: The Representation of Labour in Capitalism*, especially her renowned chapter, "The Value Theory of Labour," pp. 115–180, Atlantic Highlands, NJ: Humanities Press, 1979. See also the varied German-language debates beginning in the 1970s, often glossed as 'Neu-Marx Lektüre."

15. See David Graeber, "It is Value that Brings Universes into Being," *HAU: Journal of Ethnographic Theory* 3, no. 2 (Summer 2013): 219–243.

Afterword

Putting Pluralism into Practice: You Have To Be There

Bill Maurer

Maybe I'm feeling the aftereffects of the COVID-19 pandemic, when so many relationships moved online and conferences and classes went virtual, but it is striking to me how many contributions to this volume on the work and legacy of David Graeber reference in-person meetings, conversations, or events. David Pedersen starts with a 2001 panel of the American Anthropological Association meetings, and discusses a seminar offered by Terence Turner at the University of Chicago. Sharad Chari mentions Graeber's response to a speech at Occupy Wall Street in 2011 by Gayatri Spivak. Josh Reno recounts protesting alongside Graeber in London in 2010, with Graeber the next day presenting him with the gift of a fragment of glass from a window, smashed during the mêlée, from the Tory party headquarters. Despite his voluminous corpus, and the range and depth of his own reading, David Graeber was profoundly shaped by his encounters in the conference hall, the seminar room, or the conclave and conflict in the streets, and in turn gave back to those forums something of his practical theorizing.

The stylistic conceit of including in one's chapter "memorable moments with David Graeber" is to be expected given the unavoidable element of hagiography that will always creep into a retrospective like this volume (and for that reason, I exclude my own). But I want to suggest in my reflections on these thought- and action-provoking chapters that these moments that flash through this book and stick with the reader long after the eyes have left the page themselves have something to teach us about the specificity of Graeber's contribution to anthropology and its political praxis that he sought to realize, to enact, and to nurture. This is his repeated assertion that the way to refuse the idiocy of capitalist bureaucratic "bullshit jobs,"[1] the route toward recapturing the imagination, reawakening our "capacity to act,"[2] and realizing expansive possibilities in the face of "violent simpli-fications"[3] of white, capitalist culture, is through dialogue. "As he saw it," write High and Reno in their introduction, "if you weren't prepared to go out and encounter people and treat them as equals, you were stuck in the labyrinth of the library stacks forever."[4]

This is not to say that Graeber did not wander that labyrinth: another striking thing about these collected essays is the map they draw of his bibliographic meandering, and mainly through the classics of the anthro-pological canon, from Tylor and Lowie to Leach and Lévi-Strauss. This is also not to deny that there is a very high degree of privilege associated with access to that archive, uncritical acceptance of its own lineaments of mostly heteronormative male whiteness undergirding its authority, and facility with its historical complexity and ethnographic and theoretical nuance. Of course, Graeber developed that facility through the privilege of access to the spaces of the institutions that he, despite being characterized as having been outcast by the discipline, nevertheless occupied (Chicago, Yale, the London School of Economics, Goldsmiths ... as opposed to, say, North Carolina Central, where Zora Neale Hurston finally found an academic appointment), not to mention his career-long interaction with his own "big men," exemplified by Marshall Sahlins and Terence Turner.[5]

At the same time, however, as this volume demonstrates, Graeber's schol-arly works and his political activism evidence a continual striving toward experimentation, play even, by relentlessly holding open the possibility for dialogue. His work can be bracing—even irritating at times—given the simultaneous recitation of and irreverence toward the anthropological canon. His refusal of incommensurability and embrace of a "commonal-ity in human experience"[6] went hand in glove with the insistence that we should strive toward a politics where "humans are fundamentally equal and [should be] allowed to manage their collective affairs in an egalitar-ian fashion, using whatever means appear most conducive."[7] This applies, too, to his generous reading of those classic anthropological texts, as High and Reno discuss, alongside his general lack of attention to their colonial contexts of production, or to postcolonial and antiracist critiques of eth-nographic representation. Though he plays with the canon, you can tell he loves it. That is not necessarily a vice, though I often wish he had been more transparent about the sources of his own genealogy, and open to others.[8]

The dialogic mode of inquiry is simultaneously a mode of critique, too, though, through which people, even differentially situated in relations of power and domination, recognize the capacity to become otherwise. Insofar as dialogue is always processual, it is also potentially always open-ended, expanding the horizon of possibilities. The everyday communism Graeber repeatedly extolled in his writings—the "gestures so tiny … that we ordinarily never stop to think about them at all," like his example of tiny dinner table debt created when one asks a companion to "pass the salt"9—betrays a moral economy obscured by modern bureaucratic capitalism. Graeber's analytical and political challenge was to linger in the moment of those tiny gestures, dilate the spacetimes of their performance, to tarry in the pluralism of the present so often foreclosed by the "condition of structured ignorance"10 of the dominant mode of production. For, as I have argued elsewhere,11 that mode, considered in the statistical sense of the term, is just a central tendency. There are always other possibilities at the tails of the distribution.

In this volume these new social possibilities often take the form of inversion. The king becomes clown; the idiot, the wise man (Reno). But this is also the carnivalesque (High), the "festive misrule"12 celebrated by François Rabelais, the French Renaissance writer who figures in both *Debt* and in the work of the twentieth-century Russian literary critic Mikhail Bakhtin whose concept of dialogism Graeber so deftly exploited. This is the world upside-down sense of revolution in Edwards' chapter, an unending turning around and around, again signified by the Burmese term *taw lan ye*.13 Or the as-if quality of revolution in Eritrea, conveyed by Michael Ralph.14 Graeber, following Bakhtin, might say that if we are ready so willingly to suspend disbelief and accept the totality of the world within a novel, then why is it so difficult to do the same in the spacetime of a planning meeting, a protest, or politics?

For Graeber, what forecloses possibility is the active production of ignorance by the bureaucratic state. Graeber's anarchism rejects any rule-based order enforced directly or indirectly by violence and not of a community's active, engaged design. Oppression limits creativity, sterilizing or short-circuiting the generativity of the dialogic moment. An explicitly anarchist activism, then, strives to reanimate our dulled creative potential, to thrust us into new relations and reawaken and amplify those tiny moments of elementary communism. Activist practice reveals other ways of being/doing in the present, and anarchism amplifies this revelation, allowing us to experience, together, what we can collectively do without a state.

As Peebles demonstrates in this volume, however, the state (or its corollary, the central bank) might also be the sovereign source of a collective commons—the money supply, in this case, as a public good. And despite its "hiding behind the veneer of a 'public institution,'" the privatized public university still has the potential to "tip ... towards life-enhancing possibilities," writes Chari.[15] Rather than churn out docile "widgets," it can still afford a space for the creation of full, relational, persons precisely because, I would argue, so much of the work going on within it—even by the bureaucrats!—still often has the character of the gift.[16]

Graeber's model of "oppression" signals the belief in human creativity and potential, and also human freedom. Graeber and Wengrow make this explicit in *The Dawn of Everything*, where they ask how the potential for freedom got shunted (they repeatedly use the word "stuck") into the affairs of the state or, more specifically, the triumvirate of "sovereignty, bureaucracy, and a competitive political field."[17] Yet complex social systems do not have to be governed by the violence of this triumvirate. *Dawn* is full of examples of large-scale, stateless societies that did not evidence it, as well as societies where people took up, say, agriculture for a while, and then decided it wasn't worth it and moved on. Their point is to underscore "the possibility that human beings have more collective say over their own destiny than we ordinarily assume,"[18] that the state as we know it is not inevitable; that other ways of being are possible.

The challenge with this understanding of oppression for me, however, is that it presumes its opposite is freedom.[19] But I have a hard time seeing freedom in, for example, the aristocratic hierarchies of the Nuer.[20] For Graeber and Wengrow, because those hierarchies did not seem to pervade every aspect of a person's life, they deem them "largely theatrical."[21] "Domination," they write, "first appears on the most intimate, domestic level. Self-consciously egalitarian politics emerge to prevent such relations from extending beyond those small worlds into the public sphere."[22] When such egalitarian politics do *not* emerge, people are "free" insofar as they have the option of exit: "The freedom to abandon one's community, knowing one will be welcomed in faraway lands; the freedom to shift back and forth between social structures [...]; the freedom to disobey authorities without consequence—all appear to have been simply assumed among our distant ancestors."[23]

I mean, I guess so? Seen one way, exit is an expression of an inherent autonomy. Seen another, however, I can't help but think of Jean Briggs' ostracism from the Utku Inuit community up in the cold, far North,[24] or

Jane Collier's remarks on so-called "egalitarian" societies that "A woman, because she is defined within political discourse as giveable, may be killed by the men who give or receive her,"[25] even if women are otherwise relatively autonomous. Being killed does not sound "theatrical" to me; and if exit is fleeing the possibility of murder, is it really "freedom?" (This is partly why Collier rejects the term "egalitarian.")

My long-standing beef with Graeber is precisely this: in his search for the origins of the fusion of bureaucracy, political competition, and sovereignty that gave rise to the modern state, he presumes what Michelle Rosaldo called "a faith in ultimate and essential truths."[26] For him, it is the ultimate and essential truth of human freedom. For me, however, the opposite of oppression is not the freedom of free and equal (Enlightenment) subjects. It is the expanded possibilities for organizing inequality so as to see how others have done so, and so that we can challenge our own and create a system where the inevitable inequalities among people can be fairly, justly, humanely managed. The gift is always a debt; but a system of generalized reciprocity and mutually enmeshed debts might just sustain a society and everyone in it regardless of ability.

Josh Reno asks us to reflect on the inevitability of a condition of disability for all humans. But is the radical freedom of Reno's son, the "becoming-moron" Reno advocates as a means of throwing a wrench in the machine of bourgeois society—no matter how liberating—actually an act of equality? Reno writes, following Danilyn Rutherford, that a post-liberal disability justice is about a radical opening of "new ways of being with one another."[27] To me, this requires an expansion of our vocabulary for modes of (inevitable) inequality.

Graeber seems to have gotten this point in his activist practice—indeed, it's captured in the title of this book: not "free" but "*as if* already free." And I've noted before the tension between Graeber "in the books" and Graeber "in action."[28] High and Reno relate Graeber's experience of consensus-based decision making, and the pleasure of the sense of giving oneself over to the collective even if one's own position does not carry the day. For me this is still not "equality" or "freedom" or the absence of "oppression," but simply a decision-making mechanism that organizes the relations between winners and losers in a manner that leaves people feeling whole, heard, one might say respected. And respect is an idiom for organizing inequality; it is not the same as autonomy, or equality. It is an acceptance of difference, and a mode of honoring it.

On the one hand, my argument might be just quibbling with definitions. On the other, however, I want to hold on to Graeber's own practice—flawed, fragmentary, privileged, provoking—of "being there." I think the distinctions I am drawing are important because if anthropology and the social sciences are "the ideological arms of sociopolitical arrangements," as Esther Netwon put it in the first ethnography of queerness, changing the terms of anthropology has the potential to pluralize possibility in those arrangements (to queer them, one might say).[29] Even if "trying to change them is like to crawl out of your own bones."[30] In Newton's case, it was about trying to change the university (see Chari, this volume), and thereby change the world. I am not sure if Graeber thought the university was a proper site for activism except to abolish it (although again, see Zora Neale Hurston's professional journey, receiving a degree at Barnard and teaching at two historically Black colleges). Nevertheless, in his account of his experience in the streets the thrill of "being there" is part and parcel of the fragmentary condition of the politics of protest. Nothing is ever tied up with a bow; there are always loose ends; and it's good that those ends are loose, because that implies the give in the system—the opening of unthought of possibilities.

Perhaps that fragment of glass from the Tory HQ is an apt metaphor for Graeber's life and works, as well as where he left us after his death. Dialogue, too, is always fragmentary. There can be mishearings, misquotings, misunderstandings, contradictions and opposites held close and at the same time.[31] Picking up those fragments, bringing them somewhere new, contains the potential to create new configurations and establish alternative sets of relations among them. But you have to be there—wherever you are—to do the work.

Notes

1. David Graeber, *Bullshit Jobs: A Theory* (New York: Simon & Schuster, 2018).
2. Holly High, "Birthing Possibilities," ch. 2 this volume, 53.
3. Georgina Tuari Stewart, "Ka Mate, Ka Ora: On Truths, Lies, and Knowing the Difference," ch. 4 this volume, 99.
4. Holly High and Joshua Reno, "Introduction: David Graeber in the Library Stacks," this volume, 3.
5. Turner is particularly interesting given my argument, insofar as it was from his seminars and mimeographed papers—not his published work—that he developed his cult following. You had to be there, in other words.

6. High and Reno, "Introduction," this volume, 15.

7. Ibid., 20, quoting Graeber, *The Democracy Project*, 184.

8. Take Irma McClaurin's genealogies of Black feminist anthropology, which do not seem to intertwine with Graeber's much at all. Irma McClaurin, *Black Feminist Anthropology: Theory, Politics, Praxis, and Poetics* (New Brunswick, NJ: Rutgers University Press, 2001). And it has always amazed me that someone who so carefully pored over the ethnographic literature on "egalitarian" societies seemed to have missed the feminist debate about "universal sexual asymmetry." See Michelle Z. Rosaldo, "Woman, Culture, and Society: A Theoretical Overview," in Woman, Culture, and Society, ed. Michelle Z. Rosaldo and Louise Lamphere (Stanford, CA: Stanford University Press, 1974), 17–42. This perhaps also says something about his various institutional locations and what works were circulating where and when.

9. David Graeber, *Debt: The First 5,000 Years* (New York: Melville House, 2011), 89.

10. Sharad Chari, "Actualising the Public University: For Debt-Free, Antiracist, Accessible, Quality Higher Education," ch. 5 this volume, 123.

11. Bill Maurer, "Late to the Party: Debt and Data," *Social Anthropology* 20, no. 4 (November 2012).

12. Chris Humphrey, *The Politics of Carnival: Festive Misrule in Medieval England* (Manchester: Manchester University Press, 2001).

13. Michael Edwards, "Reading Graeber, Leach, and a Revolution in Myanmar," ch. 6 this volume, 149.

14. Michael Ralph, "Debt and Political Possibility in Eritrea," ch. 7 this volume.

15. Chari, "Actualising," ch. 5 this volume, 122.

16. On this point, I would direct readers to Frederick Wiseman's film, *At Berkeley*. This is not to deny the very real questions of labor exploitation and unfair compensation at universities.

17. David Graeber and David Wengrow, *The Dawn of Everything: A New History of Humanity* (New York: Farrar, Straus and Giroux, 2021), 507.

18. Graeber and Wengrow, *Dawn*, 206.

19. Holly High (personal communication) pointed out to me that Graeber argued something similar in his essay on cultural refusal: "Acts of creative refusal can lead to new ideals of equality, new forms of hierarchy or, often, a complicated mix of both," David Graeber, "Culture as Creative Refusal," *Cambridge Journal of Anthropology* 31, no. 2 (Autumn 2013): 4. Perhaps I can take a phrase from the title of this volume, however: where I still think Graeber held out the idea of bringing into being an actually existing equality, I would prefer analytically and politically to treat that equality "*as if* already free," simply because I see all societies as necessarily systems of inequality—though inequality plays out always in "nonnecessary" ways, as Rosaldo always put it. For example, as High also indicated to me, "The idea of up and leaving takes on a whole different dimension when

thought of through the lens of care and dependency [of children or of disability], rather than autonomous adults."

20. Graeber and Wengrow, *Dawn*, 132–133.
21. Ibid., 131.
22. Ibid., 209.
23. Ibid., 133.
24. Jean L. Briggs, *Never in Anger: Portrait of an Eskimo Family* (Cambridge, MA: Harvard University Press, 1971).
25. Jane F. Collier, *Marriage and Inequality in Classless Societies* (Stanford, CA: Stanford University Press, 1988), 56.
26. Michelle Z. Rosaldo, "The Use and Abuse of Anthropology: Reflections on Feminism and Cross-Cultural Understanding," *Signs* 5, no. 3 (Spring, 1980), 393.
27. Joshua Reno, "On Morons," ch. 1 this volume, quoting Rutherford, 48.
28. Bill Maurer, "David Graeber's Wunderkammer, *Debt: The First 5,000 Years*," *Anthropological Forum* 23, no.1 (January, 2013): 91.
29. Esther Newton, *Mother Camp: Female Impersonators in America* (Chicago: University of Chicago Press, 1971), xvi.
30. Ibid.
31. I think this would resonate with Graeber's understanding of Heraclitus in: David Graeber, *Toward an Anthropological Theory of Value* (New York: Palgrave, 2001).

Notes on Contributors

Sharad Chari teaches Geography at the University of California at Berkeley and is affiliated to Critical Theory, Rhetoric, Gender & Women's Studies, the Berkeley Faculty Association, the Marxist Institute for Research, and the Wits Institute for Social and Economic Research. His recent and forthcoming works include *Ethnographies of Power* (Wits, 2022, co-edited with M. Hunter and M. Samson), *Gramsci at Sea* (Minnesota, 2023) and *Apartheid Remains* (Duke, 2024). His brush with fame was in offering his illegal sublet at Westminster Abbey to David (c.f. the opening of *Debt*). Warm thanks to Josh Reno, Holly High and to all the contributors in this book for an engaging collective editorial process.

Michael Edwards is a Smuts Fellow in South Asian Studies at the University of Cambridge, and will be joining the University of Sydney as a Lecturer in Anthropology in 2024. His first book project, *Myanmar and the Dissonance of Salvation*, is a study of religious difference amid the country's fraught and fleeting democratic opening. A second project explores questions of transnational religion and solidarity emerging from Myanmar's unfolding revolution. For help with his essay in this volume, he is grateful to Giulio Ongaro, Nikita Simpson, and Hans Steinmüller; to audiences at Cambridge and the LSE, where versions of it were presented; and, of course, to Holly, Josh, and other participants for the gift of the "slow workshop".

Holly High is an anthropologist. She is currently an Associate Professor and Future Fellow at the Alfred Deakin Institute of Globalisation and Citizenship. She has been a specialist of Lao PDR for over 20 years. She is the author of *Fields of Desire* and *Projectland*. She is also the editor of *Stone Masters*. Holly has held Fellowships at Yale University (Program of Agrarian Studies), Cambridge University (Clare Hall Junior Research Fellow, Department of Anthropology Research Associate), Sydney University (Sydney Equity Prize, Discovery Early Career Research Award) and Deakin University (Future Fellowship). She is currently writing a book about women in the Lao revolution, and editing a collection of Kaysone Phomvihane's writings, and the *Handbook of Contemporary Laos*.

Bill Maurer is Dean of the School of Social Sciences and Professor of Anthropology; Criminology, Law and Society; and Law at the University of California, Irvine. He is the author of numerous books and articles, including the edited collection (with Lana Swartz) *Paid: Tales of Dongles, Checks, and Other Money Stuff* (MIT Press), and most recently, served as editor for the 6-volume series, *A Cultural History of Money* (Bloomsbury). He would like to thank Tom Boellstorff, Jane Collier, Holly High, Taylor Nelms, and Joshua Reno for their thoughts and inspiration for this chapter.

David Pedersen is an Associate Professor at the University of California San Diego. His first book, *American Value* (2014) explores El Salvador and its relations with the United States as both countries have been reshaped by several decades of transnational migration and remittance circulation. He is writing a new book titled *Capitol Crisis: Memory, Imagination and the Breaking of Habit*. I am grateful to Holly High and Josh Reno for patiently leading this project also commenting on my written draft. It would not have taken this final form without their fine advice and encouragement. Many thanks also to friends from the era recalled, including Chandra Bhimull, David William Cohen, Paul Eiss, Mani Limbert, Ed Murphy, and especially Julie Skurski.

Gustav Peebles serves as Universitetslektor in the Department of Social Anthropology at the University of Stockholm. Recently, he led a Mellon-funded research collaboration ("Currency and Empire") and another funded by Wenner-Gren ("The Price of Wealth"). Many of his publications (including a book entitled *The Euro and Its Rivals*), seek to track credit, debt, money, and the diverse struggles to regulate and manage these vital economic phenomena throughout human history. Most recently, he has been exploring digital currencies, including work on the Swedish Central Bank's e-currency proposal, as well as digital currency as a potential tool for fighting climate change.

Michael Ralph is Chair of the Department of Africana Studies, and Founding Director of the Center for an Equitable Economy and Sustainable Society, both at Howard University. Michael's 2015 book *Forensics of*

Capital demonstrates that the social profile of an individual or country is a credit profile as well as a forensic profile. He has two forthcoming books: *Life* explores the relationship between the history of actuarial science, slavery, life insurance, and other techniques for determining how much someone's life is worth, and *Before 13^(th)* revises the scholarly consensus about private prison labor, or convict leasing. Michael is also completing the graphic books *Fishing* and *Basketball IQ.*

Joshua O. Reno is Professor of Anthropology at Binghamton University. He is the author of *Waste Away* (2016), *Military Waste* (2019) and, with Britt Halvorson, *Imagining the Heartland* (2022), all from University of California Press. He has a forthcoming book, *Home Signs*, which examines the strangeness and importance of non-verbal communication from an autoethnographic perspective. He would like to thank everyone who participated in the slow workshop in honor of David Graeber and the staff of Pluto Press.

Georgina Tuari Stewart (Ngāpuhi-nui-tonu, Pare Hauraki) is Professor of Māori Philosophy of Education in Te Ara Poutama, the Māori faculty at Auckland University of Technology in Aotearoa New Zealand. Formerly one of few Māori-speaking senior school teachers of science, with special interests in the relationship between science and Māori knowledge, and what it means to be Māori today. Author of *Māori Philosophy: Indigenous thinking from Aotearoa* (Bloomsbury, 2021) and lead editor of *Writing for Publication: Liminal Reflections for Academics* (Springer, 2021). Deputy Editor of *Educational Philosophy and Theory* (EPAT), and Co-Editor in Chief of *New Zealand Journal of Educational Studies* (NZJES).

Tangi kau ana te hau ki runga o marae nui o Hinemoana
E te rangatira, haere atu, oti atu rā.
Only the wind cries on the vast expanse of the ocean
Farewell, esteemed one.

Index

Thanks to our Patreon subscriber:

Ciaran Kane

Who has shown generosity and
comradeship in support of our publishing.

Check out the other perks you get by subscribing
to our Patreon – visit patreon.com/plutopress.
Subscriptions start from £3 a month.